Pioneers in Popular Culture Studies

Pioneers
in Popular Culture Studies

edited by

Ray B. Browne
and
Michael T. Marsden

Bowling Green State University Popular Press
Bowling Green, OH 43403

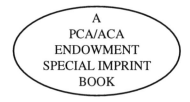

A
PCA/ACA
ENDOWMENT
SPECIAL IMPRINT
BOOK

Library of Congress Cataloging-in-Publication Data

Pioneers in popular culture studies / edited by Ray B. Browne and Michael
T. Marsden
        p.   cm.
    Includes bibliographical references.
    ISBN 0-87972-775-6 -- ISBN 0-87972-776-4 (pbk.)
    1. Popular culture--United States--Study and teaching. 2. United
States--Intellectual life--20th century. 3. Intellectuals--United States--
Biography.   I. Browne, Ray Broadus. II. Marsden, Michael T.
E169.04.P563   1999
306.4'0973--dc21   98-30244
                                                                              CIP

Cover design by Dumm Art

CONTENTS

INTRODUCTION

The Popular Culture Association and the American Culture Association were integral parts of an academic revolution that began in a time of great cultural and political upheaval. The designers of the two associations, perhaps stirred by the flashes of rapid social and cultural change around them, thought that similar improvements, which were already desired by many students and faculty, could be effected through academic organizations of like-minded individuals. Many of the prime movers were members of other academic organizations which purported to be on the cutting edge of development and improvement, but which were not, at least in the eyes of the new breed of change agents. The established organizations, sometimes clinging to the past or to the territory they colonized, had lost their forward momentum and had allowed their cutting edges to become chipped and rusty.

The new breed of change agents pushing the two new, tandem associations were comprehensive in their desires and objectives. They wanted a new evaluation of academic subject matter and a whole new attitude toward changes in the canon of the humanities and social sciences—and through those changes a broadening and enriching of all approaches to knowledge. After those changed attitudes would inevitably come different and improved teaching methods, together with a new respect for students. This enthusiasm for education of the new academic revolutionaries was founded on the belief that education is too precious to squander and the student's mind too important not to dignify and respect. More central to their argument, however, was the realization that in a democracy—even a developing democracy—all institutions need to be studied to be understood, developed, and preserved. The assumption became that one learns most about a subject by studying it directly and logically from the ground up, moving from the known to the unknown.

In a democracy, so the new pioneers believed, such an approach begins with everyday culture—everyday in the sense of life around us all the time and culture in the broadest anthropological and humanistic terms. This approach meant that established and revered approaches, methodologies, and concepts currently being circulated as coin of the academic realm should be reexamined. Some were to be found covered with encrustations which needed to be scraped away to reveal their true value. In the case of others, when the encrustations were removed, they

1

would be recognized as dross, long since having lost their value and in need of being jettisoned.

Not, however, that all lighthouses of the past still being used to cast light on the present should be shuttered and abandoned. They always should be kept in a state of readiness, and sometimes requiring periodic updating. But some continued to walk the streets of Concord with Ralph Waldo Emerson and felt that one of his most oft-quoted aphorisms if brought up to date served well in the new mixing of ideas. So one was modified for the modern academic: "A foolish academic canon is the curse of little minds, adored by little statesmen and philosophers and divines and professors." The new change agents among us felt that this American philosopher, one of the earliest in wanting to discard the shackles of European political and philosophical hegemony and academic servitude, had another general message for us today in his advice, "I hate quotations. Tell me what you know," and would emphasize the individual *you,* thus taking the responsibility away from the collective and placing it on the individual.

The success of the two resulting professional associations in tandem has been remarkable. In 1970, when the Popular Culture Association was founded, the whole notion of such an inclusive approach to education was anathema. Even the word *popular* was insulting to all "serious" educators. The feeling was that all knowledge should percolate down from the top, that academics should be properly interested only in what they had learned and that everyday life—the near total culture of America and increasingly of the world—should perhaps be tolerated but certainly despised.

But in three decades, as the popular song says, times they have changed. "Popular" is no longer a four-letter word. The study of everyday culture is commonplace. It is estimated that every year more than a million—perhaps as many as two million—students of higher learning take a course in popular culture under one name or another—in architecture, art, aesthetics, history, literature, music, religion or philosophy. The study of everyday life, furthermore, is not treated as adjunct material to a more important subject, but as integral and core to many disciplines. The rebellion within academia—or invasion, if you like—is not complete, but it is appropriate that the history of that important fight to date be chronicled.

In some ways we come to writing the history too late. Several of the leading pioneers have passed on and left the recording of their history to others, who at best can present only their version of what actually took place. There is another lamentable fact about this history of the "pioneers" of the development of popular culture studies which will become immediately apparent—it is a male-centered presentation. Such was not the intent of the editors. The development of popular culture studies has been carried in the minds and souls of women as well as men. Without their contributions the movement would be incomplete. But we were not able to collect as many contributions by and about the women who have worked so effectively in this whole enterprise as should have been the case. For reasons of death, age, sickness or other hindrances, they could not contribute. For our deficiencies, we apologize.

But we felt as editors that the task needed to be done now though it must be incomplete. Histories usually are unfinished. Perhaps the gaps can be filled in later in a supplementary volume. Meanwhile the editors and the contributors wish for the members of the two associations, past, present and future, all the best—and urge them to engage in continuous reexamination of themselves, their assumptions, and their goals. Education is too precious to squander.

Ray B. Browne
Bowling Green, Ohio

Michael T. Marsden
Marquette, Michigan

Jane S. Bakerman

JANE S. BAKERMAN:
TALKS ABOUT TALKING

Regina Calvin

Because Jane S. Bakerman spent a good part of her career conducting and publishing interviews, it seemed that the interview format would
be appropriate for this essay. Thus, most of what follows will be in her
own words.

Q: Did you intend that interviewing would be a big segment of your
professional work?

No, not at all. It came about quite naturally but as a surprise, just as
working in popular culture did. I had always assumed that I would do
traditional scholarly studies of traditionally canonized American writers.

Q: How did you get started doing interviews?

Actually, it was the old boy network. John Brady, a former colleague at Indiana State University, had become the editor of *Writer's
Digest*. He knew I had been writing about mysteries, and he wanted to
publish an interview with Ross Macdonald, so he asked me to do it.
Miraculously, Macdonald agreed, so I read everything about interviewing that I could lay my hands on and went off to California, trying to
behave as if I knew what I was doing. Luckily, Macdonald *did* know
exactly what *he* was doing, so everything went well. He was very forthcoming and even offered me some advice which perhaps I should have
taken.

Q: What was that?

He said that anyone who wanted to be a writer—meaning, of
course, fiction writer—should stop teaching because both efforts drew
on the "same creative juices." I expect he was right. But luckily, I was
happy teaching and being an academic writer.

Q: It sounds as if the Macdonald interview was a good experience.
Was it? And was that generally the case?

Yes, it was generally the case. These experiences were very pleasant. There were moments of terror beforehand, of course; I was always very nervous, but I found the writers themselves to be gracious and lively. I almost always had a very good time, as, it seems, did they. Though once or twice, I was unsure of my welcome.

Q: How do you mean?

Well, three times, I worried about actually getting *in* even though the writers had agreed to be interviewed. I remember standing on the stoop of Lois Gould's town house, getting no answer to my ring, and becoming terribly fearful that I had the date or the address wrong. (Actually, that waiting period and the dozens and dozens of tiny throw pillows decorated with buttons that she kept on her sofa are my most vivid memories of that long ago day.) But she had gone out to mail a letter and just miscalculated her time a bit. Some years later, I became well acquainted with Sara Paretsky's front porch while I waited for her—though it probably *seemed* longer than it actually was. She thought someone else would be home to invite me in to wait.

But with du Maurier I really became nervous. The innkeeper where we were staying, the taxi driver, the *cook* at the hotel (called into conference because she was distantly related to du Maurier's housekeeper) all assured me that Daphne du Maruier *never* saw "outsiders," and that I would be turned away. The cab driver even gave us explicit directions to a pub at the shore where we could while away the time until he could get back to us—between dropping us off and collecting us in time for our train, he had to get the village ladies to their hairdressing appointments.

Actually, we had trouble detaching ourselves at the end of the day. Du Maurier gave us lunch; she took us for a walk; she chatted volubly, and we all enjoyed ourselves. It was a lovely day, and I appreciated her generosity and remember her very fondly.

Q: What prompts writers to agree to interviews, do you think?

It's good business, of course. A good interview often attracts new readers to an author's work; that's a—perhaps *the* major factor. Often, writers whom I admired enormously were surprisingly flattered to be interviewed. Sometimes, they were simultaneously intrigued and a bit leery of being approached by an academic—I think that was the case with Ruth Rendell. Daphne du Maurier told me that she was interested because my request letter said that my husband would accompany me and act as timekeeper. She found that a curious reversal of roles (though it seemed perfectly normal to us) and so paid attention to the request whereas most of the time, I gather, she did not.

Q: What sort of preparation did you do besides reading about how to do interviews?

Well, one has to know the author's work very thoroughly, of course—so it became important to me to work with writers whose work I really admired. I didn't want to spend hours and hours reading fiction I disliked—that's a luxury I wouldn't have had if I earned my living by writing rather than teaching.

It was also important to touch upon the same topics more than once during the conversation—fairly subtly, if possible. This technique contributed to accuracy, of course. But also, I noticed that the interviewee's mind sometimes kept tugging at a question though we had gone on to talk about other subjects, so going back, as it were, offered an opportunity for her or him to amplify. Those amplifications were usually very good material.

Oddly enough, one teaching habit also helped me do interviews. I used to give oral exams to my students either singly or in small groups, and the close attention that required—to draw them out a bit, for instance—transferred handily to the interviews.

Q: So, good questions were the most important factor in a good interview?

Well, they are a key component, of course. They say that attorneys ought never to ask a question to which they don't already know the answer. That's a little too pat for interviewers. An interviewer has to be careful not to build an answer into the question—that cuts the subject off from her own line of thought—and it could cause some resentment, I would think.

But actually, I think that *listening* is the most important factor in doing a good interview. Very often, the subject will just touch glancingly upon a topic which turns out to be very fruitful to pursue. If I were too wedded to my notes, and if I were not listening carefully, I might miss that—and probably did sometimes early in the game. When a potentially interesting idea comes up, it's important to put the interview plan on hold and pursue the new point.

Q: What other flaws or faults did you have to guard against?

Impatience. The urge to finish someone else's sentence. It's vital to give the subject time to think about what she's saying; otherwise, you get pretty shallow material. And if I could just stay quiet long enough, I noticed, the subjects often came up with really nice little side bars—anecdotal material that wouldn't, couldn't, have come from strict adherence to my notes.

That's the golden material—and that's what can make an interview unique. After all, if a subject is honest, and most are, the answers to some questions are going to be the same time and time again. It's up to the interviewer, then, to find a way to unearth new material, to establish a slant. Listening is the key to that.

Q: You say "most" subjects are honest—are some not?

As you see, when you ask that, it makes me smile. I asked Lois Gould about her age—probably not too tactfully! But each reference work gave a different birth year. Apparently, she was fully aware of that, and she was honest about the fact that she probably wasn't being honest. That is, she said, "I'll give you *an* answer." So I didn't ever bet any money on it!

Once in a while, of course, a subject can simply make a mistake. Anyone might do so. That's why I've found it useful to let the subjects read the interview transcript of the tapes—I always tape the interviews and would be unwilling to do one otherwise. The interviewees catch things I may have misheard—or that they may even have misstated.

Offering to let them read the material before publication is also reassuring and sometimes, I think, helps prompt a subject to agree to the interview.

Q: Has that promise ever worked against you?

Yes, once it did. Toni Morrison had spoken very movingly and very extensively about the publishing industry, and Joe Weixlmann, the editor of what was then *Black American Literature Forum,* for which I was doing the interview, asked me to work that material up into a second article. I did—and she asked me to kill it. It was such good stuff that I hated to let it go. But a promise is a promise . . .

Q: You mention Toni Morrison. This interview is for a book called *Pioneers of Popular Culture Studies.* Do you consider her work popular culture?

Sure. Of course I do. Mind you, she wasn't a Nobel laureate when I was writing about her. She wasn't even extremely well known, but she had a wide following even then. Good literature is good literature, whether it's "popular culture" or "high culture," and very, very frequently the lines between those cultures are arbitrary—and probably shouldn't exist. After all, Shakespeare and Dickens were popular culture in their day. It's those of us in later generations who have canonized them.

But Morrison writes for everyone—I think that's a great compliment. I don't think she's interested in exclusivity; her ideas, her messages are far too important to be aimed at a select few. It's not a good idea to assume that excellence is associated with only one social class or with one type of art. To our deep enjoyment and great benefit, it can surface anywhere.

Q: You say when you *were* writing about Toni Morrison. Don't you continue to do so?

I haven't in a long time. She doesn't need me any longer. I like writing about authors who are underrecognized or who are at the beginning of their careers. That certainly wasn't true of Ross Macdonald or Daphne du Maurier, of course, but those were assignments someone else dreamed up. (And pleased I was that they dreamed those dreams!) But it was the case with people like Ruth Rendell and P. D. James—those interviews and articles came very early in their careers.

I really like the idea of paying attention where it is deserved rather than where it's popular to pay it. And I guess I like the gamble, also. For the most part, I've been lucky; most of the writers I've invested my energy in have become well known. But even if they haven't, they still, in my judgment, deserved the attention I paid.

Q: Can you give some examples?

Yes. Lucille Kallen did a short series of very funny, very perceptive mysteries and then stopped publishing as far as I know . . . She captured the flavor of small town life handily, I thought, and developed character very well. Earlier, Suzanne Blanc wrote a brief series of mysteries set in Mexico whose protagonist was a Native American. She was addressing very unfashionable issues and doing it well. Both writers were worthy of attention. In my view, both were successful, but the public just didn't give them enough attention—not an uncommon situation, I'm afraid.

That's one of the great benefits of the Popular Culture Association. It trusts its members to do quality work about quality subjects whether they are widely known or not.

Q: Talk a bit about the Popular Culture Association and your activities in it.

It's been one of the great joys of my life. Actually, I'm beginning to suspect that the PCA owes a debt to William Faulkner!

Q: Oh? How so?

Well, I wrote the chapter about George N. Dove for this book, and when I interviewed him, he said that when he found that half the world was writing about Faulkner, he looked around for other avenues of research and found the Popular Culture Association—to our very great benefit, I might say!

Much the same thing happened to me. I submitted an article about Faulkner to a widely praised journal, and they rejected it, saying that they got bundles of Faulkner criticism and that since I wrote reasonably well, I should find another author to write about.

So, I fired off an article about May Sarton which they returned, suggesting scathingly that I write about someone worthy of being written about. I took offense. Sarton *was* worth writing about, and the article did get published elsewhere. But those little exchanges prompted me to look around a bit, and I found the Popular Culture Association.

And to my great good fortune, I also found the Mystery and Detection Area. I've given papers in a variety of areas within PCA, but the Mystery and Detection Area is home. All this changed my life.

Q: How so?

It gave me a forum, a place to present scholarship among peers who not only understood but also appreciated what I was trying to do. And that was to call attention to a form which had been much misunderstood and largely overlooked by the literary establishment. It also meant that I could give papers which discussed writers who weren't yet widely known or who had been overlooked and be assured of an audience which might not agree with me but would give me—and more importantly my subject-authors—a fair hearing.

Actually, one of the great side benefits of going to regional and national meetings was coming away with a list of potential good reading based upon papers others had given—that led, by the way, to one of the great pleasures of the national meetings.

Some years back, I suggested that we offer a session called "Read Any Good Books Lately?" We meet at noon—some people eat their lunches at the sessions and everyone takes notes like mad. We just mention authors and titles and give very brief comments about the books' or writers' strengths—anyone who tries to tell too much plot gets quashed; we don't want the suspense spoiled! Someone takes notes formally and the following year brings a handout listing everything and everyone mentioned. Recently, Paula Woods and Fred Isaac have chaired these very informal sessions, I think, and Natalie Kaufman has prepared the lists.

It's been great fun to share ideas so informally—we really *like* each other, you see—and I've noticed that after an author has been mentioned a couple of times, we begin hearing papers about him or her. The session apparently feeds our creative juices.

Q: So the PCA gives you fun and companionship?

And much more—travel, for example. I've gone to most of the international meetings and found them stimulating and informative as well. One of the side trips during a PCA meeting took me to Stonehenge, a spot I'd wanted to visit for at least fifty years—and the spot where for the first time in my life I was called upon to identify myself as a pensioner! Well—that was important; it made a difference in the fees!

Seriously, though, the primary value has been the opportunity to present good scholarship in a nurturing atmosphere. Having the opportunity to explore a newly opening field of inquiry means that there are endless possibilities. Endless possibilities mean that petty competitiveness is pretty well obviated. That's been very important to me. This doesn't mean, however, that second rate work is acceptable. It isn't—anyone presenting it either learns better very quickly or turns to something else.

And there's another very important value to all this, I've found. When a scholar gets out on the circuit, reads her papers to informed audiences, and gets their feedback and support, it puts her own campus in perspective. One has a larger professional life that's demanding but provides direct contact with others, unlike publishing which offers different gratifications. Local campus politics don't seem quite so important in this larger context. PCA and other meetings put them into proper focus.

Q: What's the source of all collegiality in the mystery/detection caucus?

I've thought about that a great deal. One vastly important factor is, I believe, the openness and inventiveness of Pat and Ray Browne. Not to mention the enormous amount of work they've invested in the organization and, thus, in many of us as individuals. I owe them a lot. Actually, every academic who currently publishes in the field of crime fiction criticism owes them a lot.

Another thing is the genuine decency of some of the pioneers—both Earl J. Bargainnier and George Dove, for instance, have influenced me greatly. Like Pat and Ray, they were open to new ideas and to new people.

Between them, Earl and Pat invented what has become a series of essay collections out of the Popular Press. Earl edited *Ten Women of Mystery* which was followed by my own *And Then There Were Nine . . . More Women of Mystery* at his suggestion. Since then, there's been a steady flow of essay collections organized in various ways . . . Mary Jean DeMarr's *In the Beginning,* for instance, deals with authors' first works and the relationship of those works to the rest of the writers' work. Currently, Natalie Havener Kaufman and I are editing a two-volume study of contemporary women in the workplace as depicted by crime writers; these are also essay collections, and we hope that the Popular Press will publish them. Between *Ten Women* and *Hang on to Your Day Job* (our working title), have come perhaps a dozen other titles. These volumes are important for their seriousness of purpose and their sound quality. I'm proud to have been involved with so many of them.

Q: So, your activities in popular culture scholarship have included conducting and publishing interviews and being active in the Mystery/Detection Caucus of PCA. Have you done much reviewing?

Well, it seems to me that I have, but, you know, you can always find someone who has done more! I've written reviews for *The Armchair Detective* and *The MYSTERY FANcier* during its colorful existence. For a number of years, I did a column of mystery reviews for *Belles Lettres*. That column was called "The Criminal Element" and now appears from time to time in Pat Browne's scholarly journal, *Clues,* which comes from the Popular Press. *Belles Lettres* reviewed only books by women, but now the column focuses on British mysteries—and I like writing about books by both men and women.

Q: Are you a tough reviewer?

Yes, unquestionably. But you can't necessarily tell that by reading the reviews; in fact years ago, a letter to the editor in *The Armchair Detective* accused me of never *not* liking a mystery. Actually, I dislike plenty of them, but I don't see the point in giving print space or air time to bad books. I think it's vastly more important to give exposure to good material.

Q: What qualities do you demand in a book you consider to be good.

Well, first of all, not every book worth a good review is excellent in every way—that goes without saying, or should. Well, I look for graceful writing, for an appreciation for the language. Now, that doesn't mean fancy or unduly elevated language. It means language which suits the book's locale and its characters whether the setting be Cleveland, Ohio, or Kingsmarkham, Sussex.

I think that I demand seriousness of purpose; I appreciate an author's consideration of an important social question. This can be a huge issue such as child abuse or environmental concerns but it can be treated in a small or intimate way so as to suggest the importance of the great issues to all our individual lives. The issue can also be more parochial, such as the tight housing situation in London which figures in several of Ruth Rendell's novels, for instance.

Vivid settings are important. They needn't be exotic—I really do relish Les Roberts' celebration of Cleveland because I, too, grew up in what became the Rust Belt. I appreciate Cleveland's pulling itself together, and I mourn the decline of my town, Gary, Indiana. On the other hand, Dana Stabenow's portraits of the Alaskan wilderness or Tony Hillerman's depictions of the Southwest are thrilling because they take me outside myself and my own experience. I really value that when its persuasively done.

Q: Anything else?

Oh, of course—I like learning details of various jobs, for instance. Though I never plan to become a cabby, I like learning about how to do it from reading Carlotta Carlyle's adventures. And I like to laugh. I like humor. It's good to have fun amid the murder and mayhem—hanging out with Smith and Wesson, Annette Myers' continuing characters, provides both these qualities. I learn about being a Wall Street headhunter, and I laugh at Wesson's sharp wit (and sharp tongue). Those novels, by the way, make some wonderful observations about friendships with nary a preachy word in the series to date. Quite an accomplishment.

Q: You mentioned giving air time as well as print space to good writing. What did you mean by that?

For almost five years, I presented book reviews in weekly segments on WBAK-TV, now the Fox outlet in the Wabash Valley. That project covered a wide range of books. Some were mysteries, but most were not—they included cooking and gardening books, children's books, biography and autobiography, and a wide range of novels. I really enjoyed that and regretted the station's dropping their public service segments.

Q: What are your faults as a reviewer?

Well, sometimes, I suppose, I miss the point of a book when narrowness of vision or lack of experience limits my understanding. That's the big danger for all reviewers. And I do indulge one bias. I just won't work on a book that wallows in graphic violence, especially against women and children. We live in a violent culture, and crime fiction treats (and sometimes exploits) that violence, but the subject can be treated without reveling in it, and as a reviewer and as a literary critic, I demand that.

Q: What would you like to say that I haven't asked?

I always ask that question! Well, during my professional life, three great developments have enriched literary studies: the rise of women's studies, the attention being paid to African-American literature, and the development of popular culture studies as a discipline.

I feel so fortunate to have been a part of all of those movements, all within the Popular Culture Association as well as within other organizations. The Women's Caucus of the PCA (like the mystery/detection gang) has offered me opportunities for scholarship, personal support, and wonderful friendships. I think its vigor has been a key contribution to the overall strength of the PCA, and I'm proud of that sector as I am of the entire organization.

Note

Jane Schnabel Bakerman was born in Gary, Indiana, July 4, 1931; in 1971, she married Theodore Bakerman (d. 1995). She holds degrees from Hanover College and the University of Illinois and has taught in the public schools in Gary, Indiana, as well as in the English departments at West Virginia Wesleyan College and Indiana State University. Now Professor Emerita of English at Indiana State, where she served as the first coordinator of the Women's Studies Minor, she lives and writes in Terre Haute, Indiana. Bakerman was honored by the Mystery/Detection Area of the Popular Culture Association with the Dove Award for Contributions to the Scholarly Study of Crime Fiction, and the PCA Women's Caucus established the annual Jane Bakerman Award for the best feminist article published during the previous year. She is a founding member of the National Women's Studies Association and of Sisters in Crime and has also been active in the Midwest Popular Culture Association, American Association of University Professors, the Modern Language Association, the Midwest Modern Language Association, and the Society for the Study of Midwestern Literature.

Carl Bode

CARL BODE:
GENTLEMAN CANON BREAKER

Ray B. Browne

Carl Bode was the exceptional academic in being able to work with people of all backgrounds and interests, both academics and non-academics, and to dignify all with his presence. He was the born Jeffersonian democrat. From birth he stepped forth with the proper genes for popular culture studies, for he was always interested in everyday culture. But he was also interested in what he recognized some people saw as elite culture, though he tended to make exclusives inclusive, in other words to make Sunday ideas of best intentions and pretensions and behavior the actions and attitudes of everyday life. His two embodiments of proper Americans, as we shall see and understand, were Henry David Thoreau and H. L. Hencken.

Carl graduated from the University of Chicago (1933) and started teaching English at the Milwaukee Vocational School (1933-37). Methods of teaching English intrigued him. While teaching high school he managed to publish three articles and to write two more. These articles in many ways span his many approaches to and attitudes on high school education. In one article he was the bystander ("The H[igh] S[chool] Debate as Seen by a Bystander" [*Wisconsin Journal of Education*, December 1936]), in another he was seeking special help for the superior student ("Special Help for the Better Student" [*Bulletin of the Department of Secondary Education of the National Education Association*, January 1937]), in another using popular song lyrics to teach versifying ("A Popular-song Path to Verse Technique" [*The English Journal*, October 1937]). In another article he was concerned with the teacher as politician, a matter that preoccupied him through life ("The Teacher as Politician" [*School and Society*, December 1937]).[1]

The other two articles he wrote during these years which were published after he left high school teaching had to do with the domineering advisor ("Penance for a Problem Case: The Dominating Advisor" [*Wisconsin Journal of Education*, January 1938]), and Justice Oliver Wendell Holmes and the student council ("Justice Holmes and the Student Council" [*High School Journal*, May 1942]). After leaving high school teaching he kept his interest by working on an annual bibliography of articles, pamphlets and books on the teaching of high school English. His article on popular music was the sounding note of his interest in popular culture.

In 1941 Carl took his Ph.D. at Northwestern University, being fortunate to be the first Ph.D. graduate of Leon Howard, who always felt special interest in him and whose interests were always sufficiently catholic to allow him to nurture any and all interests. After graduation he taught at Keuka College (1941-44), served in the U.S. Army for eighteen months, taught at California Institute of Technology (1945-46), UCLA (1946-47), and the University of Maryland (1947-1982), emeritus, (1982-93). While at Maryland he headed the American Civilization Program 1950-57.

This American Civilization Program reflected Carl's burning intellectual interest, though he could never shape it into the courses and faculty he wanted. As we have seen, from his earlier efforts he had been interested in society's total culture, everyday and Sunday, worker's and patrician's, popular and elite. In 1949 he took the lead in founding the American Studies Association, a group of professors who knew that the study of America had to include more than its literature, philosophy and politics. Carl served as the ASA's first president (1952). In 1949 he took the lead in founding the *American Quarterly*, a publication that was to transform study of America. From the first it laid out goals and methods:

The goal was to "attempt to find the common area of interest in which specialists of various kinds and the aware reader may meet. It will publish articles of a speculative, critical and informative nature which will assist in giving a sense of direction to studies of the culture of America, past and present." (*American Quarterly* 1.1)

There had been a rift in the concept of means at the formation of the American Studies Association. Robert Spiller led a group of traditionalists who insisted that the ASA become a conventional scholarly group, merely changing their objectives. Carl, on the other hand, wanted a group who would not be "a professors' club but something wider." Carl's vision lost, and throughout his career Carl felt somewhat betrayed and quite dissatisfied with the group.

During these early years he continued working on Henry David Thoreau, one of his earliest and truest loves. In 1943 he edited Thoreau's poems, and issued an enlarged edition in 1964, with the *Portable Thoreau* (1947, revised edition 1964), selected journals of HDT, 1967 and the "best" of Thoreau's journals in 1971. During these years he also published his *Ralph Waldo Emerson, a Profile* (1969).

But from the first, as he said, "to avoid concentrating too much on one period and one person," he turned to the American popular novel. Specifically he finished "an article for one of the quarterlies on the ideas in the novel of Peter B. Kyne" (1880-1957), author of twenty-eight books on various kinds of young adventurers and their exploits, a piece which if ever published is not available. And he planned to study the novels of Lloyd C. Douglas (a study that was not to be finished and published until 1965, in *The Half-World of American Culture*).

Ever prolific, Carl started intellectualizing and analyzing various aspects of American culture. First it was the American Lyceum (1956), a study of America's intellectual leaders to spread learning through the country. Then Carl got down to the bedrock of his interests in American society, in *The Anatomy of Popular Culture 1840-1861,* with generally a comprehensive coverage of the subject. He wanted his study "To paint, in a panoramic fashion, a picture of our popular fine arts of the 1840s and 1850s in all their unexpected richness . . . and to suggest how the American character may have revealed itself through its cultural preferences" (ix). He included such unusual topics as love, aggressiveness, religion and architecture, fine arts and communication among the popular arts. But he was not satisfied with the book, and he republished it in 1970 with what he considered a more appropriate title. In his earlier study he had assumed that there was a fault line between elite culture and popular culture but by 1970 he had seen that his earlier title, "clumsy though exact," did not quite picture the culture he wanted pictured, so he changed the name to *Antebellum Culture* (1970).

In the 1950s, and thereafter, Carl had built a reputation, was aware of and much pleased with his assumed power. Having formed the American Studies Association and served as its first president and having friends in powerful places in government he could get almost anything he went after. For example, he was a Ford Foundation Fellow (1952-53), Newberry Library Fellow (1954), Guggenheim Foundation Fellow (1954-55), and honorary Fellow of the Royal Social Literature, United Kingdom. But he used his prestige sparingly. Once when I felt he might effectively apply pressure to get something that he and I wanted done, I suggested that he lean on the powers. But Carl demurred. He cautioned: "Ray, let me tell you a fact of life. The only way to have power is never to use it." At times, of course, he contradicted his own philosophy. But usually quietly and if possible indirectly. On many occasions I have seen him sit through lengthy discussions of topics and at the end suggest a way that might effect the desired results, and usually carry the day.

On other occasions I have seen him uninterested. Two examples. During the many years that I was associated with him, Carl was an active member of the American Council of Learned Societies. For some years I thought that the Popular Culture Association might profit from being a member of that learned group. On several occasions I suggested to Carl that he sound out the executives and see if we should apply for membership. On every occasion Carl cautioned me: "Not quite yet. Let's wait awhile so we can be sure to get in when we apply." He never brought the subject up to the ACLS, and apparently was wrong. In the last few years I have received several requests for the PCA to join the ACLS and on occasion have been tempted, though to date have never acted on the invitation.

On another occasion I found Carl's lack of enthusiasm for one of my suggestions startling. For years Russel Nye and I had been talking about the many academics around who for one reason or another—personal or professional—would not join the Popular Culture Association though their interests and activities paralleled those of the members of our association. Russ and I knew that there is much in a name, especially among academics, and if we could somehow dignify or decontaminate the word *popular* in our organization we could attract those people. Russ, Marshall Fishwick and I had for years toyed with alternate names, only to come up with no suitable substitute. Besides we knew we were gradually winning the war by attrition, and we probably should remain true to our principals.

But without selling our principals for the porridge of acceptability, I knew that somehow I could attract those people interested in American culture but not in working under the flag of *popular culture.*

So on a cold Sunday morning in February, 1978 I finally decided to act on my conviction that there should be a publication called *Journal of American Culture* and an organization named the American Culture Association to precisely fill the bill that would satisfy many academics. As usual I felt I would test my idea in the academic marketplace—that is, with my two associates who I knew would approve. First I called Russ Nye and explained my brainstorm. As usual he agreed it was a fine idea, giving his standard verbal stamp of approval: "Why not? Sounds like a good idea to me."

Next I called Carl, expecting an even more enthusiastic approval. I was therefore surprised at his negative reaction, not cautious but negative: "It's not a good idea," he said. "In fact it's a bad idea, the worst you've ever had. There is no need for such an association and you can't carry it off." Though I generally respected Carl's opinion I felt that in this case he was wrong. So with a two to one majority among my constituents—Nye and myself—I announced the creation of the American Culture Association and its publication, the *Journal of American Culture.* The ACA began with Russel Nye as president, me as editor of *JAC,* and both have succeeded.

It is hard to fathom Carl's opposition. He may have felt that the proposed ACA was too much like and therefore threatened the American Studies Association. More likely, perhaps, he may have reasoned that the PCA, influenced by the ACA, might slip back to being another ASA, thereby losing its edge and thrust.

The success of the ACA might have placed Carl in an awkward position. For years, as the ACA and *JAC* grew in importance Carl was silent on the subject. I said nothing, just letting things ride. Carl bided his time and on one public occasion gave his *mea culpa,* saying that he had been wrong in his assessment of the value of such a venture and I was to be congratulated for carrying out and developing it. As usual, he was unassuming in success and gracious in defeat.

On other occasions, when he knew he was right, Carl could be as cold and unrelenting as a glacier. Once, for example, when I had returned to the University of Maryland presumably to stay (1975-76) he and I decided that it was time to go to the National Endowment for the Humanities in order to get some financial help that he and I knew was being lavished on the American Studies Association by the NEH and the United States Information Agency. We called the office of the NEH and made an appointment. When we got to Washington, the Chairman of the NEH, former speech writer for Spiro Agnew, Ronald Berman, met with us to inquire what our purpose was, then told us that he and the NEH did not have time to talk with us, as he was against all we stood for. Carl turned to fire and ice and said, "Look, you may think that you are a person of strength here, but we pay your salary and support the NEH. You will talk to us." We then stepped out and demanded that the secretary schedule an appointment, and we came back for that confrontational hour. Of course we never got anything from that Chairman (and precious little ever from the NEH) but at least we had the pleasure of expressing our feelings.

Despite the cold rage against the Chairman of the NEH, generally Carl's behavior was impeccable. Perhaps the words of C. P. Snow, in his Preface to Carl's *Half-World of American Culture* (1965) best characterize Carl's personal relations to the public:

In this delicate act of presentation [of presenting America to the English] he was outstandingly successful, mainly by being integrally himself. English writers and painters found that he was wise, tolerant, and, in the best sense, very American. Long before this term of office [as Cultural Attaché] was over, people found him a friend who was like a rock in times of trouble. It is not usual for a Cultural Attaché to be called upon to solve people's personal difficulties; but Carl Bode took those on, along with his other duties, and when he left London he left a gap in our lives . . .

Bode is not easily frightened. He thinks it right—and this is very valuable—that popular literature should be examined, as well as fashionable academic topics. I have never read anything about Lloyd Douglas before, and very little about Erskine Caldwell. And yet, if we are going to understand our society, we are obliged to understand why certain books are read by millions. Quite unsnobbish, Bode applies himself as an open-minded student of our culture to matters which most of us are too genteel to touch. We all ought to wish that there were more like him.

A further example of how successful Carl could be with indifferent or hostile bureaucracies was his success with the Maryland Arts Council (1971-79; Chairman 1972-76), and the Maryland Humanities Council (1981-90; Chairman 1984-86). When he joined those groups I expected that his persuasive personality would effect changes in philosophy in a way that I, as a member of the Ohio Humanities Council for two terms, had never been able to do. As usual, I leaned on him to create a revolution. He fought me off and said that he was being effective, especially in getting funding for projects of local significance. I am sure his were fruitful years for himself and the two Councils.

On other projects he did lean heavily though graciously. One success that Carl valued highly was getting the Cosmos Club in Washington to change its policy and admit women as members. When he joined the club, it must have been for mixed reasons: meeting some of the most important people in the world; having a pleasant and convenient place to dine in Washington. But he obviously knew that the Cosmos Club did not admit women as members, and it is entirely possible that one major reason for joining was to correct that obvious injustice. Carl immediately started urging that the policy be changed. Twice he was rebuffed. In one of his newspaper columns called "Caverns for Caveman" (*Highly Irregular* 154) Carl once ironically wrote that the Metropolitan and Cosmos Club in Washington "have a sentimental value and I hope they stay. What if, sitting in their leather armchairs, the members look a little stiff?" But Carl kept on the subject until the policy was changed. "It was one of the most satisfying things I have done," he once said to me.

Personally, Carl was in the best sense of the word puritanical, or, if you like, spartan, always self controlled. I believe I never saw him drink alcohol or smoke. Milk was his favorite drink and ice cream his favorite dessert. On numerous occasions while I was on the University of Maryland campus and he was around he would call me at three in the afternoon and suggest that we go down to the University Dairy and have a dish of ice cream. It was always a pleasant thirty minutes of talk. Carl was not a person to spend time in idle chatter. Like Thoreau, Carl had no idle chit-chat in him. So though some of our lines of talk seemed irrelevant or without purpose they all pointed toward some goal. Like Thoreau, Carl considered time too valuable to waste.

He was also puritanical in his clothes, as well as his demeanor. Always physically slim, clean shaven, he always looked impeccable, no matter what kind of clothes he wore. He would bring dignity to a beggar's rags.

He would also bring dignity to a rebellious march on the streets; sometimes he might join in, as he did in marches in Washington during the rebellious sixties and seventies. He always assumed that rebellion, or at least the rebellious spirit, gave value and purpose to life. He was always therefore pleased when his daughters—Barbara, Janet and Carolyn, some or all—engaged in small or less small personal and political causes.

In the personal life I knew, Carl was always a loner, almost a Melville *isolato*, always carrying his Walden hut around with him in which to retreat for meditation. He gave of himself fully and freely during the daytime—the public hours—but liked his evenings free for his own life. In College Park this life often included some participation in public affairs but not activities in his home, not at least for his academic colleagues. I, for example, was in his home twice, once in one place while his first wife, Margaret Lutze, whom he married in 1938, was alive and once in his new home after he married Charlotte W. Smith, his second wife, a professor in the history department at the University of Maryland (1972).

Generally he lived his life as he pleased. For example, while I was on the faculty at Maryland in 1975 the novelist James M. Cain lived only a few blocks from the campus in Hyattsville. Carl had had Cain over to the campus to talk to his students. On one or two occasions when I suggested that I would like to meet Cain, Carl hinted that Cain was a retiring person but that we might get together sometime in the future. We never did.

Carl and I had an interesting association. I felt a special bond between him and me through our mutual graduate school advisor, Leon Howard. When we first met we seemed to hit it off. When I went to Maryland to join the faculty in 1957 we cemented our personal relations through our common interests. As the most powerful member of the

English Department, he told me many times that if I needed anything just to let him know.

Unfortunately for me, however, he went to London as Cultural Attaché almost immediately (1957-59) and was absent when I fell in bad with the Director of Composition and because of his blackball was fired. Too proud to ask Carl for help I tucked my tail and left. Since then Carl told me that had he known of my beheading he would have reversed the decision, since he felt that he and I were standing on a sufficiently large turtle to be able to support the whole world of popular culture studies.

Through the years, wherever I was, we cooperated on similar interests. When I no longer needed his help we remained close friends because of mutual respect and common interests. At times our association took curious, not to mention eccentric, turns. For example, at the annual PCA conferences Carl assumed that as Secretary-Treasurer it was my duty, or I would not mind, to take special care of him. At the second annual meeting, for instance, in Toledo, the first evening at 10:00 I had gone to my room in the hotel. He called and said: "Ray, I'm here. I don't have a room. What are you going to do?" To take care of what I assumed was an emergency I gave him my suite and drove the 20 miles to my home in Bowling Green. Thereafter for years Carl would not reserve a room in the convention hotel but would call on me to take care of him. So I always reserved one for him. He never acknowledged that this effort was perhaps beyond my obligations.

Through the years he supported me both publicly and privately. Though he always praised my work publicly, privately his support was even more complete. Once a month or thereabouts when we had not seen each other for a time, Carl would call me long distance to see what was new. Since generally there was nothing new, he would direct the conversation around to the importance of what I had done in creating the PCA and *JPC*. Academia, he would insist, owed much to me. The PCA had served American higher education well, etc. I was always embarrassed by these evidences of respect and tried to shift the conversation back to the great contribution he, and many of our fellow academics, had made. But he seemed single-minded. I never could decide whether Carl was feeling guilty over not being present to save my skin when I was fired at Maryland years ago or whether he felt remorseful over opposing the establishment of the ACA and *JAC* or whether he had other reasons. But there was never any doubt about his whole-hearted support from beginning to end.

One other sad final note on Carl's approval before we turn to a happier chain of events. When I retired from Bowling Green State University in 1992 Carl was coming to the retirement conference that was to last three days. As the occasion approached, his health became more and more precarious and he called several times to say that he was unwell but still hoped to come. Finally he called and said that he could not come but was sending a video tape to be played. The tape he sent was heartbreaking. Carl was obviously old and sick unto death, but still filled with appreciation for what I had done to develop the study of popular culture. His testimonial dampened the eyes and seared the heart of everyone present.

On a happier note, Carl always had a Puckish side to him. He admired the eccentric Thoreau and felt akin to *The Young Rebel in American Literature*, the name of one of his books (1959) and in life. For P. T. Barnum he had a special admiration. In editing *P. T. Barnum: Struggles and Triumphs* (1981) Carl had written in the Introduction ("Barnum Uncloaked") with obvious delight that "Barnum yearned to widen the world's eyes and bring a grin to the world's face" (10). Even more approvingly, Carl ended his Introduction with this quote and these words: "[Barnum] wanted to provide a quickener rather than a deadener for the American people. And he wanted his book to furnish a good example for them to use." He ended his preface to the 1869 and 1889 versions with:

If this record of trials and triumphs, struggles and successes, shall stimulate any to the exercise of that energy, industry, and courage in their callings, which will surely lead to happiness and prosperity, one main object I have in yielding to the solicitations of my friends and my publishers will have been accomplished." There was one added word in the 1889 versions. With a lovely and typical touch, he inserted *integrity* before *energy*. Integrity.

Like Barnum, Carl was capable of some straight-faced hoaxing himself, all for the betterment of scholars and scholarship. In the *Journal of Popular Culture* (5.1 [Summer 1971]) I had published as the lead article a bit of historical research—so-called—entitled "The Significance of 'Mother' Pillows in American History and Culture," by a graduate student, Lyell D. Henry, at the University of Iowa. Lyell had identified himself as a person whose "interest in American popular culture centers on its pathological aspects and derives in large part from a long standing addiction to the works of H. L. Mencken." Henry, giving the earliest date for "Mother" pillows as the War of 1812 suggested that other scholars should "be sufficiently persuaded of the cultural importance of such pillows to contribute new inputs to their study and to help bring into sharper focus their full significance in American history and culture." He buttressed his article with fulsome footnotes.

Carl, possibly excited by his and Henry's mutual interest in Mencken, responded in the next issue of *JPC* (5.2 [Fall 1971]) with a comment on Henry's article entitled "Fluffing the 'Mother' Pillow," in which he pointed out that he had recognized that Henry was a promising scholar since publication of his "pioneering survey 'Paintings on Velvet of Niagara Falls, 1620-1920.'" Calling Henry's article on "Mother" pillows seminal, Carl suggested its "only peril is that envious men will scheme to refute it." Carl himself, however, corrects Henry's dates. "'Mother' pillows *were* used before the War of 1812—I wonder what Mr. Henry thinks George Washington slept on." That was the end of the Great Mother Pillow Fight, and the beginning of the end of my being able to publish admitted hoaxes amid the forest of solemn scholarly articles.

But it was not the end of Carl's interest in Mencken. With an ever-rising preoccupation with the satirist-commentator and newspaper man, Carl published *Mencken* (1969), *The Young Mencken* (1973), *The New Mencken Letters* (1977), *The Editor, the Bluenose, and the Prostitute: H. L. Mencken's History of the "Hatrack" Censhorship Case* (1988), and founded and was the first president of the Mencken Society (1976-79). Interestingly Carl never asked me if I was interested in Mencken and never suggested that I join the Society. To him every person was captain of his or her own destiny. As he says in his poem "Remarks about Art: II," "the soul has only the soul to portray itself."

There is no doubt that Carl saw in Mencken a voice for an attitude about American society that he could not release in his own role as scholar. In his article "Fluffing the 'Mother' Pillow," Carl said that the realization that truth "doesn't always prevail" had driven him to coin "Bode's Third Law" which reads: "Error crushed to the Earth will rise again." This was one of Carl's oft-repeated witticisms; I've heard him say it a hundred times. He never mentioned that he had created it by turning on its head poet William Cullen Bryant's more positive poetic line: "Truth, crushed to earth, shall rise again." Mencken, like Carl, obviously felt that error always stands upright and like a weed cannot be kept down. Thus Carl's attraction to the Sage of Baltimore

Carl could also release some of his attitudes in the poetry that he published through the years in the poetry magazines such as *Accent, The Contemporary Review, The Poetry Review, The Prairie Schooner,* and *The Western Humanities Review* and were collected in three volumes, *The Sacred Seasons* (1953), *The Man Behind You* (1960), and *Practical Magic* (1981). Though they have the distant smell of the library, the poems are frank, direct, a little naive, and honest. They cover all kinds of subjects. Surprisingly, perhaps, there are many poems about historical subjects: Guy Fawkes Day, Milton, many about the Biblical saints and seasons, several about London landmarks (written while he was living in London as Cultural Attaché), about nature, and, of course about personal relations. There are poems about love, the difficulty of achieving and keeping it. Throughout there seems to be a melancholy about life, about resignation ("By God I hate to grow old," he says in "Covent Garden Market"). It is easy to think that perhaps the basic Carl spoke clearest in his poem "The Good Earth":

> He lies who says there are no saints on earth—
> Lies or as blind or ignorant as a beast.
> But who proclaims the cross? As best
> The scrawny bigot
> Rooting the red clay for his saving.
>
> The rushing April rain washes over the red
> Clay hills and floods all greenery
> Away, leaving the ugly farms
> Sterile and the one
> Dirty town naked with animals
>
> Yet there are a few saints. I even know
> More than one. But most are sows
> Defending—or devouring—what we
> Beget; malicious hens;
> Dogs mounting
> Each other at the street corner;
>
> Celebrating spring on red mud farms or muddy
> Streets. Lord Jesus, what is there,
> What can you see in most of us
> To make us
> Worth the saving?
> (*The Man Behind You*)

The grimness in some of the poems was considerably lightened in the pieces which, following Mencken in the newspaper business, Carl took to contributing to, first the *Washington Post* and, for a longer time, the *Baltimore Evening Sun*. Carl took the foibles of humankind as his subject, and approached them with Menkenesque twists though without the sharp teeth of the bitter satirist. In his *Mencken* (1969), Carl said that "It is Mencken the writer who has the chief claim on our curiosity. His style was one of the striking creations of his era, far more dynamic than his solidly conservative ideas. His genius for seizing the unexpected and amusing word, for making the irreverent comparison, and for creating a tone that was not acid but alkaline helped to make him the most readable of American essayists" (4). Carl also points out that from 1910 to 1917 Mencken "led the guerrilla warfare in this country against cultural conservatism, especially Puritanism, its most stubborn form" (5). It is these two characteristics—style and rebelliousness—that undoubtedly led Carl to admire Mencken even to the point of making him a cult hero. I often talked with Carl about his Mencken Society and found him freely and open-facedly serious and amused, or more properly, amusedly serious about his interest in Mencken. To Carl writing occasional essays for these two important papers must have seemed the goal for which he had spent a life in preparation. He could write on any subject he cared to choose, and write only when he chose. He chose to write one essay about every three weeks, and the subjects he picked were almost always, as he said, those that "nobody else writes about"—literally anything that sprang to mind and passed the test of interest and (un)importance: beauty queens, steam radio, tennis, White House sit-in, bathtubs, and gingersnaps, and on and on, plus an occasional direct appeal to Mencken to come back because he was sorely needed.

Carl was "attracted by two dizzingly different literary rebels, Henry David Thoreau and H. L. Mencken," and tried to merit their companionship. In many ways he succeeded though he could not be as firm as the former or as sharp-tongued as the latter. In truth, Carl was a moderate and sensible rebel who was, as he said, "fascinated by the popular culture of our time as it shifts or sashays around."

He did not merit the accusations thrown against him by one or two Maryland legislators who called Bode the most subversive professor on the University of Maryland campus. "Bode has tried to destroy any authority at the University," he said, a charge that Carl felt was unjustified. Carl would undoubtedly have liked to substitute for the legislative authority, for which he had little respect, that of a higher wisdom. In fact, among the many coats that Carl wore one of the most conspicuous was always that of peace-maker and compromiser; not selling out but achieving a desired end through compromise. An excellent example is the role he played at the formation of the Popular Culture Association at Toledo, Ohio, in 1969, at the national meeting of the American Studies Association.

There were two voices of dissension working in the American Studies Association at that meeting, the Radical Caucus and the Popular Culture Association. The Radical Caucus was led by half a dozen firebrands, like Betty Chmaj and Robert Sklar and Bob Merideth, who insisted that the ASA change to include blacks and women and that *American Quarterly*, the official ASA publication, be changed into "a vital vanguard journal," and other significant changes made in the American Studies Association. Carl, already having endorsed creation of the Popular Culture Association, moved back and forth between the official ASA and the Radical Caucus trying to get the two different points of view harmonized for the good of American Studies. Carl was disappointed when reason, as he saw it, failed to succeed.

But that whole business did not comprehend the full dimensions of Carl. Another side is illustrated by the subtle wisdom and wry humor in the dedication of the book *Highly Irregular: The Newspaper Columns of Carl Bode* (1974); "To John Anderson of the Washington *Post,* who started me on my downward way, and Bradford Jacobs of the Baltimore *Sun* who greased the slope." Carl was proud of those essays, and would clip nearly every one as it appeared and send it to me. The tone can be inferred from this introductory paragraph to "Steam Radio":

Steam radio is what the snide telly-boys at the BBC term the old-style radio which some of us have loved. They sneer usually out of ignorance though sometimes not. Yet it had its own absurd fascination. So cluster around your father, you rotten kids, while he tells you what steam radio was really like. (*Highly Irregular* 13)

Carl never stopped his effort to plumb the reality of American culture. When he was 79 he edited and published *American Perspectives* (1990), commissioned by the USIA in its Forum Reader Series. Carl's aim was twofold: "first to suggest what Americans have been like since the start of the century; and second, to suggest what Americans are like today." In his Preface, Carl pulls back from his earlier confidence about American popular and elite cultures being one. He accepts both high and popular culture but melds them into bourgeoisie culture, the middle class, "because the ideas and attitudes of the great majority of bourgeoisie remain the heart of American civilization" (2). In his collection of essays Carl pictures the range and dynamics of American culture.

C. P. Snow ended his Preface to *The Half-World of American Culture* with the words, "We all ought to wish that there were more like [Bode]." Indeed we should. Rebels with causes are always needed though seldom appreciated by the establishment. Like Daniel Boone, Carl Bode stood on the cultural Cumberland Gap and viewed a part of the real territory of American culture and recognized the attitude and tools needed to understand it. The general rebellion driving toward taking popular culture studies seriously was strengthened by his work. In the words of author Tom Wolfe, Carl had the right stuff. And he used it. Pioneers must not be forgotten.

Note

1. Interestingly Bode did not present his ideas in an intellectual vacuum. In the issue of *The English Journal* in which his article appeared there were five other discussions of popular culture and education. In "Literature and the Film" (1), Allardyce Nicholl, chairman of the Department of Drama at Yale, insisted that since film was becoming so important in culture, it is "patently exercising such a wide influence [and] demands that we attempt immediately to solve at least some of the questions in which it confronts us." Another, "Developing Discrimination with Regards to Radio" (120), argued for study of radio and the question, "What is this system doing to our boys and girls? What responsibility have we, as teachers, toward the 'radioizing' of youth?" Another, "Why Boys Read Newspapers" (195), suggests that the reading habits of teachers be ignored and instead study be made of what the students read and like. In another essay, "Community Resources in the English Class" (612), the author outlines the many places and activities used for instructional purposes in Detroit: "We have listed two hundred places in and about Detroit which are of special interest to boys and girls, including art centers, newspapers, libraries, historical museums, automobile factories, drug-manufacturing plants, banks, hospitals, parks, the telephone company, radio stations, theaters, and airports." Another, "Child Welfare and the Cinema" (698), urges understanding and use of the movie in education: "There is a danger that we may claim too much for the effect of the cinema. But there is a greater danger at the present time that we shall claim too little as the share of the cinema in this process of educating children (using education in the broader sense of the term)." Finally, in "The New Vogue of Historical Fiction" (775), Harlan Hatcher, professor of English at Ohio State University, examines older historical novels and new, insisting that the old are better.

The awareness of the importance of popular culture studies at this time and the subsequent and still on-going arguments over introducing such subjects into our school curricula reminds us of the academic and intellectual's fatal flaw: that of contentment with ignorance and half-knowledge. Our intellectual warehouses are filled with reinvented wheels long since discarded as superseded and useless. Yet we continue to study their physics and to polish them when such exercise is worse than useless. "A little knowledge is a dangerous thing," said Alexander Pope. Contentment with a little knowledge is even more dangerous. Academics need less arrogance in what they do know and more shame that they don't know.

Ray and Pat Browne

RAY AND PAT BROWNE:
SCHOLARS OF EVERYDAY CULTURE

Gary Hoppenstand

No two people have meant more to the study of popular culture than Ray and Pat Browne. Like careful, nurturing parents, they gave birth to the movement, lent direction to its development, created publications and an academic program to strengthen it, and after a long and arduous battle with those hostile to its growth, they brought it respectability. Ray and Pat Browne's great accomplishment is, in actuality, a story of many accomplishments. For example, they founded the *Journal of Popular Culture* in 1967, the Center for the Study of Popular Culture in 1968, the Bowling Green State University Popular Press in 1970, the Popular Culture Association in 1970, and the Department of Popular Culture at Bowling Green State University, the only one in the world, in 1972. In addition, they established the *Journal of American Culture* and the American Culture Association (both of which have been closely aligned with the popular culture movement) in 1978. Ray and Pat created the Popular Culture Library at Bowling Green State University in 1967 and have been contributing to it ever since, currently contributing some 50 to 100 books a week toward its development.

These many accomplishments were achieved after Ray and Pat Browne moved to Bowling Green State University in 1967, but Ray's larger mission—his drive to study and catalogue the everyday aspects of our life and culture—had been developing for many years in his own life.

Early Life
It is a truism that the most significant social movements in our society are often directed by significant people, as with Ray and Pat Browne. Ray's interest in the study of everyday culture resulted, in large part, from his upbringing. Who he became was due, in large measure, to who he was. He was born in Millport, Alabama, on January 15, 1922, to an upwardly mobile family. He was the youngest of four children, two girls and two boys, whose names are Lydia, Mevalene, Byron (named after the British poet), and Ray. His father was a banker who had moved to

Alabama from rural Kentucky in 1909 and who worked in a number of states in the South. Though Ray's father was from the South, he did not seem to be of the South. His attitude and philosophy about life, which had a tremendous influence on the young Ray Browne, was not consistent with that of many Southerners of that time and place. In 1909, for example, Ray's father (who was named Garfield after the 20th President of the United States), was "color blind" in his dealings with people, treating everyone he met, regardless of their ethnic background or skin color, with fairness and respect. Ray's mother, who was a devout Southern Baptist, also was not troubled by these concerns, trusting God to sort out such minor problems in Heaven. Ray's father was an agnostic, and he taught Ray to develop a critical view of the world and to question what may be all too obvious to others. Ray learned at a young age that things may not always be what they appear to be.

The stock market crash of 1929 reversed the tide of financial fortune for Ray's father. He was forced to move his family back to Millport, where they at least owned a home. Ray thus grew up in Millport during the 1930s which, in many ways, was a typical Depression-era Alabama town. It lacked many of the necessities of modern-day life (including running water and sewage), as did most communities of only 700 people in that region of the country at that time. In fact, the WPA project directed by the Roosevelt Administration provided or improved the infrastructure of most of these underdeveloped towns.

If he was not the Huck Finn of Millport, Ray was certainly the Tom Sawyer. He loved fishing and hunting, was an independent spirit, and often went against the grain of community expectations. His father serving as his role model, Ray became an independent thinker. He questioned those social conventions that defended the abuse of African-Americans, seeing in such behavior, exhibited by his childhood friends (and by their parents), a great injustice. Though surrounded by stark poverty, Ray knew that he could better his life through hard work and determination. He had the utmost respect for mental labor, as well as physical labor. Ray believed, as his father taught him, that if one possessed intelligence, then he or she should use it productively. Indeed, Ray's parents instilled in him an appreciation of both compassion *and* intelligence that, as an adult, he translated into good citizenship and a life of service. From his earliest memory, Ray was resolved to succeed in life.

Millport, at that time, was a typical small Southern town. Children—black and white—played baseball and football by themselves and with adults. Despite the fact that there was no town movie theater, films —mostly Westerns, starring such popular screen personalities as Tom

Mix, Hoot Gibson, George O'Brien, Bob Steele, and Ken Maynard—were frequently exhibited in a tent, which was filled with kids drenched in sweat from the hot Saturday afternoons. Sometimes the circus stopped in town, but more often traveling amusement groups entertained the local residents. Saturday afternoons and evenings also saw the performance of medicine shows with their hucksters offering prosaic entertainment and selling their snake-oil medicine. The only real medicinal quality of this concoction was its high alcoholic content, which made anyone who drank it feel "cured" for a brief period at least. Ray fondly remembers his mother, a teetotaler, feeling better after she took her "medicine" broth from the slick salesman.

Sometimes there were other less traditional forms of entertainment available. One Saturday, for example, a light one-motor two-seat airplane landed in a cotton field about a mile outside of town and, after paying the owner of the field for the destruction of his crop with a ten-minute flight, the pilot took other excited townsfolk for a ride at two dollars a trip, a large sum of money at that time which purchased the experience of a lifetime.

Less constructive activities sometimes occupied the thoughts and actions of the town's young people. On holidays and, occasionally, for no particular reason, the town's children enjoyed playing practical jokes, such as hoisting a wagon to the top of a building, placing someone's bicycle on the top of a pole, and soaping windows. Such excess energy and youthful enthusiasm were frequently punctuated by lengthy periods of philosophical speculation on the meaning of life. The popular spot for this deep contemplation (on issues ranging from the definitions of truth and beauty to the meaning of life) was the street curb, long after the town had shut down business for the day.

University Life

Following his graduation, he fortunately landed a job with the National Youth Administration at the University of Alabama that paid him 15¢ an hour. Using this income and all the money that his sister, Joan, could spare from her paycheck, Ray attended the University of Alabama, eating for 60¢ a day and renting a room for $4 a month.

At the university, Ray was profoundly influenced by one English teacher, William P. Fidler. Fidler had played football at Alabama with the star athlete, Johnny Mack Brown, and later earned his Ph.D. at the University of Chicago. Having just returned to Alabama as a faculty member, Fidler was a delightful and irreverent iconoclast who believed that no dean or university administrator was going to tell him how to teach or how to conduct his research. Leaving the University of

Alabama, Fidler moved to Washington, D.C., to become Secretary of the Association of American University Professors. When Fidler retired, Ray wrote him a brief note stating how much he had influenced his life, receiving a kind note of reply in return. Without a doubt, William Fidler exerted the strongest academic influence on Ray during his four years as an undergraduate at Alabama.

Following on the heels of Ray's university days came four years of service in the U.S. Army. When Ray was discharged from military duty, on his return trip home to Alabama from New Jersey, he saw firsthand how unevenly justice was administered in American society. His bus had stopped at the Greyhound station in Columbia, South Carolina at 7:00 in the morning during a torrential rain so that the passengers could disembark to eat breakfast. But not all of the passengers were allowed to enter the restaurant. A black soldier, still in uniform, had to eat his meal while standing in the rain. Other soldiers, white or otherwise, were, no doubt, perplexed and concerned over this harsh treatment of a veteran, and perhaps wondered if their own personal sacrifice for their country was undermined by what they had witnessed. Ray vowed that such prejudiced thinking and behavior must be eliminated. Like Abraham Lincoln—who while witnessing an act of injustice against a slave woman was quoted as saying, "When I can I'll do away with that"—Ray knew that he could never engage in such despicable behavior, nor live in a part of the country where such actions were tolerated, or even countenanced.

With the financial support of the GI Bill of Rights, Ray entered graduate school. In England, after the war, he attended one term each at the University of Birmingham, studying Shakespeare and early Greek philosophy, and Nottingham University, studying literature in general. Upon returning to the States, he was determined to continue his graduate studies and selected Columbia University in New York over his other preference, the University of Chicago, primarily because Chicago demanded a $35 fee to accompany the application and Ray did not have $35. Columbia did not ask for a fee.

Receiving his Master's degree from Columbia in 1947, Ray went on to teach at the University of Nebraska (earning $2400 a year), where his ever-present interest in the study of everyday culture was beginning to produce results. The University of Nebraska was the home of Louise Pound, a seasoned teacher and a widely respected folklorist. She had just retired when Ray arrived, but she was still professionally active. Her position at Nebraska was assumed by Lowry Wimberly, a folklorist who was editing the *Prairie Schooner*. Ray was fascinated with life on the prairie. Two areas of particular interest to him were the study of pioneer society and the study of several ethnic cultures that had settled in

Nebraska. He was especially impressed by the fact that around Lincoln there were lands that had never suffered the plow. Though the English Department where Ray worked was controlled by those whose primary interests were in literature, Ray found enough stimulation to develop his interests in culture—the everyday culture of people outside literature and elite culture.

In 1950 Ray and a friend traveled the West Coast, starting in Seattle. Their purpose was to review various universities for advanced graduate study. For his Ph.D. work, Ray selected UCLA, primarily because he was intrigued by the beauty of the UCLA Westwood campus, the proximity of the beach and the mountains, and the fact that everyday when he went to school he could walk through orange groves. In a number of ways Ray's choice was fortunate. Though the English Department at UCLA was encumbered with a number of conventional thinking scholars who felt somewhat inferior to the English faculty's reputation at Berkeley, it had as the head of its American literature program Leon Howard, as well as the star of the folklore program, Wayland Hand.

Ray desired to work in American Studies, which he felt would allow him the greatest freedom in studying everyday culture. Though UCLA did not have an American Studies program, Leon Howard insured that the Department allowed research which could be tied in with the folklore work of Wayland Hand (who was an internationally recognized folklorist), which could then result in a Ph.D. degree.

Ray discovered that association with these two mentors was fortunate in every way. Howard had just arrived at UCLA from Northwestern, where he had worked in American Studies. Though he had no experience in what Ray was calling "popular culture," Howard understood the concept of Ray's research and determined that he get the training he needed. When Ray informed Howard that he wanted to do his dissertation on the origin and dissemination of Alabama folksongs, Howard was most pleased, especially when told that Ray had collected folk versions of the Lord's Prayer.

Ray's association with Wayland Hand was a little different. Hand understood precisely when Ray explained his interest in studying Alabama folksongs. He assisted Ray by directing him to all the proper reference books, as well as assisting him with the various theories and methodologies of folkloring. But Hand never quite understood Ray when he told him that he wanted to explore the "folksongs and folklore of everyday America—Hollywood, New York, radio, and architecture," in other words the popular culture of everyday life. Even though Hand never fully comprehended Ray's scholarly interests, he tolerated Ray and respected what he was doing insofar as he could comprehend it. He did not understand, but he trusted. Sadly, just before Wayland Hand died in the Pittsburgh airport at the age of 80 while on his way to a folklore conference, Ray learned in a visit with Hand that he was still somewhat puzzled about the study of popular culture.

Scholarly Interests

As a Ph.D. student, Ray recognized the importance of scholarship and publication, so he directed his attention to these areas. Initially, he drew on his interest in the folklore of Alabama, where he had grown up. Folk expressions called orations fascinated Ray. These popular orations were used in school, were published in nineteenth-century textbooks, and were employed in what passed for "elocution," or getting students to stand before the class and make speeches. Thus, statements such as "I long to be a candidate for the next legislature and don't care who knows it," or "I was born long ago in an old log cabin that had no doors or walls and no place to cook," became standard bits of elocution and were disseminated into the folk culture. Ray was fascinated with the cultural use and permanence of such rituals.

He was also interested in the folklore of children's taunts and teases, in such sayings as "I'm a bug and you're a thug." In addition, Ray studied Negro folktales, the investigation of which brought an entire culture to life for the scholar. Some of this culture was a holdover from the days of slavery; the rest of it was of recent origin and was extremely promising. Ray felt that no history of Alabama, or of the U.S. itself, could be complete without an understanding of the contemporary expression of African American history and culture. His research in these areas was published in *Southern Folklore Quarterly* and *Western Folklore*.

Ray, however, was intrigued by the more conventional areas of scholarship too, especially John Milton and John Dryden. He was interested in how much the common culture of England remembered Milton's and Dryden's works. In 1958 he published an essay in the *Bulletin of Bibliography* entitled "Milton and Dryden in 19th Century Popular Songbooks." Yet, of the traditional authors Shakespeare was, of course, his greatest love. Ray was fascinated by how much Shakespeare's work had permeated the world, particularly American culture and specifically in popular songs. One essay, which grew out of a seminar paper of which Ray was especially proud, was "The Satiric Use of 'Popular Music' in *Love's Labour's Lost.*" As Ray remembers the incident surrounding his research in this area, the professor of his class, Tom Clark, was not overly impressed with the validity of the paper's argument, but felt that it otherwise had some merit. Ray's thesis was that in this play Shakespeare, involving himself in the famous Harvey-Nashe quarrel of the period, ridiculed Gabriel Harvey mercilessly. The journal, *Shakespeare Quarterly*, was not interested in the piece, but the essay finally found publication as the lead article in the September 1959 issue of the *Southern Folklore Quarterly*. The original critics of the paper may have been correct in their assessment for, to say the least, it never revolutionized the study of *Love's Labour's Lost* or the Harvey-Nashe quarrel.

Ray's continued interest in Shakespeare and culture did have a greater impact in the academic community, as evidenced by his growing list of publications. One 1957 essay, "Shakespeare in the 19th Century Popular Songbooks," which appeared in the *Shakespeare Quarterly*, was used as the foundation for several subsequent studies. Ray's "Shakespeare in American Vaudeville and Negro Minstrelsy," published in the Fall 1960 issue of *American Quarterly*, has been used as the basic scholarship in the fields of Shakespearean and American research ever since.

Early Professional Difficulties

Ray's academic career after graduation from UCLA in 1956 began, as he says, "with a bang and ended with a fizzle." Carl Bode, Leon Howard's first Ph.D. graduate at Northwestern University, was professor of English and American Studies at the University of Maryland, College Park. Ray wanted to come to Maryland, not only to work with Bode but also to be near the Library of Congress in Washington. Bode arranged to have Ray hired, and thus began a close association between these two scholars that lasted for some thirty years. Both were interested in the study of American culture and popular culture. Bode had published widely in both areas, and he thought he saw in Ray someone who would help develop an American Studies program at Maryland.

Such a plan would have likely turned into reality in the normal course of developments. However, at the beginning of Ray's second year at Maryland, Bode left to become Cultural Attaché at the American Embassy in London. In Bode's absence, Ray developed an adversarial relationship with the Director of Freshman Composition. The kindest thing that could be said about this relationship is that vinegar and gasoline do not mix, and the resulting explosion cost Ray dearly. When the question of tenure came up at the end of his third year, Ray was summoned to the Chairperson's office on a Friday afternoon and was informed that he was going to receive tenure. Subsequently, the following day Ray bought a house in the College Park neighborhood. On that Monday, he was again summoned to the Chairperson's office and told that the Friday decision had been revoked, that Ray had been denied tenure. The Director of Composition had vetoed the earlier decision.

Ray could have appealed to Carl Bode, who was in London at the time (and Bode frequently chastised Ray over the years of their association for not informing him of the denial of tenure, for he would have intervened and had the decision reversed). Instead, Ray, without a deep-felt bitterness, began searching for another position. Because of this episode, Ray has since often said that being fired is something that every academic needs as least once in his or her career, since it is a humbling experience that helps build character. Perhaps it is, but with his self-image somewhat wounded he obtained a position at Purdue University where, from 1960 to 1967, he enjoyed success with his developing career.

At Purdue, under the leadership and direction of Chairman Barris Mills, scholarship was highly valued, and there was tremendous interest in American Studies and in American literature studies. Ray continued his work in what could be loosely termed conventional American Studies, while he taught four classes a term (two of which generally met on Saturday morning). His main interests in American literature centered on Mark Twain and Herman Melville, research that was an extension of his work at both UCLA and the University of Maryland.

Melville and Twain Scholarship

His book-length study of Melville, entitled *Melville's Drive to Humanism* (1971), initially appeared as several papers as the book was developing. These essays addressed the question of how Melville's thinking fit into an evolving American democracy and how Melville's work reflected his commitment to that democracy. In his book Ray examined *Moby-Dick,* discussing the ways Melville had used the popular theater—burlesques, extravaganzas, farces, variety acts, curtain raisers, entr'actes, melodramas and Negro minstrelsy—as well as folk humor in this powerful novel. One of Ray's more compelling arguments about the relationship between popular and folk humor and *Moby-Dick* appears in the chapter entitled "Epilogue," in which Pip says "'Here's the ship's navel, this doubloon here, and they are all on fire to unscrew it. But, unscrew your navel, and what's the consequence?'" The consequence, according to the folk/popular theater joke of the day, is that if you unscrew your navel, your rear end will fall off. Yet, as Ray argues, from such a catastrophe (as Ishmael swirls toward the "button-like black bubble at the axis of that slowly wheeling circle"), he springs forth on the coffin that saved his life. Ray's conclusion thus states that Ishmael is "resurrected from the belly button of the world."

Ray's thesis about Melville's development of the common-man hero was further expanded in his paper, "Israel Potter: Metamorphosis of

Superman," which was published in the anthology *Frontiers of American Culture* (1968). Ray's argument in this essay points out that, while pondering the question of human liberty, Melville unites the superhero and common hero, transforming the former into the latter. As Ray states, "By the end of the book the superman of the beginning has disappeared and been replaced by the common man."

Of his various impressive studies of the works of Melville, however, the one that Ray is proudest of (and continues to think as one of his most searching essays), is *"Billy Budd:* Gospel of Democracy," which appeared in *Nineteenth-Century Fiction* (1963). Though most critics of the time saw Melville's short novel as a study in ambiguities, Ray, on the other hand, read it as a clear development of the conflict between authoritarianism and liberty, between the political ideologies of Edmund Burke (representing the conservative), and Tom Paine (speaking for freedom). During Melville's writing of his novel, the conflict between these points of view was problematic. According to Ray, Melville resolved this conflict in the ballad appended to the story, which describes (in what Melville called "popular verse") how the common people carry the burden and triumph of democracy and the rights of man. These essays (and others), collected and published in *Melville's Drive to Humanism,* reflect Ray's belief that Herman Melville was the American Shakespeare.

Another one of Ray's early and lasting scholarly subjects was Mark Twain, which was possibly due, in part, to the similarity between their respective backgrounds. What is more likely, however, is that Ray's interest was based on what he perceived to be Twain's purpose and accomplishments in his writings. For example, Ray views the conclusion of Twain's *Huckleberry Finn* differently than do many critics. These critics argue that, at the end of the story, Huck heads west to escape civilization. Ray perceives a more immediate object of scorn in Huck's desire to get away from it all, to flee the civilization of St. Petersburg, and, more importantly, the company of Tom and Jim. Having achieved intellectual freedom, Ray maintains, Huck could exercise his physical freedom and continue his intellectual and moral growth. "He can be true to himself," Ray concludes, "because there is no reason to be false to himself in order to be true to society."

Another subject in Twain's works that has intrigued Ray over the years is Twain's quarrel with Heaven, and with the man who, if he did not inspire that quarrel, at least fed it, Captain Wakeman. Ray published a full profile of Wakeman in an article that he wrote for *American Literature,* entitled "Mark Twain and Captain Wakeman" (1961). Ray's keen interest in Twain's Captain Stormfield developed while browsing through the stacks of the Library of Congress. Ray had uncovered an anecdote in the book, *Old Abe's Jokes: Fresh from Abraham's Bosom. Containing all his issues, excepting the "greenbacks"* (dated 1864), which appeared in a two-page story called "Old Abe's Slap at Chicago." In this story, a man from Chicago died, went to heaven, and tried to gain admission. St. Peter questioned the man, asking where he had expired. "I died in Chicago, in Illinois," the dead man replied. Shaking his head, St. Peter stated "Chicago . . . there's no such place." Finally, the man is admitted to Heaven as "the first man who ever came here from that place." The similarity between this anecdote and Twain's "Captain Stormfield's Visit to Heaven" is so obvious that Ray deduced that Twain must have gotten his inspiration from "Old Abe's Slap at Chicago," or some version of it. Subsequent scholarship on the topic, especially by Howard Baetzhold, attempts to refute Ray's conclusions, but Ray continues to stands by his argument.

Vision of American Studies

While these scholarly initiatives at Purdue were maturing, Ray believed that too many important ideas were not being fully addressed in the study of American culture, especially in so-called American Studies, which mainly concentrated attention on a few, narrow dimensions of American civilization, rather than on the entire spectrum of the American experience. He believed that these omissions seriously weakened this field of study. He wanted American Studies to discuss and analyze all levels and all elements of our society. Having worked with the American Studies Association for years, Ray was afraid that the organization's officials, as well as the larger body of American Studies faculty, were somehow glued to the concept of myth and symbol (a concept that is not necessarily confining, but which can be when hammered into the pedagogical frame of "major themes and developments"), a methodology that he felt was quite restrictive. Having also worked for years in the American Folklore Society, Ray saw a similar problem in this organization in which conventional ways of looking at folklore were valued in such a way as to cut off new thinking and new ideas. Ray thought that these two disciplines—American Studies and American Folklore Studies—had much more in common than members of either group realized (and surely more than either group cared to admit). He felt that the respective faculty should be introduced to each other and encouraged to address the general topic of American culture.

To achieve this end, in the spring of 1965 Ray organized a Mid-American Conference on Literature, History, and Folklore that was held at Purdue. In a fashion not yet totally clear to Ray's co-hosts—Donald Winkelman and Allen Hayman—nor even to Ray himself, the conference's inclusion of such areas as American Studies, folklore, sociology, philosophy, and popular entertainment, represented for Ray what he was beginning to define as popular culture studies. Publication of the conference papers in the collection, *New Voices in American Studies* (1966), elicited at least one negative review in which the reviewer stated rather resentfully that there was "nothing new in these voices." The truth of the matter was that the disgruntled reviewer was looking at the anthology through short-sighted glasses.

Another conference was held at Purdue in 1967 that again focused on the question of what new theories and new methodologies should be used in a fully integrated study of American culture. The conference essays were collected in *Frontiers of American Culture* (1968), and this volume tended to define more clearly a direction that a number of scholars in American Studies felt needed to be pursued.

Following these successful efforts to expand the field of American Studies, Ray decided that it was time, in his words, "to get to the heart of the American Studies Association." At the first independent meeting of the ASA, which was held in Kansas City from October 26th through the 28th in 1967, Ray talked to Robert F. Lucid, Executive Secretary of the ASA, about holding the second meeting in Toledo, Ohio. This conference would be sponsored by Bowling Green State University, with the avowed purpose of establishing a Popular Culture Association. Lucid had attended the 1967 conference at Purdue and liked what he saw there. He fully agreed with Ray that a Popular Culture Association should be formed at the Toledo meeting. Thus, from the some 800 people who attended the Toledo American Studies Association conference, 200 attended a session that dealt with the creation of a Popular Culture Association. Though it was made perfectly clear at this formation meeting that the PCA was designed to supplement and augment the efforts of the ASA, there were many in the ASA who saw the PCA as a threat and acted belligerently against it. One of Ray's former colleagues at Purdue, for example, was infuriated when told that the PCA had been formed, because he viewed the upstart organization as a danger. He was correct in a sense, because the PCA was dangerous to the ASA.

Directions in Popular Culture Studies

Originally, membership in the PCA was about 40% ASA constituency and 30% English department constituency, with the remaining 30% comprised of academics scattered across the disciplines, from sociology and speech communication to music and home economics. This rate of dispersal remained fairly consistent throughout the first ten years of the Popular Culture Association's existence.

From its modest beginning of 200 members, the PCA has grown into a vibrant organization of 3500 scholars, and the national PCA meeting alone draws 1500-2000 participants annually. The existence of these impressive figures confirmed the belief of those who saw the PCA as filling a need that the ASA was unwilling or unable to meet. Initially, there was a great deal of so-called "bad blood" between the ASA and the PCA. And though there are still many current and ex-members of the ASA in the Popular Culture Association, negative attitudes concerning what the ASA was doing or not doing have dropped rather sharply in recent years, as the PCA confronts more important initiatives in its future.

But, during its first decade of existence, criticism of the Popular Culture Association, and the study of popular culture in general, was raucous and vitriolic. There were many academics who would not understand or tolerate the study of everyday culture. In a number of publications, including the *Journal of Popular Culture,* Ray defined the term "popular culture" as those elements in culture which are used everyday and by a majority of people. He suggested that, to the modern world, popular culture is the same thing as folk culture was to the pre-literate world. In today's society, Ray argues that some 80% of culture is popular, some 10% folk and some 10% elite. As an illustration of these percentages, he employs a drawing of the CBS eyeball to illustrate his point.

Ray thus contends that the 80% of a society's culture should be the object and subject of study and understanding. But such reasoning drew angry fire from many educators. The purpose of education, in their minds, was to separate the elite from the everyday and to elevate students from the level of the uneducated. The goal of the educated person, these teachers reasoned, was to be different from (and superior to) the uneducated. Ray discovered that there were many academics and media people who, ironically, having worked in their nation's popular culture, had otherwise felt that the academy had sunk to the pits in studying everyday culture. These individuals tendered many jokes about students getting degrees in comics, or about students wasting their time studying movies, or about students sinking so low as to take Disney seriously. Academics in such fields as sociology, communications, and theater and cinema (as it liked to be called) were contemptuous of popular culture studies, never realizing that popular culture, under whatever name it masqueraded, was precisely what they had majored in and worked in. Such academics, Ray felt, were trapped in the "heroic syndrome," or the belief that anything that "shimmered" was automatically and unquestionably important. These scholars would have felt that majoring in Anaximander and Anaxagoras was far more important than understanding the impact of U.S. movies on global cultures.

An important moment in the development of Ray's professional career occurred when he moved to Bowling Green State University in August of 1967, and, with the approval of the University's President, founded the *Journal of Popular Culture*. At least the importance of this move was recognized by the powers that be at Bowling Green. Within the next twelve months, the BGSU administration called upon Ray to discuss with the Board of Trustees his plans for the future development of "Popular Culture Studies" at the University. It was at this meeting that he outlined his plans for the "Center for the Study of Popular Culture," as well as several related initiatives.

The establishment of a program in the study of popular culture was radical, and the world took notice. He was first written up in the *Chicago Tribune,* and the reporter was surprised to discover that Ray did not look like a hippie, but instead like a "square" academic. As a result of that article and other journalistic reports published over the years, Ray appeared twice on the CBS Evening News. He also appeared on most television stations in the Northeast, twice on the *Phil Donahue Show,* and twice on *Geraldo*. Ray's interviews were featured in *Newsweek,* the *New York Times,* the *Wall Street Journal,* and *People,* as well as in most of the newspapers across the country. He has been interviewed by the international media, including the BBC News, Australian radio and New Zealand radio. He is still regarded as being the country's foremost authority on all aspects of popular culture. His two journals—the *Journal of Popular Culture* and the *Journal of American Culture*—are known worldwide.

Bowling Green Disappointments and Triumphs

During the early years, however, administrative approval of Ray's initiatives in popular culture studies did not carry much weight in the English Department. Ray had been hired to develop the folklore program that a folklorist named Donald Winkelman had begun. Ray viewed popular culture studies as precisely that, an updating of folklore studies. But the English Department did not agree with this interpretation. To them, folklore meant ballads and folksongs and folktales, not comic book heroes, rock 'n' roll, nor movie stars.

So, while Ray persisted in teaching popular culture as folklore and best-selling novels as contemporary literature, the clamor within the English Department became strident. Several charges were leveled against Ray by the department's more conventional faculty. They accused him of 1) wasting students' time by teaching them worthless material; 2) wasting the taxpayer's money; and 3) embarrassing the department by teaching non-canonical subjects. Ray did have a few supporters on his side, including Philip O'Connor (Head of the Creative Writing Program), Fred Eckman, John Gross (whose premature death from a stroke deprived Ray of a strong champion), Richard Carpenter (an influential member of the department), both Ralph Wolfe and Ed Daniels (who saw merit in new directions of scholarly study), and Stanley Coffman, Jr. (Chairperson of the English Department, whose elevation to Provost deprived Ray of an important voice in that unit). Unfortunately, the votes of these supporters counted for too little. Finally, the hue and cry against Ray in the English Department became so clamorous that the administration allowed him to create a Department of Popular Culture.

This resolution seemed to be, on the surface, an ideal one, but in academia (as in governments of all types) nothing is easy. One would think the creation of a new academic department could be accomplished with the stroke of a pen. However, when academics are asked about such an action, one invites a thousand strokes of the sword. The Dean of the College discussed the creation of a Popular Culture Department with the chairs of the other College departments for a year before getting the idea approved.

It is ironic that, many years later, when the study of popular culture has permeated all aspects of the humanities and social sciences, some of Ray's colleagues who formerly fought so hard against him now secretly admit that they were wrong in their earlier opposition, that they should have assisted the popular culture program rather than trying to kill it. Even though hindsight is always 20/20, it is not always purgative. Some of Ray's earlier detractors have never seen the errors of their way, or had the grace to admit their faults.

Though he bitterly resented his "retirement" in 1992, Ray has thought subsequently that perhaps the time was right for such a move. He had been Chairperson for 20 years, with some of his faculty being with him from the start. Perhaps Ray's opponents were tired of his liberal approach to the administration of the department. Perhaps they simply wanted a change in leadership. Whatever the cause, there was no doubt that the University's Administration wanted a change.

When he left the Department of Popular Culture, Ray says he experienced several feelings, and perhaps several regrets. After his retirement, he wanted an office outside the department, so that he would not be around to be tempted to offer advice; the faculty would rightfully resent this "ruling from off the bench," to use Ray's phrase. He was saddest about not having achieved a Ph.D. program in popular culture studies, a favored project that he had been working on for years.

Back in 1969 when Ray was still a member of the English Department at BGSU, he had been offering a Master's degree in popular culture studies and had graduated 100 students. As such, this program was quite successful, but Ray knew that no academic program can really succeed unless it is dignified by having a Ph.D. as its terminal degree. Hence, through the years he kept urging his colleagues to join him in proposing a Ph.D. in popular culture studies to the University's Administration.

In 1988, the proposal for the Ph.D. program was drawn up. Three distinguished scholars, John Cawelti, Neil Harris, and Lawrence Levine, came to the BGSU campus twice, finally approving the proposal. The Council of Deans of Ohio also approved the proposal, saying that it would add greatly to the academic offerings of Bowling Green. The Dean of the Graduate School concurred.

This approval, unfortunately, had arrived too late. The State of Ohio had just begun its cutback in the funding of higher education and declared that there would be no new Ph.D. programs created, which placed the proposal for a Ph.D. in popular culture studies at BGSU on hold. Initially, there was some hope that this proposal would be forwarded to Columbus "soon." In his history of the popular culture movement, entitled *Against Academia* (1988), Ray gave the proposal a 50/50 chance of success. He now admits that he was overly optimistic at this point and now believes that it never will be approved. In retrospect, Ray thinks that such a degree is no longer required, since scholars get their Ph.D.s in dozens of disciplines that study popular culture. But, by not attaining a specific Ph.D. in popular culture studies, this, in Ray's view, will surely change for the worse the course of the development of the field as an academic discipline.

The denial of the Ph.D. degree, however, was not a total loss. Throughout Ray's career at Bowling Green State University, the English Department allowed a concentration in popular culture within its own Ph.D. program, as did the American Culture program. In both, Ray directed the research and dissertation work of several dozen students. Other faculty members in the Department of Popular Culture have also directed dissertations in English, History, and Communications, among other academic areas. The Popular Culture program at BGSU has produced hundreds of Master's degrees granted to students who have gone on to work successfully in a variety of areas, from teaching, to the entertainment industry, to creative writing. The Department of Popular Culture has thus had an influence far greater than its relatively small size would seem to predict.

The Philosophy of Popular Culture Studies

To a certain extent, the problem in introducing popular culture studies to the academic community lay in designating everyday culture as popular culture. Carl Bode had published his *The Anatomy of Popular Culture 1840-1861* in 1959, but when his book was reprinted in 1970, he changed the title to *Antebellum Culture,* thinking this as being more appropriate. Ray insisted on keeping the term "popular culture" to describe the study of everyday culture, because one of his favorite authors, the seventeenth-century scholar Sir Thomas Browne (no ancestral connection) had used it in his magnificently baroque book, *Pseudodoxia Epidemica, or Enquiries into Very Many Received Tenents and Commonly Presumed Truths* (1646), which was otherwise usually entitled *Vulgar Errors.* Determined to examine and refute a number of errors then normally held, Thomas Browne studied such topics as mineral and vegetable bodies, animals, man, geography, history, illustrations, and many other subjects. As one noted authority said of the book, "[Thomas] Browne has here confuted dozens of false ideas which some educated persons have even today not thought of questioning."

Conversely, to certain academics of the late 1960s, anything having to do with the general public—the people—was by definition contemptible. The Americanists of this decade thought that Emerson, Thoreau, Eliot, and Hemingway were models of learning. But they forgot that Emerson (who was loved by those academics who did not have the imagination to advance beyond what they had been taught) counseled "A foolish consistency is the hobgoblin of little minds." Ray, in his dealings with academia in general and with Bowling Green State University in particular, was determined to use his training as a prelude to continued development. His thinking was that academics tie themselves to their learning and training, rather than using this education and knowledge as a springboard for leaping into the unknown. He still strongly believes that American students deserve a better education than they are receiving, and that improving education means having better educated (and better educating) instructors.

Having such a belief indicates that Ray was nothing if not self-confident. Indeed, when he arrived at BGSU, he felt his scholarly accomplishments were the equal of any of his colleagues in his new English Department (or anywhere, for that matter). He therefore was secure in his professional equality. In addition, Ray also thought he was strengthened by his vision and by the courage of his convictions. There may have been a tinge of arrogance in Ray's self-confidence; certainly there was courage. He was willing to gamble his present academic security, his reputation, and his future on what he felt should be done.

Nevertheless, very much aware of the ever-present hostility of academic criticism, Ray, along with Russel Nye, Carl Bode, Marshall Fishwick, John Cawelti (and others) worried many hours over what the Popular Culture Association should be named. They pondered the question: "Was there a term that meant 'everyday culture' that could be disguised, or rendered less inflammatory, than 'popular culture'?" No term or name was discoverable, so the organizers of the PCA let the term "popular culture" stand. By the time they could figure some way out of their dilemma, the term had ceased to be a pejorative expression, and thus there was no need to replace it. The designation of "popular culture" was left alone, and now has achieved for many scholars a new dignity and importance, as well as a better understanding.

Before the study of popular culture had become respectable, Ray realized, and felt keenly, the sharp edge of academic criticism directed at the Popular Culture Association. He knew that there were numerous academics throughout the land who wanted to study everyday culture, but who were reluctant—because of peer pressure or the disfavor of their superiors—to join the PCA. Ray wondered what might be done to improve this situation. As he remembers the moment, on a cold, snowy Sunday morning in February of 1978, he hit upon the idea of forming a parallel organization to the PCA, to be called the American Culture Association, which would be comprised of like-minded individuals who would not be encumbered with the heavy stigma of those who are interested in popular culture studies. The ACA, then, was designed for those persons who were interested in studying an aspect of American culture not generally covered by the American Studies Association, but who also wanted to be affiliated with a "more respectable" sounding name than the PCA.

Ray immediately contacted Russel Nye, who said (as he usually did), "Why not? Sounds like a good idea to me." Then Ray contacted Carl Bode, assuming that since Bode had been so enthusiastic about the PCA that he would also readily endorse the concept of the ACA. To Ray's surprise, Bode replied, "No. Never. That's the dumbest idea you've ever had, Ray." He was not discouraged, and with a 2/3 majority approval from the PCA membership, he immediately went ahead with the creation of the ACA, quickly establishing the *Journal of American Culture* to support the new organization. Ray swiftly worked out a rationale for the new Association and journal, one that supported the study of everyday American culture, both past and present, so although there was a philosophical basis for the new ACA, in reality its formation was political. The ACA was designed basically, in Ray's words, "to capture those people who, for one reason or another, did not want to be seen in the company of PCA scholars." Ray was pleased that his "ruse" worked. John Cawelti, for example, reported that one day he stepped into the hallway at the University of Chicago to be greeted by several of his colleagues in anthropology proclaiming in effect, "Glory be! Now there is an organization good enough for me to join!" Ray's conclusion to Cawelti's story: "If you can't hoist them on one petard, use another!"

Ray admits that the long-term success of the two organizations—the PCA and the ACA—was attributable in large measure to the fact that they both had successful, supporting publications. Because of his many years spent writing and publishing scholarly articles and because of his experience working with academic associations, Ray knew that the success of any new academic association was predicated on a solid publication outlet.

Luckily, the Popular Culture Association was able to build its foundation on a successful journal. While still at Purdue, Ray had been toying with the idea of developing a new type of scholarly journal, and when the opportunity presented itself for him to move to Bowling Green, he chose the *Journal of Popular Culture* as the name of this new scholarly periodical. Ray had no articles ready for publication. He did not even have a clear notion of what he wanted to publish or where to obtain his essays, but he was confident. During his six years at Purdue, Ray had often talked with Russel B. Nye, who frequently came down from Michigan State University to discuss with Ray the various aspects of the study of American culture. Nye's role had been significant in the two conferences Ray had organized at Purdue, and he and Ray had often talked about the need for a journal which would feature scholarship about everyday culture. When the job offer came from Bowling Green, Ray immediately went to BGSU's President, William T. Jerome, III, and asked for $4000 to establish a new journal. President Jerome approved the idea, and the money was granted. Incidentally, now long since retired from his post at BGSU, President Jerome recently said that Ray's $4000 was the most fruitful money he had ever invested.

With approval for his new journal in hand, Ray got to work locating articles to be published in the first issue. Essays for the *Journal of Popular Culture* were forthcoming from Russ Nye, as well as others who, upon being written to by Ray, wrote articles that fit the broad definition of popular culture studies. Concurrently, Ray (who was given a free hand in these matters) established a Center for the Study of Popular Culture (with a mission statement not yet finalized) and a supporting press called the Popular Press (which also had no mission statement, nor any manuscripts). Realizing the value of the *JPC* in furthering the cause of everyday scholarship, Ray then began publishing the *Journal of Ameri-*

can Culture, following his own plan that he earlier had established with the *JPC;* he solicited articles from people he knew.

Ray reports that the history of editing and publishing the *Journal of Popular Culture* is filled with amusing and enlightening anecdotes. From the start, being the only refereed journal of its type, the *JPC* both enjoyed and suffered from a mixed reception in the scholarly community. It commanded considerable respect, despite the fact that there was considerable suspicion of the field of popular culture studies itself (and of its publications). To appear in the *JPC* meant a great deal to its authors, because it allowed them to publish materials that otherwise would not see print. This success has translated into the number of submissions the *JPC* receives annually, which has been far more than it can possibly handle. Overall, the acceptance rate for articles submitted to the *JPC* has been less than 10%.

Academics, Ray notes, seem to assume a great deal regarding their scholarship. They think that because they have written an article the editor of a journal (and presumably the world) should be glad to have the chance to read it and publish it. When Ray has turned down articles, for one reason or another, he has received many irate letters and telephone calls accusing him of being a fool and guaranteeing him that he does not have the faintest idea what he is doing. Others have expressed additional complaints. After Ray had accepted a 40-page paper from a Canadian scholar at the University of Winnipeg and edited it to 25 pages, he received a blistering telephone call from the author saying that he would not accept the editing, and that, in fact, the article should be at least 20 pages longer! Ray has also had to deal with the problem of multiple submissions and publications. Once he published an article and within the week it also appeared in a Canadian journal.

Yet, by and large, *JPC* authors and would-be authors have cooperated. The *Journal of Popular Culture* has been responsible for many scholars from around the world (especially in the U.S.) obtaining promotion and tenure in numerous departments. Usually accompanying the submission of a paper is the statement, "If you will accept this article, I will get tenure with promotion." Of course, such tugs at Ray's heart have carried no weight; he, in fact, sees these remarks as a type of academic scam. Nevertheless, over the years Ray has been pleased to be asked to assess the academic worthiness of scholars who are up for promotion. And he has always taken these external reviews very seriously.

Pat

The story of Ray's academic career must pause for a moment, in order to recount the darkest time in his life. As a student at UCLA in

1952, he had married Olwyn Orde, who was also a student in English. During the happy years of their early academic careers and their time together, they had three sons: Glenn, Kevin, and Rowen. Olwyn was pregnant again when, during the Christmas holidays in 1965, the family was returning from visiting Ray's sister in Roanoke, Alabama. A fifteen-year-old, driving a stolen car on the highway just south of Huntsville, collided head-on with Ray's car. The resulting impact instantly killed Olwyn, Rowen, and the unborn baby. The accident devastated Ray. Weighed down by the loss of his wife and two children, but with his two young sons still requiring attention, when Ray was released from the hospital he dedicated himself, above all else, to raising his remaining children. Whatever time was left over he would devote to his career. Luckily, he was able to find time for the pursuit of that career.

Luckily, too, Ray was able to meet and marry the sister-in-law of one of his colleagues in the English Department at Purdue. Pat Alice Matthews, a Southern woman whose interests parallelled Ray's and whose energy was almost as unbounded as his own. Following their marriage in 1966, their two careers were almost inextricably intertwined with regards to the development of the PCA and ACA, the management of the two journals, the advancement of the Center for the Study of Popular Culture, and the Popular Press. Without Pat's support, Ray probably would not have dared so many ventures, nor succeeded in them. Often, Ray's and Pat's opinions conflicted on certain issues, with Pat observing that a number of Ray's ideas were too radical or advanced for the moment. However, when they decided to move forward on a venture, she gave it everything she had. For three years, Pat worked without pay for the two journals, and for one year she worked without pay for the Popular Press. One day, an enlightened administrator at BGSU, Sheldon Halpern, who was Ray's former colleague in the English Department and was then currently Assistant Provost, gave Pat a contract. Even though the financial terms of this contract were fairly meager, at least Pat's contributions were finally officially recognized. Her career since has been inseparable from Ray's.

As with Ray, Pat's numerous professional accomplishments have not been easy, since she has suffered from agonizing migraines for most of her life. Never knowing when one would strike, she and Ray always had to make two sets of arrangements for each occasion—one if things went right and another if Pat was stricken with a migraine attack. Because of these unpredictable attacks, Pat and Ray have visited some of the best and worst emergency rooms in the United States, as well as in foreign countries (such as Great Britain). Once she has recovered, though, Pat has dived right back into the fray of PCA/ACA business.

The team of Ray and Pat (which sounds something like a comedy act) over the years has worked well together. They are a pair dedicated to the same end. Pat, who is a realist and a skeptic, has acted well as a counterweight to Ray, who is a dreamer and a perpetual doer. When their opinions have conflicted, sometimes Pat is proven right in her negation, and sometimes Ray has the correct idea.

Journals and the Popular Press

Ray has always believed that if two journals are successful, then other new journals should also succeed. To this end, he has established several thriving new scholarly periodicals beyond *JPC* and *JAC*. Though Pat has felt that two are sufficient, she has supported Ray's initiatives and has even created her own journal. In 1980 she established *Clues: A Journal of Detection,* selecting this name because she wanted the publication to feature work on the art of detective fiction, not just crime fiction. *Clues* continues to flourish. In 1971 Ray and Pat's friend and colleague in BGSU's Department of Sociology, R. Serge Denisoff, established *Popular Music and Society* (which is now edited by Gary Burns at Northern Illinois University). In 1980 Alvar Carlson, Ray's and Pat's colleague in BGSU's Department of Geography, commenced his prestigious *Journal of Cultural Geography* (which is now edited by Lewis Seig at Oklahoma State University). And in 1974 Ray and Pat subsidized a new publication, the *Journal of Popular Film,* that was run by two of Ray's Ph.D. students; today, this periodical is called the *Journal of Popular Film and Television* and is published by Heldreth.

Ray discovered that the advantage to running a press is that you can start a new journal whenever you please. Thus, when Ray thought the occasion warranted a new journal, he created one. Through the years these have included the *Journal of Regional Cultures* (1981-84), the *Journal of Canadian Culture* (1984-85, working as editor with Russ Nye and a Canadian academic), and the *Journal of Popular Literature* (1985-91). All of these publications folded after a few years. Ray's conclusions drawn from this situation is that one person can only edit so many journals. Otherwise, these publications tend to lose their credibility. In addition, readers and institutions can only subscribe to just so many periodicals. Had there been time, Ray probably would have experimented with other new journals, and might have even established associations to support them, but even his tremendous levels of energy had some limits.

One of Ray's wildest ambitions regarding his work in scholarship was his *Abstracts of Popular Culture* (1977). It was his intent to abstract every article on popular culture ever published in the United States and the world and have these abstracts published quarterly, or monthly. His plan was to provide a general index to all the scholarship covering popular culture studies, so that academics around the world could keep up on the various topics of everyday culture. It was a noble ambition, and it could have succeeded if Ray's resources had been ten times as extensive as they were. After one year, he had to admit that this project was too big even for him, and *Abstracts* thus closed its last page.

Meanwhile, the Popular Press, despite these abortive drains on its resources, continued to flourish. Its first book publication was John Cawelti's *Six-Gun Mystique* (1970), a study that brought fame to its publisher and continues to remain one of its bestsellers. Now in its third printing, Cawelti's book continues its success into the twenty-first century. The Popular Press was initially confronted with a shortage of manuscripts and a lack of money, but as it had access to more and more top rate manuscripts (many of them setting the scholarly standards in their respective fields), the Press quickly became self-sufficient. Another book that followed the success of Cawelti's was Susan Cornillon-Koppelman's *Images of Women in Popular Literature* (1972), which was the first book published in women's studies and subsequently helped to define the area. This book, too, has brought acclaim to the Popular Press and demonstrated the Press' policy of being a trend-setter. From its inception, Ray served as the Director of the Press until his retirement. Pat is now Director and general factotum. In addition to publishing eight journals, the Press has averaged about 20 books a year, a commendable accomplishment.

It has not proven easy persuading academics to study popular culture, although nowadays many scholars in most humanities and social science disciplines are turning to it. Further, a glance at the publishing lists of the university presses and commercial houses will reveal that a significant portion of their catalogues consists of some type of popular culture study. Often, the words "popular culture" are in the title, though the subject may be otherwise obscure. When the Popular Press began its existence, it was quite alone. Soon, however, other presses followed Ray's and Pat's pioneering efforts, which has advanced the field in general.

While managing the journals and the Popular Press, Ray and Pat were also spending a great deal of their efforts running the Popular Culture Association and the American Culture Association. At the start, Russ Nye had consented to be the first President for a two-year term; he wanted, in Ray's words, "to set the right precedent." Ray opted for the Secretary-Treasurer position, so that he could remain in office for a longer period of time and see that the two organizations developed as they should. Whether that arrangement has been best for the association might be open to debate, but Ray has continued through the years in his capacity as Secretary-Treasurer of the PCA, with Pat doing much of the work as employee without portfolio. She has always managed the yearly program, and generally helped out in every way she could. Her experience and knowledge have been indispensable in the selection of the cities for the annual national meetings, the choice of the hotels, the design of the programs, and many other countless details. With a few notable exceptions, generally the yearly pick of city, hotel, and program has been quite successful.

Because of their enthusiastic support and development of the PCA and ACA over the years, at times Ray and Pat have seemed to neglect other areas of their life. Ray laughingly notes that he and Pat have often concluded that the cohesive force that has held their marriage together has not been personal love, not love of children, not love of marriage, but an obsession with the success of the PCA and ACA, as well as the journals into which they have poured so much of themselves. "The effort," Ray states, "was too important to let weaken or fail." In any event, Pat still discovered time to create and edit her *Clues: A Journal of Detection* and edit four books: *Heroines of Popular Culture* (1987), *Making the American Home* (1988), *Digging Into Popular Culture* (1991), and the monumental *Encyclopedia of United States Popular Culture,* now scheduled for publication in 1999.

The PCA and the ACA

Ray and Pat have been successful in maintaining the original philosophy of the PCA and ACA. From the beginning, the two associations have been run on the assumption that universal participation by all involved members would be beneficial in developing popular culture studies as an academic field and that the publication of articles in the journals would help to foster and disseminate knowledge. The founders of the PCA realized that faculty members from around the country (not just the "stars" or the privileged few) instruct our future leaders. Anything that can be done to increase their effectiveness should also result in better effectiveness in the classroom. In other words, the founders of the PCA felt that scholar-teachers are more effective than teachers who are not scholars. They believed that all instructors benefit from professional participation in scholarly conferences.

One of the major products of the national PCA and ACA has been the spawning of regional chapters. Ray has always dreamed of the time when every region would have a strong chapter that would serve scholars in that area and also serve as a recruiting device for the national meeting. In his more naive years, Ray thought of the possibility of there being representatives in every state and on every campus. The PCA/

ACA in the South has very successfully used State Representatives. But on the national level, these micromanagers have never materialized. The PCA/ACA in the South has always been the healthiest regarding its size and complexity. Stemming from this thriving organization is the notable journal, *Studies in Popular Culture,* now in its 18th year of publication and appearing quarterly.

In all, there now exist eight regional chapters of the PCA/ACA. Three of these chapters (the Far West, the Mid-Atlantic, and the Popular Culture Association in the South) have their own journals—the *Popular Culture Journal* (edited by Felicia Campbell), the *Mid-American Almanack* (edited by Margaret King), and *Studies in Popular Culture,* respectively. After years of unsuccessful effort, one new international chapter of the PCA/ACA—the Latin American Popular Culture Association—was formed in 1996 in Puebla, Mexico. To this day, Ray continues developing chapters throughout the world.

Although the study of popular culture is more prevalent in the United States than elsewhere, it has long been a staple in England, France, Italy, and (to a lesser extent) in other European countries. A few scholars have been working in the field in Australia and New Zealand, as well as several in South and Central America, and Mexico. Ray feels that there are more academics in these foreign countries who work in popular culture; they are just difficult to reach. He thinks that perhaps they are studying popular culture and calling it by a more conventional name, such as anthropology, sociology, religious studies, film studies, and so on.

Scholarly Pursuits

With his goal of encouraging participation by all, Ray has been blessed with an open and democratic mind. As he says, "I never met a subject that I did not like," and in his opinion, all subjects are worthy of consideration. If one were to title the philosophy behind his academic scrutiny, the name of this philosophy would most likely parallel the name of the NPR radio show, "All Things Considered." To that end of having all things considered, Ray has spent countless hours at PCA and ACA national and regional meetings listening to the research projects of hundreds of proposals. His attitude about scholarship reflected that of his friend, Russel Nye, whose favorite statement was "Why not?" when asked about the pursuit of knowledge in offbeat areas.

A great deal of the time, Ray's suggestions for topics of study in popular culture have met with success. But on one subject he has failed to get anyone's attention. When the eighth meeting of the PCA was held in Cincinnati in 1978, a reporter from *Newsweek* commented to Ray that with so many subjects being studied that he must be satisfied. Ray replied that even with some 200 topics under analysis, he still regretted not having anyone discuss wall coverings. To this day, Ray is disappointed that nobody seems to be interested in the social and cultural impact of wall coverings. A number of scholars, of course, recognize the importance of furniture, or architecture, or floor coverings, or pictures as art, but nobody recognizes the importance that wallpaper and objects on walls have on people's actions and attitudes. Shakespeare, for example, is full of references to walls and the things hanging on them, but scholars in literature and the humanities, Ray feels, seem indifferent to such aspects of culture. Trying to stimulate interest, Ray wrote the entry on wallpaper coverings for the *Encyclopedia of United States Popular Culture.*

Indeed, Ray has always insisted that all subjects are worthy of some degree of study. As a graduate student, Ray did research on children's taunts, teases, jump-rope rhymes, and games, believing that in the verbal expressions of children there are significant symbols of aggression, hopes, and dreams which provide a key to understanding children's thinking. Folklorists have known the importance of this category of folk culture all along, well before it was popularized by Peter and Iona Opie in their work on children's lore. But other academics did not bother to study children or their culture. "Judging from present-day violent behavior among children of all ages," Ray states, "it is time we started reading the signs and symbols of their life."

Ray has also insisted that the apparent density of a subject is not as important as the depth of perception. "Anyone can read the obvious signs in so-called elite literature," Ray argues. "The everyday and obvious require greater subtlety, skill, and perception."

Ray has always continued his study of the meaning of folklore (not of folklore itself, but its meaning and its place in society, its function). He completed his first major publication while a student at UCLA, a book-length study entitled *Popular Beliefs and Practices from Alabama* (1958). While conducting field research for this book, Ray ran across many interesting and unique people. One individual, in particular, has since stuck in his mind. Ray had advertised in all the Alabama newspapers for informants, receiving a written response by a lady in southern Alabama. Ray's visit with this lady turned out to be a surprise for him. When, in 1951, he finally drove to her farm address, he was met at the door by a little woman who was five feet tall and pale as flour. She said, at first, that she would sell him material at $5.00 per item. After she learned that Ray was but a "poor student working his way through college," she then volunteered to give him all she knew. And for months afterwards, she got out of bed at 4:00 a.m. every morning to write down her beliefs, practices, and stories she remembered. One of her more remarkable qualities was her undying faith in God. She pointed out that when she and her husband had moved to their farm, they had to hitch up the wagon every Sunday and drive five miles into town for church, then drive the five miles back home. Though the trip was arduous, it was worth the effort because, as she stated, one day God would build a church much closer. "And just last year [in 1949]," she said, "some people had built a church just up at the end of the lane—after only thirty years!" Ray noted the axiom that states "all things come to those who wait."

Regarding the study of folksong—the subject of Ray's dissertation and subsequent publication, *The Alabama Folk Lyric: A Study in Origins and Media of Dissemination* (1979)—Ray discovered how much music has always meant to Alabamians. He was intrigued by their willingness to take any song they hear (folk, popular, religious, classical) and remold it to suit their needs. As Ray says, "The folkways of Alabama were alive, and still are, with the sounds of music."

In an earlier publication, *"A Night with the Hants" and Other Alabama Folk Experiences* (1976), Ray examined the dynamics of a folk experience: a "happening." Searching through the countryside around Cullman, Alabama, Ray located a family that carried on the tradition of holding gatherings at least once a week, usually on Friday nights, at which neighbors were invited for an evening of storytelling, song singing, and folk experiences of all kinds. Ray attended one of these meetings and recorded it from beginning to end. He later published this experience verbatim, and in doing so was the first to present folklife in precisely its entirety. As Ray says of the accomplishment, "It was folklife, powder and paint and warts and all."

Continuing his study of medical folk practices that appeared in *The Indian Doctor: Frontier Pharmacology* (1964), Ray edited an earlier book of folk medicine that was used on the American frontier. His interest lay, again, in things other than the remedies themselves. He wanted to know what the effects of these practices were on the patients, either helpful or harmful. With the aid of a famous pharmacologist—who reported that of the 100 remedies used, 60 were beneficial, 39 were neutral, and only one was actually harmful—Ray learned a new respect for the wisdom of folk tradition.

In addition to his books, Ray also expanded his research in folklore by writing a number of articles on the topic. He published an essay on the Southern "holler," a unique vocal exercise which may have developed from the Rebel yell and which is pure lyric. Still practiced among some Indian tribes in South America, the "holler" can carry up to a mile in distance. Ray also wrote about how superstitions were used as propaganda during the American Revolution. Then, combining his dual interest in both folklore and literature, Ray demonstrated that Hawthorne's *Twice-Told Tales* gained their effect from the fact that they were literary developments of folk motifs. Ray says, "That made them not twice-told, but oft-told." Expressing his fascination with authors of the American Midwest, Ray wrote an article about how Hamlin Garland's stories were held together by popular folk songs.

Meanwhile, Ray has kept up a rapid-fire series of publications. He has written perhaps a thousand book reviews on virtually every subject. In addition, he has published two hundred articles and some sixty books. Thematically, these articles and books can be divided into four categories: 1) efforts to persuade people to study popular culture; 2) efforts to establish workable definitions of popular culture; 3) studies that indicate the breadth, depth, and complexity of popular culture analysis; and 4) studies of other subjects that interested Ray.

Philosophies of Popular Culture Studies

Ray notes that there are, of course, a number of ways to look at popular culture, and each discipline has its own useful method, though often these methods parallel and overlap one another. The Frankfurt School offered perhaps the most iconoclastic analysis of popular culture studies. This approach was later supplemented by the Birmingham School, and is now followed rather closely by American adherents who are largely theoretical in their thinking.

The Frankfurt Institute for Social Research contributed such names as Theodor Adorno, Max Horkheimer, Herbert Marcuse, Erich Fromm, Leo Lowenthal, and Walter Benjamin. The Birmingham School offered Richard Hoggart, Raymond Williams, and the two second generation critics, Stuart Hall and Tony Bennett. The Frankfurt School looked down on the "Masses," as Marxists are wont to do. The Birmingham School, though sometimes calling the "Masses" members of the popular culture community, also felt that no good could come from them. American Marxists, Neo-Marxists, and pseudo-Marxists (the most influential being Fredric Jameson) have likewise looked upon popular culture as being manipulated by an all-powerful capitalism which has nothing but contempt for the desires and accomplishments of the so-called masses. A number of American critics have also taken this position, as best illustrated in R.B. Kershner's *Joyce and Popular Culture* (1996). One American Marxist critic, Michael Real, on the other hand, has pointed out the Marxists' debt to popular culture studies:

Popular culture analysis has contributed significantly to Marxism as well. The peculiarities of human activity and expression generally grouped under the label "popular culture" have proven complex and elusive enough to have forced some of our best contemporary Marxist thinkers—Raymond Williams, Stuart Hall, Pierre Bourdieu, among many others—to move away from the doctrinaire danger [outlined by Arthur Asa Berger]. Marxist critics who have seriously engaged in analysis of popular culture have seemed to emerge more subtle and sensitive in their definitions and distinctions.[1]

In keeping with his adherence to democratic subjects, Ray has tried to convince scholars of the value of the humanistic approach toward subject matter and method; this approach consists, according to Ray, of any and all methods, as long as they contribute to our understanding of culture. Ray's humanistic view of everyday culture tends to frown on the doctrine of so-called Marxists (and other post-modern theories), though they happily embrace such fields as feminism, multiculturalism, and Native American studies, among others. Ray has always urged scholars to think of popular culture studies as the "New Humanities," or the old humanities modernized.

A far greater task has been the attempt to develop some common understanding of a definition of popular culture. Many misconceptions regarding this term exist. Ray notes that the expressions "popular culture" and "culture" are so ingrained in the human psyche that it is very difficult to get scholars to reexamine their definitions and alter these definitions as logic and new understanding seem to dictate.

For Ray, the first misconception about popular culture is that it is only entertainment. To a large extent, this confusion resulted from a superficial reading of Russel B. Nye's monumental and pioneering study, *The Unembarrassed Muse: The Popular Arts in America* (1970). In his discussion of the popular arts, Nye sometimes failed to clearly distinguish between these and the much broader culture. As a consequence of the seeming equating of the two, during the early days of popular culture studies if you mentioned the words "popular culture," your listener might laughingly reply that movies are great. If someone wanted to insult you about your field of academic research, you might be told that comics are silly and childish and surely not worthy of critical attention. Ray believes that it has been (and continues to be) difficult to correct people of the notion that popular culture is exclusively entertainment and to get people to realize that popular entertainment is only one aspect of a total culture. "Popular culture," Ray states in his essay, "Notes Toward a Definition," first published in *Popular Culture and Curricula* (1970) edited by Ray Browne and Ronald Ambrosetti, "thus embraces all levels of our society and culture . . . It includes most of the bewildering aspects of life which hammer us daily." This was an explanation that Russ Nye found most satisfactory.

Ray's definition of popular culture resembles the similar anthropological definition of culture. Since the publication of "Notes Toward a Definition," Ray has gradually modified his view, now concluding that folk culture should also be classified as popular culture. The majority of elite culture, as well, Ray feels should be reconsidered. In a capitalistic democracy such as the United States, where human action is driven by money, the vote, and lust for power, Ray thinks that virtually all culture (except the most extremely elitist) is popular.

Ray's conclusion, as of the writing of this essay, is inclusive. He argues:

Popular culture is the way of life in which and by which most people in any society live. In a democracy like the United States, it is the voice of the people—their likes and dislikes—that form the lifeblood of daily existence, of a way of life. Popular culture is the voice of democracy, democracy speaking and acting, the seedbed in which democracy grows. Popular culture democratizes society and makes democracy truly democratic. It is the everyday world around us: the mass media, entertainments, and diversions. It is our heroes, icons, rituals, everyday actions, psychology, and religion—our total life picture. It is the way of living we inherit, practice and modify as we please, and then pass along to our descendants. It is what we do while we are awake, and how we do it. It is the dreams we dream while asleep.

Ray thinks that it has, likewise, not been easy to convince scholars that "popularity," in the sense of being widespread, has absolutely nothing to do with popular culture. These two similar expressions mean entirely different things. Large nations have dominant popular cultures. Small groups of people (say, one or two, provided they are to some degree separate from other cultures) have their popular culture. They serve the same purposes but are entirely different in degree of measurement. Ray believes that it is a serious flaw to think that only those elements of culture disseminated by the mass media are popular culture. Objects or thoughts that are innocent of any electronic dissemination, including coffee-table gossip, for example, are genuine and useful popular culture subjects. Perhaps the best graphic representation of this concept is the inverted pyramid (see illustration). Each level of culture has its own dynamic, which may or may not include features of the others.

In his attempt to further the study of popular culture by defining it and by demonstrating the wide-ranging subjects in the field that require further analysis, Ray has published at least 60 books. Some of these have been collections of essays edited with Marshall W. Fishwick, a long-standing national authority on a variety of cultural topics. With Fishwick, Ray has been particularly searching in his attempt to define heroes

Popular Culture

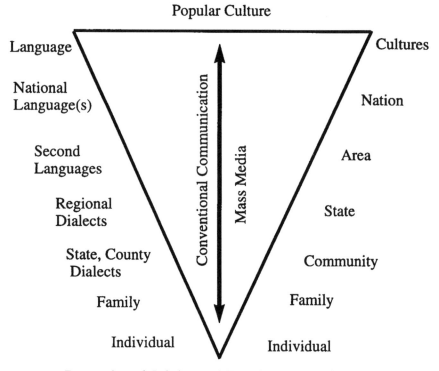

Dynamics of Origins and Developments of Culture

in general, and American heroes in particular. Heroes have naturally developed in the creation of icons, symbols, the Humanities, and they have been another natural outgrowth of religion.

Ray has always been interested in the offbeat and unusual characters found in literature. Folklore is, of course, full of weird, outsized, outcharactered personages and monsters. Being different, the unusual in society levels out the democratic impulses, serving as a counterweight. Ray and I, for example, edited a volume of short stories from the pulp magazines about such characters, *The Defective Detective in the Pulps* (1983) and, with Garyn G. Roberts, another two volumes, *More Tales of the Defective Detective in the Pulps* (1985) and *Old Sleuth's Freaky Female Detective (from the Dime Novels)* (1990). In addition, Ray and I published an anthology of scholarly essays on Stephen King, *The Gothic World of Stephen King: Landscape of Nightmares* (1987), and in 1996, *The Gothic World of Anne Rice,* one of the first collections on Anne Rice, who is one of the most popular authors of gothic horror fiction in the 1990s. All such writers and stories appeal, in Ray's opinion, to the dark underbelly of human existence, a subject almost overwhelming in the 1990s.

In his edited collections, Ray has also covered such wide-ranging subjects as Abraham Lincoln, popular culture and the expanding consciousness, rituals and ceremonies, fetishisms, and related topics. In nearly every one of his edited volumes, Ray has contributed significant essays on the subjects being discussed. He is especially proud of the anthologies, *Laws of Our Fathers: Popular Culture and the U.S. Constitution* (1986, edited with his son, Glenn Browne), and *Lincoln-Lore: Lincoln in the Contemporary Popular Mind* (1974). In both of these books, Ray more fully addressed the subject that many of his previous efforts had been driving at: the voices of democracy creating democracy. Concerned with the ever-growing communication media swirling around us in today's society, Ray (paraphrasing Thomas Jefferson on education) states that, "A democratic people that is not fluent in the media of communication cannot create a society that will stand." But, Ray observes, the media are more than just the electronic media. "They actually consist of all the flora and fauna which communicate through sound or sight," he says, "all the human creations which reflect individual and society's notions about creation and expression." Ray feels that only by learning all of these media of communication can humankind fully understand the universe, and with that understanding fully develop itself. "It is imperative," Ray argues, "that an educated public understand the many tongues of languages that are speaking to them."

Ray has long felt that a common theme running throughout literature (especially the most effective literature) has been the popular culture which authors have used to strengthen their subjects. In this vein, he has been especially pleased with his book, *Heroes and Humanities: Detective Fiction and Culture* (1986). Writers of crime fiction, Ray argues, since they deal with such obviously anti-social subjects (if they are doing their best work), must also include the life-affirming ideas of compassion and empathy in their fiction. Among the contemporary authors of such fiction, Ray discovered many who used their stories to illustrate how society is threatened, and may be saved, if their heroes can generate enough empathy to energize the reading public. Crime fiction, Ray suggests, carries on the drive to democratize power in society, a movement that has been developing since the beginning of society, one that received a dramatic impetus with the invention of gunpowder. When all people are made equal in their power to destroy, Ray believes that, hopefully, a study of such instincts and practices can reveal how violence might be countered, through empathy and love. In many ways, then, Ray argues that crime fiction has perhaps the heaviest social and humanistic obligations of all art forms.

In *The Spirit of Australia: The Crime Fiction of Arthur W. Upfield* (1988) Ray took his notions one step further. Arthur Upfield was the leading Australian writer of crime fiction during the first half of the twentieth century. Upfield had lived the life of a drover through the Australian Outback. He knew Australia's weather, its flora and fauna, and its people. He believed, as many do today, that the real Australia was not Sydney and Melbourne, but the Outback, the land of the Aboriginals and the cattle drovers.

So, Ray's approach to Upfield's fiction was unconventional, since he felt the subject of Upfield was considerably larger than what has been usually written. Instead of placing Upfield in the context of Australian crime writers of the period (and there were dozens of these), Ray placed him as an author of the Outback who came to writing crime fiction. Upfield, Ray advances, in publishing crime stories was really writing Australian literature that examined all aspects of Australian life, particularly life in the Outback. Ray believes that Upfield thus achieved a much broader, more significant and more universal literature, a literature of the "spirit of Australia."

Conclusions and Directions

Ray published *Against Academia* in 1988, which is an account of the development of all dimensions of popular culture studies. He thought that the various struggles and triumphs of the Popular Culture Association and the American Culture Association, as well as the initiatives at Bowling Green State University and in the regional chapters, should not be forgotten. Ray was responsible for describing the developments of the national PCA/ACA, in addition to the events at BGSU, but in order to do justice to the regional chapters, he invited their respective directors to write their own histories.

In many ways, *Against Academia* was a forerunner to the current project, *Pioneers in Popular Culture Studies,* of which this chapter is a part. Here, as in the earlier book, the authors hope to state for posterity the valiant early attempts by far-sighted scholars who were willing to follow their dreams and see what lay over the mountain, no matter what the risk. Sometimes (as reported earlier in this biographical essay) the costs were heavy, as many worthy scholars were denied tenure, or were belittled and ignored by their colleagues. At times, these accounts are poignant, at times amusing, but they are always saddening. As Ray claims, "The pioneer's life is never the comfortable one."

Recently, Ray and Pat have set out on another grand adventure, the publication of the *Encyclopedia of United States Popular Culture,* a collection of entries that discusses the representations of the daily life of

Americans. Their belief is that this book will impact the direction of popular culture studies for years to come. As Ray and Pat state, "[the *Encyclopedia*] demonstrates just how widespread, varied and complex the popular culture of the United States is." They end their Introduction with these words:

Reading through or browsing in the entries will at times be an adventure in the safe country of nostalgia, or, at other times, a daring venture into a virtually unknown country. But mainly it will be a trip in our world. It will be like holding up a giant mirror before ourselves and seeing in that reflection a whole society with ourselves in the center. At times the view may be frightening but it will always be educational. It's our world, so let's understand it . . . Welcome to a great adventure of discovery and recognition.

On this trip of discovery and recognition, Ray and Pat have often been in the lead. The paths they marked pointed out ways and means for radical changes in the way academia does business, where radical is often defined as being needed but not necessarily welcomed. Their journey reveals that academics tend to be territorial and essentially self-centered. Ray states, "No matter how eccentric or mainstream, no matter how anachronistic or outmoded, the academic is certain that he or she is at the center of the universe, the spindle on which learning spins. The academic fights blindly and savagely to maintain his or her position. In many ways, the American academy houses the royal family of America." Ray firmly believes that students in particular, and American society in general, deserve more enlightened behavior from their educators. Ray notes that as the world has turned it has not gotten very far from the world that Sir Thomas Browne observed in *Religio Medici* (1642). Sir Thomas Browne's observations are as valid today as when he first made them. His thesis was that man should inquire into God's [and humanity's] works because, "tis the debt of our reason we owe unto God [and humanity], and the homage we pay for not being beasts."

The more things change, the more they remain the same, unless one makes a herculean effort to interrupt the circular flow. To do so, in Ray's mind, is a moral imperative.

Note

1. Real, Michael, "Marxism and Popular Culture: The Cutting Edge of Cultural Criticism," *Symbiosis: Popular Culture and Other Fields*, ed. Ray B. Browne and Marshall Fishwick (Bowling Green, OH: Bowling Green State University Popular Press, 1988) 146.

John G. Cawelti
Photo by Nikki Swingle

JOHN G. CAWELTI:
RHETORIC OF MOTIVES

Stephen Tatum

The fundamental purpose of criticism, then, is to play a vitally important role in the formation of culture; it is responsible for the shaping of our perceptions, the way in which we understand contemporary existence, and the awareness which future generations have of their heritage.

—John Cawelti, "With the Benefit of Hindsight" (1985)

The Secret

At the beginning of *Adventure, Mystery, and Romance,* his most important contribution to the development of popular culture studies, John Cawelti accomplishes two tasks. In the first place, he provisionally defines what he means by the phrase "formula stories," the book's key concept. In the second place, he speculates about the reasons various formula stories in literature and film have appealed to various popular or mass audiences in this nation's history. Interestingly, Cawelti advances his speculations about both the adult production and consumption of formulaic stories by assuming that adults share unforgettable, common childhood experiences. As he puts it,

As children we learn new things about the world and ourselves from stories. By hearing about creatures and events that transcend the limits of space and time allotted to us we widen the range of our imagination and are prepared to deal with new situations and experiences. But children also clutch at the security of the familiar. How often a child rejects a new story, preferring to hear one he has already been told a hundred times. And as he hears again the often-heard, his eyes glaze over with pleasure, his body relaxes, and the story ends in peaceful slumber. . . .

In that well-known and controlled landscape of the imagination the tensions, ambiguities, and frustrations of ordinary experience are painted over by magic pigments of adventure, romance, and mystery. The world for a time takes on the shape of our heart's desire. (*Adventure, Mystery, and Romance* 1)

The key words and phrases in this somewhat lyrical passage cluster together for us Cawelti's basic approach to popular culture studies throughout his career. From the early publication of his *Apostles of the Self-Made Man* through his defense of the study of popular culture during an earlier moment in "the culture wars," *Why Pop?*, and on through his epitomizing remarks in *The Spy Story*, and his more recent reflections on western films in revised editions of his influential 1971 publication *The Six-Gun Mystique*, Cawelti has sought to define both the function and the use value of popular culture texts. Throughout his career, whether in such books or in his numerous article publications, Cawelti grounds his analyses with references to a human psychology of "needs" and to an elemental human thirst for pleasurable activity. As the above representative passage from his work indicates, Cawelti inclines toward viewing the human psyche as attracted, on the one hand, to the security of the familiar and, on the other hand, as attracted to adventurous escapes from the boredom and ennui of everyday life. In his view the function of what he terms the "magic pigments of adventure, romance, and mystery" is basically to synthesize these two basic human needs or desires and, as a result of the consumer's repetitive experience with formulaic stories, to resolve in the "landscape of the imagination" the conflicts, contradictions, tensions, and anxieties which cannot be reconciled in the patently non-formulaic world of "ordinary experience."

At first glance, both Cawelti's phrasing and his imagery of "magic pigments" here seem to focus the question of formula stories' value primarily on their therapeutic enhancement of a solitary individual's interior life. So powerful is the physiological image of "peaceful slumber" as a resolution to the stresses and anxieties produced by adventurous disturbances of received knowledge and habits, it is easy to overlook his modulated insistence that an important function of formulaic texts is *not* simply that of providing some compensatory "escape" from the ordinary. Far from being mere wish-fulfillments which have no purchase on everyday experience, formulaic stories for Cawelti significantly function to prepare consumers of such stories to handle or to get leverage on emergent situations and experiences. Thus, in his various writings about popular culture texts and criticism, Cawelti situates the use value of popular formulaic stories both in the interior realm of an individual's cathartic release from tension, ambiguity, and conflict, and in the exterior, more public and social realm, to the extent that such texts provide a formal and thematic mechanism for consumers to adjust or accommodate themselves to the accumulating changes in their everyday lives.

More specifically, as we can see by reading the whole of *Adventure, Mystery, and Romance*—as well as by reading *The Six-Gun Mystique* or the numerous essays published from the mid-1970s through the mid-1980s with titles using such expressions as "Notes Toward," "Some Reflections on," "Trends in," and "Prolegomena"—Cawelti perceives any changes or evolution in a formula story's basic features and narrative patterns as constituting a strategic adjustment to the changing contours of a modernizing industrial culture. Taken together, Cawelti's writings argue that the very popularity of formulaic stories—their commercial success; their longevity as viable aesthetic forms—provides two important things beyond that of fulfilling any particular individual's wishes or escapist fantasies: 1) they give critics "a means of making historical and cultural inferences about the collective fantasies from one cultural period to another" (*Adventure, Mystery, and Romance* 7); 2) they further function "to ease the transition between old and new ways of expressing things and thus contribute to cultural continuity" (36). In thinking particularly about the cultural significance of the gunfighter and hard-boiled dick heroes in the formulaic western and detective stories which have occupied his attention for three decades, for instance, he comments that in "a complex, pluralistic society, popular heroes and their myths perform an important *integrative* role by providing *common* objects of vicarious identification and admiration for people with very diverse attitudes and backgrounds" ("Gunfighter" 52; emphases added).

"Transcendence of ordinary experience" and *yet* "integration with"; "diverse attitudes and backgrounds" and *yet* "common objects of vicarious identification and admiration": Cawelti's thinking about the form and content of formula stories consistently establishes a series of dialectical oppositions which, as my above pairing of his phrases suggests, want as their own "heart's desire" to metamorphosize into syntheses, mergers, transactions, and integrations. Though for the past several decades politically conservative critics of popular culture have lamented the way its procession of dazzling entertainments and artifacts has supposedly eroded traditional moral foundations and has fostered a celebrity culture dismissive of sobriety and thrift, loyalty and honor, Cawelti has fearlessly argued for our understanding the powerfully conserving and integrating dimension of popular culture texts. As he claims in his meditation on evolving mythologies about organized crime in this country, "one of the major functions of popular literature is to humanize and give order to disturbing phenomena by relating them to conventional views of the world" ("New" 346). The concept of culture advanced by such statements, like the characteristic Cawelti sentence, delights in the give-and-take, the trying out of various perspectives or alternative explanations as a prelude, typically, to a homeostatic self-adjusting or self-regulating balance emerging to produce an equilibrium.

Since the beginning of his scholarly career Cawelti's writings on formula stories have been invested, perhaps because of the dominance during his training of the Talcott Parsons method in sociology, in functionalist explanations of popular culture texts. But beginning particularly around the time when *The Six-Gun Mystique* was published, Cawelti's interdisciplinary thinking about culture, itself linking popular culture scholarship in its early academic form to the developing project of American cultural studies in higher education, increasingly focused on research in psychology centering on issues of audience identification and response. As the quotations already introduced here indicate, for Cawelti an abiding interest in the psychology of audience identification and the sociological import of formula stories is not in itself logically incompatible, for his central concern throughout his career—or so it seems to me now upon rereading his work—has been precisely to establish what has been "continuous" and abiding for the democratic polity and mass culture we have in "common."

Cawelti's own anatomy of the "what" and the "why" of formula stories, his methodological imperative for pursuing a "broad structural approach . . . seeking to define those basic elements and relations" ("Gunfighter" 53) populating formulaic stories, depends on the critic's first recognizing and then organizing the connection between individual and collective fantasies in relation to some general "good," and, secondly, in tracking the varied definitions of what that general "good" has been in the United States. For Cawelti, the general "good" connotes not only the continuity and health of the larger community, but also the very progression (or regression as the case may be) both popular texts and the larger community express toward an ideal of social justice. "We might speculate," he notes in discussing American mythologies of violence, "that the presence of this myth [the vengeance motif] in most of our stories of violence reflects a deep underlying commitment to a primitive sense of justice latent in all of us under the veneer of civilization and close to the surface in those who face the most frustration and powerlessness in their actual lives, the young and the poor" ("Myths" 531). With this point in mind, then, we can better understand the trajectory of his career-long investment in those gunfighters, detectives, spies, and mobsters whose existence and whose violent actions in American culture and in popular cultural texts crystallize the tensions, ambiguities, and contradictions inherent in the American democratic polity and its social contract. Such stories and mythologies about such figures simultaneously provide the *critic* of popular culture a "special place . . . to be concerned with the shaping of culture in the present and for the future" ("With" 377).

A typical Cawelti book chapter or essay begins by introducing key features of a particular formulaic story and by documenting the trajectory of its popularity in the dominant culture. It then moves to sketching in how these features' particular contours relate to particular social experiences and audience needs, as well as to inherited generic conventions. Since Cawelti's interest in formulaic stories centers largely on their evolution, the transformation of their forms and themes in response to the course of history, his chapters and essays devote considerable space to the variation and change of the formulaic story forms' features. This method largely succeeds because of Cawelti's nuanced grasp of generic changes and his provocative accounts of what such changes in formulaic stories mean with regard to the collective fantasies operative at a given cultural moment. Given as well his appointment at the University of Chicago between 1957 and 1980, I find it understandable how and why certain critics and reviewers have identified his contributions to popular culture studies in this country as representing the most-accomplished of a neo-Aristotelian or a formalist approach to popular culture texts (See Strine). Indeed, Cawelti's extensive typology of various formulaic stories in print and on film and television alone constitutes a pioneering effort in popular culture studies during the past three decades.

Now I have intentionally used the word "anatomy" above because at the outset of Cawelti's career the critic-theorist who seems most closely aligned with Cawelti's "broadly structural" approach is Northrop Frye. But regardless of how accurate certain labels are in characterizing the tenor of his work, and regardless of attributing any specific theoretical influence informing the work, I find myself drawn to understanding what I take to be Cawelti's consistent desire to examine (and account for) 1) the perennial human "yearning for transcendence and transformation" ("Trends" 78), a yearning we particularly witness in those formula stories involving the search for justice (i.e., the western and the detective stories) and the search for the most suitable love interest or mate (i.e., the romance); 2) the kinds of rhetorical persuasion popular texts deploy that *move* people (prepare them to act as well as affect them emotionally); and 3) the link between such persuasion and the human experience of desire as it emerges during childhood and is recapitulated in formula stories which are likened to "magic" for adolescents and adults.

If we hold at bay for the moment the signal importance during the 1960s and 1970s of Cawelti's typologizing of formula stories in literature, film, and television, and if we consider the thematic concerns advanced by his scholarship as I have enumerated them above by building on the introductory quote from *Adventure, Mystery, and Romance,* then I believe we can appreciate better the richness and depth of his contribution to the development of popular culture studies by considering his critical project with that of another forebear besides Northrop Frye or even, say, R. S.

Crane. That is, given Cawelti's important contributions towards understanding the fluidity of audience identification, the work of popular symbols and icons as bridging devices forging a community, and in tracking how cultural texts always disclose strategic responses to particular historical moments, I find the cluster of his preoccupations are kin to those of Kenneth Burke in his *Attitudes Toward History* and *A Rhetoric of Motives*. Consider, for instance, how Burke in *Attitudes* identifies how literary efforts to "encompass" their particular situations are driven by and achieve power according to what he calls various "offices," or *motives*. Burke identifies the office or motive of the cultural text as that of teaching, entertaining, or cathartic redemption via "sympathetic magic" (See *Attitudes Toward History* 353-75). These particularly Burkean motives informing the rhetorical strategies of literary works are certainly ones that Cawelti, in his own fashion, has identified as important functions of formulaic stories. As I have indicated earlier, for Cawelti these kinds of stories work through their imaginative resolutions to redeem the community (e.g., "Gunfighter" 51) and, by dramatizing exemplary human actions, work to teach appropriate moral values and codes of conduct.

In his *The Rhetoric of Motives,* Burke argues that what he more specifically terms the "Order, the Secret, and the Kill" are the three primary motives in "the nature of rhetoric" and rhetorical persuasion (265). Such terms cluster together for us not only the problem of violence but the key issue of sacrifice in his theorizing. Burke's argument centers on how the motive of the "secret" or what he sometimes calls "the enigma," along with that of the "kill" organize the production and reception of literary texts. This argument bears parallels with Cawelti's own analytical focus on representations of violence in American culture, to the role of enigmas in the plotting of detective and spy stories, and, in his view, to the formula stories' general function of fostering cultural continuity and cohesion through the examples of individuals who are sacrificed as a result of justifiable violence—or what Cawelti labels the "moral necessity of violence" ("Myths" 525). Finally, in the light of Cawelti's linkage of formula stories' appeals with childhood pleasures following on or bound up with ritualistic repetitions of sounds, images, and plots, consider how Burke connects a symbol's "persuasiveness," its "magic" or "mystery" with regard to moving audiences, to its "enigmas" and "secrets." The appeal or persuasiveness of these secrets Burke in turn links to what he calls a state of "infancy," defined as "a kind of 'intuition' that overlaps upon the realm of the 'unconscious' in dreams" (*Rhetoric of Motives* 175), and an intuition that is typically suppressed by a mechanistic and commercial society except in its popular entertainments' voicing of utopian possibilities.

For Burke, the "secret" in particular is a fundamental "motive" for a symbolic text's work of audience persuasion in that the secret, however it is specifically defined in a text, brings us toward or reminds us vividly of the realm of the inexpressible, that realm which exists beyond rational explanation (hence his interest in "intuition" and the "unconscious in dreams"). In my gloss of this concept, the "secret" motivating literary texts of all kinds forces readers to confront the fact that there is indeed a space *beyond* ourselves and our experiences. This imaginative space of text-audience interaction that resists territorialization or colonization resembles Cawelti's theory of adventure stories as perennially appealing to audiences because they offer an expansion or broadening of the known, a widening of the range of the imagination, a rebuke to the quotidian. Though Burke and Cawelti might well disagree on the extent to which the "landscape of the imagination" is a "well-controlled" one, to use Cawelti's phrase, my point is that the potentially liberating nature of texts which circulate the magical motives of secrets and sacrificial kills draws their critical projects together.

Cawelti's and Burke's critical projects stress secrets, magic, and mystery—Cawelti in *Why Pop?* deploys the word "delight" as well—as a counterpoint to what they perceive to be in their respective historical moments a restrictive, censorious, and ultimately deadening military-industrial political economy. In any case, whether the primary motive for a symbol's work of persuasion in a literary or cinematic text is identified as that of articulating secrets, or providing order, or redeeming via a sacrificial kill, Burke regards the symbol itself as a kind of container or vessel, one produced as a result of various combinations of this triad of motives and capable of holding ideological opposites and thematic contraries together in the same space. Burke also calls the cultural symbols regarded as kinds of vessels "bridging devices" which allow audiences or consumers of them to transcend a conflict enacted by the cultural text which houses them. At this point I want to recall not the formalist or typologist Cawelti but rather the Cawelti who argues that the "integrative role" filled by popular heroes and their myths develops because the hero and the mythic narrative associated with him or her "must be, in effect, a container into which various meanings can be poured without breaking or changing the basic shape of the container" ("Gunfighter" 52).

Though Cawelti here is discussing a way of understanding the process by which some individuals in history become not only regarded as cultural heroes but become cultural icons as well with lasting cultural significance, his imagery of container/contained aptly describes his sense of formulaic stories in general as having a basic shape into which particular artists at particular moments pour various meanings. For a variety of reasons, Cawelti's deployment of container/contained imagery seems fairly impartial or neutral, devoid explicitly of class and gender relations that have more recently attracted the attention of other commentators on such popular genres as the western (See Tompkins). Reading Cawelti's interest in enigmas, violence, and redemptive acts alongside Burke's motive of the secret, the kill, and the order, however, brings me to consider Burke's further supposition that the "secret" inherent in any symbol's persuasiveness accrues because, whether regarded as a vessel or container, it "possibly" involves "furtive identifications between monetary and genital treasure" (*Rhetoric of Motives* 174). Cawelti's appeal to the resonance of our childhood experience of hearing stories read aloud, as well as his more explicit arguments regarding either the romance formula's appeal or the post-World War II western's address to gender and sexual relations, begins to assay this same complex dynamic.

"Secrets" conceptualized as being contained by symbols, or formulas and myths, and "secrets" linked, however furtively or openly, with both sexual and property desire and with the mysterious intuitions and pleasures first experienced in childhood—I think here of the imagery in numerous children's books or even popular music of the secret garden or that special place under the boardwalk or up on the roof; of the glass coffin in which Snow White lies; of the glass slipper for Cinderella's foot; of the underground hideout of Peter Pan and the Lost Boys; of the scalloped seashell as locket containing Ariel's voice in *The Little Mermaid;* of the cupboard housing the toy figures in *The Indian in the Cupboard;* of the glass cover over the rose in *Beauty and the Beast;* of the chests of various sizes housing coins or currency or—in Disney's version of "Jack and the Beanstalk"—the magic beans and the female singing harp that Mickey, Donald, and Goofy must rescue from Willie, the giant, in order to revive the landscape and their village.

To these instances from popular texts centering the pleasure of magic or mystery with containers allegorizing sexual desire, I would add, following Cawelti's lead, that the hero as container is the obverse of the hero or heroine as contained. The trajectory of numerous formula stories for children for whom parents desire slumber is for the latter condition (being contained) to give way to the former (hero as agent who contains) as a result of a magical act, spell, or antidote: thus, Pinocchio must go through Monstro's mouth and be baptized by water before being cured by the blue fairy's magic wand which has been summoned to action as a result of the prayers of his adoptive father-creator. Or, to take an example closer to Cawelti's focus on the western, Shane and Joey Starrett must go through the dark interior of the saloon and its attendant priapic and violent evils before redeeming both the family and the community. I think of these things because of Cawelti's probing of the connection between childhood pleasures and adult fantasies as dramatized in formula stories—and because the "secret" associated with toys and children's entertainments is, I believe, identical with the "secret" of Cawelti's arguments in a variety of essays and books about the meaning and function of popular culture texts. Formula stories for adults as well as toys and entertainments for children represent transitional objects helping bridge the various instances or recapitulations of separation anxiety confronted throughout our psychic lives.

The Repair

Pinocchio's adventures illustrate the aptness of Cawelti's general claim that the "basic moral fantasy" associated with the adventure formula is that of a "victory over death" (*Adventure, Mystery, and Romance* 40). On its surface, the narrative trajectory of the text of *Pinocchio,* like that of the cowboy song "The Cowboy's Lament," suggests an inherent hostility on the part of some cultural producers toward popular pleasures, since these pleasures potentially seduce audiences away from a disciplined work ethic or reaffirm occupational and regional identities instead of promoting assimilation to a bourgeois and national model (See Tatum). As one of the many toys and dolls in Gepetto's workshop, Pinocchio the character serves as a prompt for readers' narration and play, "opens an interior world, lending itself to fantasy and privacy," to quote Susan Stewart from her *On Longing* (56). And in Pinocchio's case, where magical transformation occurs after the uttering of wishes and the touching by a luminous wand, a specifically masculinist fantasy of reproduction without the need for a mother's physical body is on display. Pinocchio as a puppet could be said to represent what Stewart calls the world of the "miniature," as opposed to that of the "gigantic" as represented, by, say, Paul Bunyan and Pecos Bill legends. And the miniature, Stewart further suggests, dramatizes a deep-seated nostalgia in industrializing cultures for a pre-industrial artisanal labor of the hand.

But of course Pinocchio's "yearning for transcendence and transformation," to use Cawelti's phrasing to describe the basic appeal of formula stories, his becoming at last a "real" boy after a series of moral tests which culminate in a heroic sacrifice revealing a developed superego, more accurately can be said to promote instead a desire to erase the traces of artisanal production—the wooden limbs and joints; the painted facial features—in order to enter the modern world of mechanical reproduction and prosthesis. According to Roland Barthes in his *Mythologies,* to cite another key text in the development of academic popular culture studies in this country during the past few decades, such a world, unlike the close confines of Gepetto's toyshop, toils ceaselessly to remove "all soiling trace of origin or choice. . ." (151). For Barthes, in short, what we see and experience in the presence of manufactured objects is the luster of the produced commodity, not the evidence of labor (and alienation) involved in production. Following Barthes' general logic about toys, we could go on to say that Pinocchio's "magic" persuasively works for audiences because in Cawelti's words it strives to "ease the transition between old and new ways of expressing things"—or in Burke's words because it serves "as an active way of maintaining cultural cohesion" (*Rhetoric of Motives* 174) during the advent of the modern industrial nation-state. William Dean Howells said as much about the pedagogical work of literary realist texts produced around the time of the Pinocchio story.

As a narrative essentially about an animate toy whose adventures recapitulate the child's transition away from narcissistic preoccupations to the larger social world, *Pinocchio* prepares us for understanding the more recent and commercially successful cinematic updatings of the Nutcracker theme, *The Indian in the Cupboard* and *Toy Story,* in the popular culture of the United States. Toys, dolls, and other miniature objects we collect for ourselves and our children represent a kind of "dead among us," Stewart comments, and she further argues that the perennial desire to animate the toy in both folk and popular cultures constitutes "the desire not simply to know everything but also to experience everything simultaneously" (57). Like the reruns of canceled television shows from the 1950s and 1960s which appear now on the Nickelodeon cable channel's "Nick at Nite" listings, the animate toy motif dramatizes the triumph of life over death, a triumph which illustrates Cawelti's conceptual understanding of the basic moral fantasy associated with adventure stories through time. Thus, this particular "secret"—that toys come to life when our eyes glaze over and we are in peaceful slumber (like Sid's father in *Toy Story,* fast asleep in his recliner when the Buzz Lightyear action figure sneaks into the family room)—is rhetorically persuasive because it "projects the potential of continuing life on the other side" (Stewart 57). Indeed, *Toy Story* near its conclusion literalizes this theme of death's reversibility when the mutant toys created by the sadistic child Sid's mixing and matching of their various parts converge on him in his backyard just like the corpses in the cult movie *Night of the Living Dead* converge on the isolated rural house in search of fresh human prey.

Barthes specifically argues elsewhere in *Mythologies* that the world of life-like or mimetic toys always "prefigure[s] the world of adulthood" and always functions to prepare the child to accept that world as a passive consumer (53). In statements that recapitulate in short form a century's worth of debate on the subject of the lure of entertainments,

Barthes instead privileges wooden blocks and more non-representational toys for two reasons: 1) they are more tactile and sensuous than the mimetic toys made of plastic, and hence are more closely aligned with nature than culture; 2) they are more likely to bear traces of their production and their link with the artisanal modes of labor. I suspect if Barthes were to see *Toy Story* he would prefer the cowboy doll made out of cloth and wool and named "Woody." And I suspect he would be particularly interested in that movie's primal scene of interpellation, when Buzz Lightyear, the astronaut action figure trying to escape from the clutches of sadistic Sid, walks into Sid's father's den or family room and sees on the television set a commercial advertising Buzz Lightyear action figures and displaying an image of a toy store's aisle filled with countless boxes containing Buzz Lightyear figures inside them. At this moment, Buzz can no longer deny what Woody has been telling him: he is not a unique, distinctive subject but in fact a mass-produced commodity. This recognition leads not to his "peaceful slumber" but to his abjection.

The remainder of the movie, some popular culture critics would argue, works to contain or manage this potentially subversive moment during which a subject gains consciousness of his very subjection to the commodity form. As *Toy Story* proceeds Buzz is "repaired" from what I want to call his symbolic castration. His literal repair occurs first as the mutant toys in Sid's room re-attach his left arm that had fallen off as a result of his trying—and failing—to fly. Secondly, Buzz is repaired as he becomes able to internalize Woody's teaching that, even though he is "a child's plaything," not a unique human on a special mission, he is nevertheless "cool" within the family of toys. Once he internalizes the claim that he indeed does have "cool" features that the other standard toys don't, Buzz successfully loses his funk about only being a mass-produced commodity by noticing the personal name of his owner written on the sole of his boot. This scrawled signature interestingly deflects the matter of property and ownership inaugurated by the Buzz storyline into a matter of identity formation. That is, Buzz assumes Andy needs him [Buzz] in order to be all that he can be in this world. Thus, Buzz is repaired to the extent that he is able to substitute for the production of his own self-image the more fulfilling destiny, according to the movie's logic, of seeing his self-image reflected in and of assessing his self worth through the eyes of Andy, his "owner." And in turn Woody himself is repaired from "laser envy" by turning away from his impossibly narcissistic identification with Andy and toward the nascent erotic possibilities represented by a very mature Bo Peep.

From this perspective, Woody's plan to reform Sid simply underlines Disney's version of the deconstructive logic of the supplement.

Woody's stern injunction to Sid to "play nice," uttered as the other toys converge on Sid in the backyard and as the secret life of toys as animate creatures with feelings is thus revealed, discloses how humans and commodities are equal and identical: humans need commodities in the form of toys in order to fulfill themselves and their destinies; and commodities need humans in the form of humans in order to fulfill themselves and their destinies. In the world of *Toy Story*, in short, while an ideology of "difference" is affirmed—the toys are different from each other in terms of personalities and functions—there is no true "otherness" possible. Seen rightly, then, toys in their secret lives express similar desires, emotions, conflicts, fears, and anxieties, which means that they are after all an unacknowledged but vital part of the human family.

Barthes' theorizing about popular culture in *Mythologies* advances a stylish version of the "containment" thesis with regard to how popular culture texts work ceaselessly to legitimate the political, economic, and social *status quo* of industrial capitalism. With the above analysis of *Toy Story* in mind, I don't think it too difficult to understand how the movie works—in a fashion similar to the advertising and marketing campaigns of such corporations as Coca-Cola and Nike—to promote the liberal mythology Barthes calls "The Great Family of Man" (150-52): regardless of our different cultures, skin colors, and, in this context, histories of sleep, we are all essentially alike in facing similar joys and sorrows in life. Nevertheless, however sympathetic I am with leftist or post-Marxian critiques of commodity consumption bent on theorizing the conditions for an expanded, truly democratic society, I ultimately find Barthes' interpretation of the bourgeois myths promoted by toys and advertising to be both seductively and reductively predictable. Is it truly the case, for instance, that mimetic toys analogous to the sleek lines of Buzz Lightyear action figures solely and inexorably prepare children for entry into the world of adult work and consumption? Isn't it possible, if not probable, that such toys also provide opportunities for children to mimic or parody that adult world invested in accurate representations, to read it against the grain, if you will, in their play? And in the second place, is it always the case that the "play" authorized by non-representational wooden blocks and toys will ineluctably provide an alternative to the bourgeois adult world of work and consumption? What are we to make, for instance, of the development that Wendy's play with "the lost boys" and Peter Pan in "Neverland" evolves into that of playing at the role of the good mother she has learned about from her own good mother back in London?

In its emphasis on the values of continuity, stability, and integration, Cawelti's version of how formula stories function presents itself as a *humanist* version of the post-Marxian containment thesis which for the past decade or so, I think it fair to say, has dominated, due to the influence of the University of Birmingham cultural studies group and to theorists such as Barthes, critical thinking about popular culture. But what continues to intrigue me about Cawelti's thinking on these matters is how his writing, as is the case with Burke's writings on the grammar and rhetoric of motives, is characteristically alert to the fluidity and varieties of identification that can occur during the triadic interaction of author, text, and reader (or listener or viewer). In several instances in his work Cawelti cautions us not to rest with any "single key interpretation," and as he says in one place, "in making cultural interpretations of literary patterns, we should consider them not as simple reflections of social ideologies or psychological needs but as instances of a relatively autonomous mode of behavior that is involved in a complex dialectic with other aspects of human life" (*Adventure, Mystery, and Romance* 26).

The notion here of a "complex dialectic" helps us understand why Cawelti is drawn to thinking about the ambiguities and paradoxes present in a variety of popular culture texts and the grounds of their appeal. Coupled with his healthy respect for the vagaries of audience response, Cawelti ends up in his analyses refraining from conceiving, say, the Disney project as only promoting the kinds of mystification that Barthes sees working in the production and consumption of mimetic toys, and refraining from reducing, say, the popular western story to expressing what Jane Tompkins has called a predominant "sadomasochistic impulse" (107).

While Disney's investors would probably not mind the Disney empire's continuing interest in mystifying commodity fetishism, the popular texts themselves, to repeat Cawelti's nuanced phrasing, do behave relatively autonomously and are always situated in a complex dialectical space of production and consumption. Regardless of our ability to identify predictable intentions and ideologies in their production, popular texts leak out potentially alternative or oppositional meanings at their seams, forcing critical audiences to recognize at some point that the ideology or the politics of the text cannot simply be deduced from a summary statement of theme and an identification of corporate sponsorship or authorial backgrounds and class affiliations. Thus in discussing the popularity of *The Godfather* movies and what they tell us about an evolving mythology of crime, Cawelti claims that "crime serves as an ambiguous mirror of social values, reflecting both our overt commitments to certain principles of morality and our hidden resentments against those principles" ("New" 352). His own extended attention to the structural patterns in formula stories has not allowed him to extend analyses into how audiences for popular culture texts use and interpret such stories in ways not intended by their producers, a more recent focus of popular culture scholarship influenced by more anthropological perspectives. Still, Cawelti's understanding of the complex place and function of "needs" on both the sociological and psychological level all but asks for the kind of ethnographical and interpretive direction taken by such scholars as John Fiske and Janice Radway in their work with reading and viewing audiences. And his speculations on these issues also suggest that as teachers and critics of popular culture texts in his wake we need to attend responsibly to the multiple and at times conflicting or contradictory connotations possible in any text. My use of the word "responsibly" in developing this point intends to remind us of what I believe to be the fundamentally *moral* nature of Cawelti's extensive anatomies of the "what" and "why" of formula stories.

"Play Nice"

John Cawelti's writings have made several key contributions to the academic study of American popular culture. By focusing on the thematic ambiguities of formula stories, he has insisted on the complexity and variability of a formula's ideological orientation, in itself a decidedly major contribution in an era of litmus test criticism from the right and left sides of the political spectrum. Secondly, as much as he sees the work of formula stories as stabilizing and working to ensure continuity in cultural life, his thinking has importantly contributed to our understanding the what, how, and why of formulaic structures' variation and change. Thirdly, at bottom Cawelti's work has resisted reifying "the popular": he conceives of the "popular" both as an "attitude" of tolerance and as an unstable, contestable space inhabited by provisional orthodoxies (see *Why Pop?* 3). Fourthly, Cawelti's scholarly project has been not only to construct an influential typology of literary formulas (particularly the western story form), but in the process to create also what he calls "a pluralist aesthetic of popular culture" ("With" 363). In his articles and books he has thus argued for the need to define an aesthetic suitable to the different kinds of experience and pleasures associated with different popular culture texts and genres, and he has argued for popular culture critics themselves to develop a "canon" representing the best that has been thought and said among popular texts.

In short, Cawelti's importance to the development of popular culture studies resides not only in his taxonomies and interpretations of popular culture texts and traditions. It resides also in his various meditations on the value of including popular culture in the academic humanities curriculum at a time when such an inclusion was regarded by some as either a lowering of academic standards or as a cynical use of popular texts as a way to motivate students to study more sophisticated literary works. As his own meditations have developed through the years, Cawelti's ostensibly pluralist aesthetic, I want to stress, has proved to be neither weakly relativistic nor uncritically populist in its orientation. Cawelti has argued throughout his career that teachers and sympathetic critics of popular culture not reject out-of-hand "high" cultural or serious artistic traditions, and he has reminded those defenders of the traditional canon about the very historicity and fluidity of cultural boundaries defining the divide between so-called serious and formulaic literature. In the end, the key term defining his work, as he says in *Why Pop?*, is *culture,* which Cawelti mostly defines in the anthropological manner as a "whole way of life," as the general domain of "the works that men create, the things that men do, the patterns of life they create which lead *toward the enrichment and betterment of life*" (24, emphasis added).

For Cawelti the purpose of studying culture whether high or low, mimetic or formulaic, is to understand ourselves more fully and as a result to become "increasingly capable of fulfilling our various potentials" (*Why Pop?* 3). He often in his writings, as the above quote suggests, defines the process of achieving this individual and collective fulfillment as the "enriching" or "enrichment" of life. In effect, this emphasis means that the content of study is not as crucial for him as 1) the motivation to study, the curiosity that leads one to appreciate "value in as many things as possible," and 2) the skills gained as a result of one's newly interpreting and articulating the "depth" and "richness" of many different aspects of culture (*Why Pop?* 10; see also "With" 373-74). The imagining of variousness and possibility in both the individual and the collective life; the notion that we each have a self that deserves the freedom to develop and be expressed, a potential to be fulfilled; the tolerance for a wide range of needs and pleasures, which translates into an advocacy of sympathetic understanding; the faith in reason as a tool and criticism as the pedagogical scene of instruction for articulating the individual's affective realm of consciousness—these assumptions inform Cawelti's specific contributions to the development of popular culture studies in the academy, and they indicate his characteristically liberal pluralist perspective.

Pluralism, as Ellen Rooney has recently suggested, always depends on the possibility of persuasion, what in this context I have called, following Burke's lead, a "rhetoric of motives" involved in moving people to act or accept. Because its approach basically assumes competing views should have equal access to a discursive arena and that values, knowledge, and a consensus—however provisional—will emerge as a result of "free" deliberative discussion by a literate, educated public, the pluralist is always interested in pedagogy, in talking to somebody about something with an instructional purpose in mind. This pluralist emphasis on conversation and dialogue—and persuasion—as a means of affecting behavior and belief means that the pluralist's strategies are always directed toward the *social* situation, are always directly concerned with the problematic of defining who "we" are, in establishing and maintaining a "community" (See Fischer 529-30). In the wake of Foucault's writings and other versions of a materialist criticism interested in asymmetrical power relations and issues of gender, race, and class, several critics (such as Rooney) have pointed out in recent years major limitations with the pluralist approach as it has been appropriated and forwarded by liberal humanists. As Michael Fischer remarks in his review of Rooney's critique, the pluralist approach too often fails to acknowledge that the "community" is exclusive not inclusive, which is to say that others are allowed in, if at all, insofar as they begin to assimilate and conform to the ideological orientations of the dominant group controlling both the means of production and the symbolic means of production (media; cultural access; education apparatuses); it fails to note that the supposedly "free" marketplace for discussion in the culture is predicated on a system of unequal resource and power allocations; it does not understand how a tolerance for allowing contending partisan perspectives to coexist appears often in the service of avoiding conflict and dialogue; and it fails to admit how a desire for achieving some higher synthesis or reconciliation of contending perspectives as a result of deliberative discussions in actuality expresses one group's hegemonic power (Fischer 532). From this perspective, for instance, the plan hatched by Woody on Sid's bedroom floor to free Buzz Lightyear by capitalizing on the special skills for which each mutant toy is capable of performing represents a kind of equal opportunity/affirmative action liberal pluralist ideal—and belies for the moment the space of competition and struggle between Woody and Buzz for status in Andy's and the other toys' eyes that has set the toys' adventure in motion in the first place.

A social constructionist or perspectival view which challenges pluralist approaches relentlessly emphasizes the contingent nature of reason, selfhood, human nature, and values, and thus asks us to recognize how all truths are partial, and how some truths masquerade—like Barthes' notion of "The Great Family of Man" myth we see enacted in the congregations of toys in Sid's and Andy's bedrooms in *Toy Story*—as universals by relying on some essential concept of a common humanity shared by all who live on what IBM now calls our "small planet." Now at moments in Cawelti's writings his language suggests a traditional liberal humanist's notion of some basic human essence that provides the opportunity to bridge differences. For Cawelti this basic human essence appears to be the creative instinct he champions as a way "to get outside ourselves and to think about that which unites us with other men and the world," or that other instinct prohibiting or constraining unity, integration and community—that basic "part of man's nature" to "exploit and destroy, to overpower, or to ignore the human reality and appeal of other individuals and other groups" (*Why Pop?* 25). Such comments gleaned from Cawelti's work, regardless of its many insights, would seem obviously to be open to the charges levied against pluralism or Cawelti's brand of liberal humanism by those who advertise themselves as being even more intent than Cawelti on promoting social justice.

Even so, we should factor into the mix here how Cawelti's writings in several instances stress the need for us to understand "broadly" and "sympathetically" and "almost in an intuitional way" (in a phrase that recalls Burke's notion of the state of "infancy" as being super rational) "things in the past," "these traditions," "their cultures," and "the patterns of life they create" (See *Why Pop?* 2-3; "With" 374-77). My point here is that regardless of, perhaps in spite of, any reading and labeling of Cawelti's critical project, and regardless of whether one still delights in or resists the liberal pluralist assumptions and formalist reading strategies that inform Cawelti's scholarship, I think it important to recognize that in the world of contingency and irony we inhabit, to adopt Richard Rorty's terminology, the two major problems Cawelti's writing consistently addresses center on how creative expressions, on whatever level of aesthetic brilliance and in whatever form and genre, can help forge solidarity or community, can help us achieve a coherent self-awareness, and at the same time how a responsible criticism of such creative expressions can prepare audiences themselves to critique whether artforms achieve or fall short of the goal of enhancing or broadening life. As Cawelti says in *Why Pop?*, "the basic thing we are up to as humanists is to enrich life, and this is not simply a matter of getting people into museums. It's a matter of getting people to see their own experience with some depth and richness and to be able to articulate for themselves and discover value in as many things as possible" (5).

As Rorty for one points out, the post-structuralist or post-modern ironist who takes to heart all the various challenges to metaphysical thinking about "essences," and who labors to point out the illusory foundational beliefs others labor under, promotes in her claims for contingency "something potentially very cruel. . . . For the best way to cause people long-lasting pain is to humiliate them by making the things that seemed most important to them look futile, obsolete, and powerless." As Rorty adds, "Consider what happens when a child's precious possessions—the little things around which he weaves fantasies that make him a little different from all other children—are described as 'trash,' and thrown away" (89). Rorty's overall point, one which I believe we can see developing in parallel fashion in Cawelti's 1970s theorizing about the functions performed by popular cultural texts, is that individuals in an intensified consumer culture can in fact construct meaningful solidarity with others even in an era of contingency and irony and of identity politics. The important point remains that "we" accomplish this task as both consumers and critics of popular culture by capaciously expanding our sense of community, not by founding it—that is, "it" regarded as the magic feeling of consubstantiality found in a genuine community—primarily on some spurious claim to a common human essence (See Fischer 533).

In comments in various works too numerous to quote here, Cawelti too stresses that our task as teachers and as students of popular culture texts is precisely that of enhancing our own and others' ability to see others as specific humans who likewise endure pain, and experience pleasure, and feel the pull of longing in a variety of tradition-specific ways. Cawelti's utopian hope is that such enhanced sensitiveness through various audiences' immersion in the particular features of accessible popular formula stories—for instance, a desire for redemption or a yearning for justice—will make it difficult for individuals to marginalize or to scapegoat people whose cultures and histories are different or alternative. As Cawelti says, in a comment that bears thinking about in connection with Rorty's observations on this topic, "I think the more broadly we can understand human creativity and appreciate it and come to love it, the less capable we are going to be of brutally treating men" (*Why Pop?* 25). In other words, the less capable we are going to be of calling others' precious collections "trash," the less capable we will be of acting like Sid in *Toy Story,* whose creativity is brutal, not redemptive. Expanding our awareness, through a delight in being in front of creative expressions, of what various cultures at various historical moments constitute as kindness or cruelty, excellence or trash, can provide a knowledge of alternative values and alternative traditions. One result of this greater knowledge of alternative values and alternative traditions is an expanded sense of community. Cawelti's rhetoric of motives, his interest in the persuasive strategies deployed by formula stories whose "secret" is that of aiding humans enduring transitions in their individual and social lives, exemplifies itself as a capacious space of critical transformation, one which has importantly enabled the work of numerous popular culture scholars for the past three decades.

Works Cited

Barthes, Roland. *Mythologies*. 1957. Trans. Annette Lavers. New York: Hill & Wang, 1982.

Burke, Kenneth. *Attitudes Toward History*. 1937. Berkeley: U of California P, 1984.

——. *A Rhetoric of Motives*. 1950. Berkeley: U of California P, 1969.

Cawelti, John. *Adventure, Mystery, and Romance: Formula Stories as Art and Popular Culture*. Chicago: U of Chicago P, 1976.

——. *Apostles of the Self-Made Man*. Chicago: U of Chicago P, 1965.

——. "The Gunfighter and the Hard-Boiled Dick: Some Ruminations on American Fantasies of Heroism." *American Studies* 16 (1975): 49-64.

——. "Myths of Violence in American Popular Culture." *Critical Inquiry* 1 (March 1975): 521-41.

——. "The New Mythology of Crime." *Boundary* 23 (1975): 325-57.

——. *The Six-Gun Mystique*. Bowling Green, OH: Bowling Green State University Popular Press, 1971.

——. "Trends in Recent American Genre Fiction." *Kansas Quarterly* 10 (Fall 1978): 5-20.

——. *Why Pop?* San Francisco: Chandler and Sharp, 1973.

——. "With the Benefit of Hindsight: Popular Culture Criticism." *Critical Studies in Mass Communication* 2 (1985): 363-79.

Cawelti, John, and Bruce Rosenberg. *The Spy Story*. Chicago: U of Chicago P, 1987.

Fischer, Michael. "Perspectivism and Literary Theory Today." *American Literary History* 2 (1990): 528-49.

Rooney, Ellen. *Seductive Reasoning: Pluralism as the Problematic of Contemporary Literary Theory*. Ithaca, NY: Cornell UP, 1989.

Rorty, Richard. *Contingency, Irony, and Solidarity*. Cambridge: Cambridge UP, 1989.

Stewart, Susan. *On Longing: Narratives of the Miniature, the Gigantic, the Souvenir, the Collection*. Durham: Duke UP, 1993.

Strine, Mary. "The Humanities and Media Criticism: The Impact of Literary Criticism." *Critical Studies in Mass Communication* 2 (1985): 167-75.

Tatum, Stephen. "The Heart of the Wise Is in the House of Mourning." *Eye on the Future: Popular Culture Scholarship into the Twenty-First Century in Honor of Ray B. Browne*. Ed. Marilyn F. Motz, John G. Nachbar, Michael T. Marsden, and Ronald J. Ambrosetti. Bowling Green, OH: Bowling Green State University Popular Press, 1994: 57-72.

Tompkins, Jane. *West of Everything: The Inner Life of Westerns*. New York: Oxford UP, 1992.

George N. Dove

GEORGE N. DOVE:
GENTLE REBEL

Jane S. Bakerman

George Dove likes to eat breakfast and so do I. That's been a lucky break for me because the Dean of the Mystery/Detection area and I have shared a number of breakfasts (though not the same menu—I've never really developed an appreciation for grits) during Popular Culture Association meetings. Conversation during these meals has helped to cement our friendship and has certainly expanded my grasp of crime fiction.

Interestingly enough, George and I don't read many of the same books, though we've often both contributed to the same essay collections. His taste runs toward the police procedural, and his discussions of it, both in papers and in informal chats, have kept me informed about his field. Those exchanges are very typical of the Mystery/Detection area of the PCA—members' tastes range widely, but we all pretty much believe in a Big Tent where all sorts of ideas and opinions can flow freely. We can learn from one another and, when necessary, agree to disagree.

Many of us believe that to a considerable degree, this tolerance is a result of George Dove's influence. Symbol of that belief and of the high regard in which he is held is the George N. Dove Award,[1] established in 1986, which is presented intermittently to scholars who have made major contributions to the serious study of crime fiction. Those who have won the award cherish it, of course, and feel honored to share in the respect accorded to George Dove.

George N. Dove was born on October 28, 1913, in Bristol, Tennessee. He took his BA and MA (1935, 1936) at Western Reserve University and married Helenhill Sherrod in 1939. The couple had two daughters, Ellen Dove Lyle and Jane Dove Cox (d. 1969). From 1936 to 1939, Dove taught in his hometown high school and then served as principal of the Brenton Junior High School from 1939-43. From 1945-47, he was principal of a twelve-year rural school in Ashland City, near Nashville.

In 1947, George Dove accepted an invitation to join the English faculty at East Tennessee State where he also served for three years as chairperson of the English department. He took a leave in 1950-51 to work on his doctoral requirements at the University of Tennessee, his doctorate in education being granted in 1952. The focus of Dove's doctoral work was the training of teachers of English, a field in which he expected to specialize during much of his career, for he recognized a great need for a coherent, effective program. He was intrumental in developing such a program for teacher training, and it was going very well when his career took a different turn.

In 1956 George Dove was lured into administration, and he held the office of Dean of Arts and Sciences for twenty-three years; that work was exacting, of course, and often absorbing, but, he says, it also left him "hungry for scholarship," and the Popular Culture Association filled that need. Though he was also active in many church and civic organizations and is a devoted gardener and an avid walker, Dove has always defined himself as an educator.

During his productive retirement, George Dove has continued to produce scholarly books and articles which are important contributions to the study of crime fiction. His other contributions to the Popular Culture Association have also been important. In addition to delivering sterling papers marked with acuity and wit, Dove has served as Area Chair, on the governing board, and as President of the PCA (1989-91). These activities, like his scholarship, have earned him wide respect, and he is an important contributor to the organization. However, the organization is also important to him. He says,

As I remember it now, there were two strong forces that drew me into the serious study of detective fiction. The first was that it offered just what I was searching for at that time [the early Seventies], a field to work in. After several attempts, I had become aware that Henry James and William Faulkner criticism were badly overstocked, and I was finding no comfort at all in the arid desert of administration, where scholarship was about as tasty and nourishing as sawdust.

Around 1973, I made the discovery that papers dealing with the study of popular fiction were not only welcomed but sought after. I developed a topic I had been thinking about, sent it off to *The Armchair Detective,* and there it appeared in print. There followed a regular production of two papers a year, one for the Popular Culture Association and one for the Popular Culture Association of the South. I was a scholar.

The other factor which attracted me to the PCA was the friendly warmth and enthusiasm of its members, not at all like the types encountered in associations of administrators. I felt the difference with special force in the spring of 1975, when I went directly from the PCA meeting in St. Louis to an administrators' gathering in Chicago. The contrast was shocking. At PCA, you see somebody leaning against a wall, you introduce yourself and strike up a conversation, and the next thing you know you two are having lunch together. With the administrators, one of those lynx-eyed people with his back to the wall is looking for prey, not friendship. It was with nothing short of joy that I went to the 1976 PCA, to the association of such wonderful people as Earl Bargainnier, Jane Bakerman, Don Wall, and Barrie Hayne. Besides, there were Giants in the Earth to be found there, like Pat and Ray Browne, John Cawelti, and Marshall Fishwick, as friendly and approachable as the rest.

Like many other members of the Mystery/Detection area of the Popular Culture Association, George Dove often presents papers which later appear as chapters in one of his books or as essays in topical collections. And, like many other members, Dove is also often able to make his special interests congruent with others' preoccupations. One good example of this is the essay, "Dorothy Uhnak" which appeared in *And Then There Were Nine . . . More Women of Mytstery*. The collection was designed to showcase female mystery writers, but Dove, along with Martha Alderson and Neysa Chouteau, who wrote about Lillian O'Donnell, incorporated the concept of the police procedural into the work. This expanded and enriched the offerings considerably, contributing to readers' overview of the various forms available in mystery writing.

The organization Dove used for the Uhnak essay established a pattern which he later adapted to good effect in *The Police Procedural*. He discusses, compares, and contrasts various units of Uhnak's work as separate segments rather than in one long piece. This method works quite well in that it dramatizes the differences between Uhnak's various efforts, and—as my students informed me—aids the reader in scanning for specific information.

In this essay, Dove sets out the characteristics of the police procedural, the form which so interests him. These include investigation by professionals rather than by "gifted amateurs" or private eyes, focus on one officer "who bears the burden of narrative interest" but the overall emphasis is upon team effort, and attention to the protocols and devices available to professional officers, the latter including such diverse aspects as informants and crime laboratories. He notes that cops' family relationships generate subplots. Further, he points out that the officers tend to protect one another to the point of covering up "each other's derelictions [as well as] the complicated one-upmanship involved in the system of favors and revenge" (38-84).

In observing that Uhnak's primary interest is people rather than puzzle (98), Dove identifies a quality that many crime fiction critics demand in writers they admire and praise. The heights and depths of human nature are the factors that capture our interest most intensely; good writers (and good critics) know that and emphasize it.

Links between the Dorothy Uhnak essay and Dove's later work, the invaluable *The Police Procedural,* are clear to any reader. His definition of the procedural, not surprisingly, isn't much different from the one Dove established in the earlier work, but he adds an important qualification—"the police procedural is the only kind of detective story in which the detective has a recognizable counterpart in real life" (3). Thus, he goes on "the procedural is the only kind of detective fiction that did not originate in a purely literary tradition" (4). *The Police Procedural* explores and analyzes the values as well as the limitations that these qualities impose.

In relatively short chapters, Dove deals with the subgenre as a whole, discussing such topics as the history of the subgenre, procedures, the police subculture, and the differences between European and American styles. Attention then turns to a group of superior practioners of the form—John Creasey, Maurice Proctor, Hillary Waugh, Ed McBain, Bill Knox, Nicolas Freeling, Maj Sjowall and Per Wahloo, Collin Wilcox and James McClure. This selection makes the study seem expansive, for it includes British, Swedish, American, and South African writers—and Nicolas Freeling who is British-Dutch-French! Dove handles each author's variations smoothly, and *The Police Procedural* is a valuable resource.

The introduction to the Freeling chapter also provides a very nice example of Dove's writing style:

Anybody seeking to construct a model of the "typical" policeman in procedural fiction would be well advised to stay away from Nicolas Freeling's Peter Simon Joseph Van der Valk of the Amsterdam police, the reason being that very few cops can quote Baudelaire, or would undertake to wear down a suspect by means of a series of social calls, or would refuse to call the lab boys to a murder site because police technology isn't his style. (211)

Here, as in most of his work, Dove combines sharp observation and emphasis on the telling detail with an informality which invites rather than demands the reader's attention and contemplation. Pared down and seemingly simple, the style is the result of careful attention and self-discipline. Typically, Dove takes his subject but not himself seriously. It's a fly-catching example of the effectiveness of honey over vinegar.

Cops and Constables: American & British Fictional Policemen, edited by George N. Dove and Earl F. Bargainnier, is another approach to the procedural. Here, George Dove handled the Cops, the American authors and characters; Earl Bargainnier handled the British. Paying attention to the great diversity of protagonists who were emerging by the 1980s, Dove selected Anthony Abbot (Fulton Oursler), Joseph Harrington, John Ball, Hillary Waugh, Dell Shannon, Collin Wilcox, and Tony Hillerman as subject-authors. This selection allowed for some ethnic diversity among the subject-protagonists who include an African American, an Hispanic, and a Native American. Dove and Bargainnier don't make a fuss about this diversity, but the point is made—shifts in social consciousness are being felt in even the most traditionally conservative form of popular fiction.

In the introduction to this book, Dove and Bargainnier make three points which may be especially important: the officers' "constant exposure to corruption," their alienation from society—many of these characters "feel more at home with the criminal element than with the public they are expected to protect"—and the importance of the family relationships motif in procedurals (4-6). The editors make a particularly interesting point when they note that officers' families "belong to the 'guilty community' and are themselves potential victims or criminals" (6); this factor, coupled with the theme of cops' alienation, can lend enormous complication to an otherwise simple plot, and it certainly allows for complexity of characterization.

The editors' careful attention to such patterns illuminates readers' understanding even as it entertains them. Moreover, without belaboring the point, Dove and Bargainnier indicate some of the intricacies inherent in a form many suppose to be simplistic and formulaic. By implication, then, Dove and Bargainnier suggest one of the great attractions of crime fiction: to see how much flexibility a skilled writer can tease into a formula. They also stimulate their readers to produce good criticism, a gratifying outcome of yet another sort.

The Boys from Grover Avenue; Ed McBain's 87th Precinct Novels, which earned a special Edgar Allan Poe Award from the Mystery Writers of America, is clearly a labor of love, though it is important to note that Dove doesn't lose his critical perspective, despite his affection for his subject. He notes, for instance, that

there was little in these first 87th Precinct stories to distinguish them from other police procedurals, except that they were much better written than most. When we re-read them now, we may be struck by the absence of those qualities that have come to distinguish the 87th Precinct stories, and to be impressed by the similarity of their tone to that of the more conventional cop story. The changes that have been worked into the series are the marks of Ed McBain's maturing style. (2)

In one stroke, Dove establishes his fairness as a critic and whets his readers' curiosity about just what kinds of excellence McBain was to unveil as he matured.

Dove begins his study by putting the series into historical context:

The year 1956 was a particularly good time for starting a police series, because public taste at that point was running in favor of the police mystery. Television featured several shows with cop detectives, including especially the fabulous *Dragnet,* which had captured the public fancy as few broadcast series ever have. (1)

Moving gracefully from that widely known icon, *Dragnet,* Dove goes on to explain the influence of Lawrence Treat whose work might well not be known to readers. By defining Treat's methods and comparing them to those of the *Dragnet* writers, Dove establishes a workable context for his commentary on the 87th precinct.

Here again, in the *Boys from Grover Avenue,* Dove of course must address the subject of the police procedural. Once more, he distinguishes between the use of "police routines (like stakeouts, laboratory analysis and informants)" (41) as opposed to the lively fireworks available to the creators of eccentric amateurs or private eyes. He notes that McBain's

understanding of the intricacies and involvements of police work, together with his awareness of their limitations, has consistently attracted favorable notice of readers who delight in those absorbing descriptions like that autopsy report in *The Mugger,* which culminates in a surprising revelation abaout the victim. (41)

As is so typical of his style, Dove here makes two points at once. He notes admiringly that McBain (who is really Evan Hunter) turns what could be a handicap into a strength by his deft handling of detail, and he also draws the reader into the inner circle of McBain admirers. If the reader already knows the scene in *The Mugger,* he's flattered to be one of the "in crowd"; if he doesn't, he's flattered to be mistaken for an aficionado and will soon know the scene very well indeed. Seems so simple; is so clever; works so well.

The complexity of time and place in the McBain novels is a potentially thorny issue which Dove handles nicely, explaining how to impose a map of McBain's city upon a map of New York City and have it all make sense, and how to correlate real time with McBain's fictional time. Dove uses both the geographical information and the time sequence to reinforce "the sense of 'tilt' . . . the special slant on reality that needs to be recognized in order to gain full appreciation of McBain's narrative technique" (30). It would be unfair to both McBain and to Dove to steal those explanations and incorporate them here, but it's important to note that both the author and his critic recognize these devices as crucial to the merging of the imagined and the actual which is so important to crime fiction. McBain pulls off a very sophisticated series of auctorial tricks, and Dove demystifies them without diminishing them.

A McBain quality that Dove particularly values is

The refusal to stereotype, the insistence upon the distinctiveness of each individual in the story [this] is a conscious element of the McBain craftsmanship, which has also successfully resisted the temptation to fall into an easy formula. (68)

Having made that point, Dove goes on to look at groups of characters—Criminals and Victims—as well as important individual characters—Steve Carella, Meyer Meyer, and Bert Kling, for example. These analyses point up McBain's skill at characterization. Dove's readers enjoy his pointing out details they've noticed and are intrigued to note those they may have missed. Here, as always, the key to good analysis is to inform the reader without patronizing him, and Dove does exactly that.

In *Suspense in the Formula Story,* which examines several types of popular fiction, Dove shifts gears, examining the ways suspense—keen interest in what may happen next—functions in stories whose endings (according to common belief) should be fairly predictable. That's what "formula" means, one would suppose. Yet, suspense is popular fiction's stock in trade, formula or no formula. Dove approaches the question of formulization/novelty from the critics' point of view, assuming that the critic evaluates the work according to how well the author has met his postulated reader's needs, thus raising the question of the "faithful reader."

This "faithful reader" is the figure whom the author postulates and whom the critic tries to picture in order to evaluate the work. Dove says,

We will lay it down as requisite, then, that the critic seeking to interpret a popular story will hold some kind of conception of the typical/average/representative reader the author had in mind as he wrote it. . . . what the critc projects is the author's image of his reader. Now, whether any given reader—or all of them—fits that image is really irrevelevant. What the critic wants is a perception of that process by which the author achieves his artistic purpose with that reader, "real" or projected. (3)

As always, Dove fortifies his point with a relaxed but appropriate example. Here, he cites a running gag from the 87th Precinct novels having to do with Meyer's Jack-Benny-like habit of stalling his age; Meyer always insists that he's thirty-seven years old. Long-time series readers catch and relish these jokes, of course. Dove uses this example to suggest that "The reader projected by McBain is sympathetic to Meyer, has a sense of humor and a good memory, and has read at least some of the other novels in the series" (3).

This is tricky business since many writers maintain that they keep no image of a reader in mind when they write. Rather, they claim, they write to please themselves or write to suit the demands of the plot or of the characters as the story unfolds. But Dove uses ideas of various projected readers to analyze persuasively the several aspects of suspense as employed in a variety of works. In this way, he demonstrates "Process Criticism," stressing the concept that

Every reading is an exercise in interpretation; the difference between the eager fan who snuggles up with the latest Dick Francis and the academic critic searching out Freudian implications in "The Purloined Letter" is the difference in the network of expectations each brings to the act of reading. (121)

Though Dove's style is rather more formal in *Suspense in the Formula Story* than in *The Boys from Grover Avenue,* he still maintains his keynote intimacy with his reader, producing stimulating criticism gracefully presented.

In 1997, The Bowling Green State University Popular Press, which has been Dove's publisher throughout his career, released *The Reader and the Detective Story,* which Dove maintains is his last (rather than his latest) book, declaring that developing these studies is "hard work." Well, it is hard work, of course, but Dove's readers can but hope that he will continue to undertake it.

The Reader and the Detective Story is an examination of reader response theory. The premise requires

the assumption of the uniqueness of the detection formula, with the reservation that the sense of "differentness" of the detective story is to be found to a greater degree in the manner in which it is read and only secondarily in the text. (5)

As even this brief quotation suggests, the demands of this topic impose a more formal style than that Dove usually uses; the "original" Dove voice sounds occasionally, however, as in chapter titles such as "The Mean Streets and the Mall" or "Are We Supposed to Take this Stuff Seriously?"

By examining formula, method, and the similarities and divergences between English and American mysteries, then, Dove further defines crime fiction in this most recent work. He raises questions about the mystery's form and purpose and suggests intriguing answers to them, drawing *The Reader and the Detective Story* to a close with these words,

> A detective story that lacks movement, intrigue, cross-purposes, and the elucidation of character [is] not worth reading. At the same time, however, it must never be forgotten that the underlying structure of transformed play, or what we [in this study] have called the mystique of the tale of detection, is the real source of its differentness among popular genres.

At the beginning of the last chapter of *The Reader and the Detective Story,* Dove reports that a student asked him, "Are we supposed to take this stuff seriously?" and that his answer was, "a suitably professorial, 'It depends'" (167). It does depend, of course—the seriousness of almost everything "just depends" upon a "hundred million" factors. What is clear, however, is that George Dove takes "this stuff" seriously; so do the 60-some writers who created his primary sources, and so do about the same number of writer/critics who produced his secondary sources. And so do I, and so, no doubt, does anyone who reads this book.

While there is no special persuasiveness in sheer numbers, there is a certain persuasiveness in the quality of the minds whose works Dove has consulted, and there is great persuasiveness in the quality of the mind and of the work that George Dove has presented in his literary criticism. In the hands of skilled writers, crime fiction is serious (and seriously entertaining) fiction. Clever minds realize that; sound critics—George Dove among them—point it out.[2]

Notes

1. The Dove Award, established at the Atlanta convention in 1986, is the brain child of another respected Pioneer of Popular Culture, Earl Bargainnier, one of George's good friends and his collaborator in editing *Cope and Constables; American & British Fictional Policemen.* Earl suggested that an award be established to recognize excellent scholarship in the field of mystery/detection criticism, and he recruited Don Wall and Jane Bakerman to help bring the idea to fruition. The original award, presented to George Dove, is a ceramic dove wearing a beat cop's cap. Subsequent models are plaques etched with a picture of the police-officer dove. Active in both the national organization and the Pop-

ular Culture Association of the South, Earl Bargainnier, now deceased, was a prolific scholar and is much missed by his many friends and associates.

2. One further question should be addressed: does this discussion do full justice to George N. Dove's work? No. This essay is merely an introduction, a tribute, and an invitation to others to learn from him as I have done. I'm very pleased to have been asked to prepare it.

Marshall W. Fishwick

MARSHALL W. FISHWICK:
A MAN FOR ALL REASONS

Daniel Walden

In mid-career Marshall Fishwick wrote in "A Commonplace Intro-duction," that "We have much in common." Coming from the "right side of the tracks," enjoying "better" people and "superior" schools, he went to the University of Virginia (1944) and then to Wisconsin and Yale (1950). Donning the robes of Platonism, exposed to the best that has been thought and said, a member of a Greek-letter fraternity, he forged on until he got a Ph.D. and a spot on that icon of icons, the Academic Ladder and that trade-title, Professor.

In the 1960s, Marshall bloomed. Like many academics he was forced to rethink the meaning of radical. The origin of the word is radix, root. The radical tries to get back to his roots, to seek out the original and fundamental things. In so doing, Marshall came upon common cul-ture and the great tradition. He found that the concrete is chosen over the abstract, and the "meanest things" are not despised. Intuition and emo-tional attachment rate higher than rational analysis; intellectual fads are ignored. Here one finds, as Conal Furay noted in his *The Grass-Roots Mind in America,* "A mind of staid judgment but easy credulity, that moves not in the intellectual's fashion of idea to idea but of thing to thing." Such thinking posits a knowable, workable world in which people live hour by hour, day by day, showing a basic composure in the face of the wrenching influences of the twentieth century.

What Marshall wrote might be called Confession of an Ex-Elitist. It is a lifelong pursuit that has led me to describe Marshall Fishwick as a man for all seasons, *and* a man for all reasons.

Popular culture became a recognizable academic movement in the 1960s. The Popular Culture Association, led by Ray Browne, Marshall Fishwick, and Russel Nye, challenged the "new critical" orientation that was dominant in much of the humanities. The popular culture orienta-tions held that artifacts in social context challenged the assumption that intellectual discourse could take place abstracted from life. It was the democratizing of scholarship that was taking place. As the United States, in the years from Theodore Roosevelt to Ronald Reagan, shifted from mass industrial to an information society, as American Studies was emerging and maturing, as decentralization butted heads with centralization and individual and ethnic diversity became major themes, popular culture courses began to explore and extol the multiple option society.

As Fred Schroeder and others have told us, there is such a thing as preindustrial popular culture; indeed, there is such a thing as ancient popular culture. The point is that without knowing what was popular yesterday, and why, we can never hope to understand what is popular today. True, we do not yet have a method of studying or classifying common culture. One concept that is helpful is formula, which allows us to analyze the conventions and inventions used in the popular arts and to devise new categories and meanings. But, Fishwick asks: is method what we need? "Is not the real meaning of culture outside of any precise method, tied into the understanding of the erratic and irrational world that people inhabit and relish?"

If American Studies can continue to debate whether it is a discipline and whether it can develop a method, then so can Popular Culture. When Marshall McLuhan died in 1980 we realized he'd been a catalyst who'd set many of us into action and reaction. When John Lennon was murdered we remembered that, in one of his last interviews with *Playboy* magazine, he'd said: "It wasn't me, or us. It was the time and the place. Whatever wind was blowing at the time moved the Beatles, too. The whole boat was moving." The fact is that, as Ralph Henry Gabriel put it in 1974, "What the end will be only the future can disclose." Instead of worrying about that end, "let's follow the advice the King gave Alice in Wonderland, and begin at the beginning, defining key terms, examining tradition, land and lore, myths and dreams." As Fishwick told us, "Let's act on [Captain Ahab's] bold resolve: not to stay close to shore, where minnows dart, but to sail out into the deep—into living waters, and keep a sharp lookout for whales."

Starting in the 1950s Marshall Fishwick published a book on *American Heroes,* a *Bibliography of the American Hero,* a book on *Virginia,* and one on *The Virginia Tradition.* That early he was laying the groundwork for the breadth and depth of an extraordinary career. In Penn State's Pattee Library we list 28 books; a new one will be out later this year, titled *The Hero: Lost, Strayed or Stolen?* And each time he has reinvented himself, gone into the deep waters, invented new concepts.

Marshall Fishwick, after a one-year stint as an instructor in American Studies at Yale University, where was awarded his Ph.D., taught at Washington and Lee University from 1950-1962, directed the Wemyss Foundation from 1962-1964, chaired the Art Department and the American Studies Department at Lincoln University, from 1964-1970, was a professor of Mass Communication at Temple University from 1970-1976, and since 1976 has been professor of Humanities and Communications Studies at Virginia Tech. For him the study of popular culture has been a process of stripping away, for often underneath the surface of things that are popular or celebrated is a larger message of society. On its face, McDonald's is a fast-food place to eat. But the chain has also wrought what Fishwick terms a McDonaldization of life in the late decades of the twentieth century, a time which "standardization, rapid turnover and dehumanization" are prized (*Common Culture*).

Popular Culture, according to Fishwick, holds a mirror up to the times. It doesn't claim to be discipline, but it does claim to work with and between the disciplines. Thus, from the 1950s to the present, to three custom-designed books, *Go, and Catch a Falling Star: Pursuing Popular Culture* (1994), *Preview 2000: Popular Culture Studies in the Future* (1995), and *An American Mosaic* (1997) Fishwick has tried to present a holistic view, a convergence of forces, to counter those who think the end is coming; for Fishwick the thrust of his books is figuring out how the challenges of tomorrow are to be met. It is also the basis of democracy: if people have enough of the right information, they will make a wise decision. In this context, Tom Wolfe (who was Marshall's student at Washington and Lee) has written that Marshall Fishwick was an "omnimaniac," in that "His scholarly interest knew no bounds, and he was determined to *teach it all* . . . all with the glittering eye and a glistening smile that seemed to come not so much from down-home happiness as from the exhilaration of the quest for knowledge and the challenge of getting it through our skulls."

It is this Marshall Fishwick, who has been one of the initial pioneers, along with Ray Browne and Russel Nye, of the study of popular culture, that I am writing about. Interestingly, Marshall Fishwick's interests have overlapped mine, in the study of minority cultures, and urban ethnic studies. As Fishwick wrote in explaining why the respected Oliver W. Larkin, author of *Art and Life in America,* was not a racist, he noted that Larkin's omission of black artists, except in passing, merely reflected the zeitgeist. Had Larkin's book emphasized the creative life, rather than "fine art," the content of the book would have been different. The exhibit of "Art and Life in Black America" that Fishwick sponsored at Lincoln University in 1968 showed that the recognition of art is a human as well as a technical problem. These are the dimensions of Marshall Fishwick that I am writing about.

In October 1958, in a lecture at Stetson University, Professor Fishwick presented his thoughts on the beginnings of American Studies. Pursuing the ambiguous, he spoke on "Where Do American Studies Begin?"

One starting point was Joe Clark, who left Henrico County, Virginia, for the Irish Creek district of Rockbridge County, covering the western slope of the Blue Ridge Mountains. It was free land but it was remote, rocky and rugged, inaccessible even by mountain standards. But Joe and his brother Nelson were determined to make a go of it. They married Native American women, built log cabins, and cleared trees for a patch of corn. Joe had twenty-four children and before long his progeny outnumbered everyone else from Wigwam Mountain to Norwell Flats. They still do (Fishwick and Browne).

No one has written the history of the Clarks. But there is much there for all of us: a lively body of folklore, indigenous, dewy-fresh, satisfying. "The distilled experience of two centuries of birthing, living and dying is passed on orally, in tales, proverbs, and songs," as Fishwick sees it. They tell of the mystery and wonder of the earth; they are history transmuted into poetry." For generations the Clarks have sung about their tribal patriarch who came to the Unpromising Land; the song marks Joe Clark as a genuine king-sized cockalorum demigod:

> Old Joe Clark had a mule
> His name was Morgan Brown;
> Every tooth in that mule's head
> Was sixteen inches around.

> Old Joe Clark had a cow
> She was muley born;
> It took a jaybird a week'n half
> To fly from horn to horn.

> I went down to old Joe's house
> He was sick in bed;
> Rammed my finger down his throat
> And pulled out a wagon bed.

Although not many of the movements of the period penetrated Irish Creek, the Great Awakening did. The gospel got back into the hills, and Joe himself became a preacher of sorts.

> Old Joe Clark set out to preach
> He preached all over the plain.
> The highest text he ever took
> Was high low Jack and game.

Ole Joe Clark had a yaller cat
She'd neither sing no pray
She stuck her head in the buttermilk jar
And washed her sins away.

With Joe the law of love did not prevail. Not were all those who followed him distressed by it:

Old Joe Clark killed a man
Killed him with a knife.
I'm damned glad he killed that man
Now I'll have his wife.

The song took hold and grew because it was a good song. In his *Treasury of American Folklore* (1944), B.A. Botkin lists verses heard in Cleveland County, Oklahoma. Back in Rockbridge County, new verses were contrived to meet new situations and times. When lumbering became the major enterprise in the district, such verses as these became popular:

Sixteen horses in my team
The leaders had no line
I whip them around a rocky road
To see that gal of mine.

Driving my old mule team
Leading Old Gray behind
Before I'll see my true love wake
I'll pull Old Nellie blind.

Eventually book-learning came up creek, and a school teacher appeared on the local scene. If this verse of "Old Joe Clark" is any indication, she was not treated in a way befitting Virginia Cavaliers:

I wouldn't marry a school teacher
I'll tell you the reason why;
She blows her nose in yaller corn bread
And calls it pumpkin pie.

In his *Treasury of American Folklore,* Botkin lists these and other verses heard in Cleveland County, Oklahoma. Many Virginians grew up with "Old Joe Clark" ringing in their ears. Charles Vardell, Jr., wrote a symphonic piece called "Old Joe Clark Steps Out," which the National

Symphony orchestra played in 1956. Then they set out to find Joe Clark's grandson, an 86-year-old mountaineer, who came, sat in the front row, and listened to the concert. Undoubtedly, Joe Clark is a single tree in the vast forest of American culture. Hopefully, our concern with size, spectacle and generality, Fishwick writes, will not blind us to the glory and truth contained in the ordinary and immediate.

It is significant that Ralph Waldo Emerson understood this danger when he advised us to discover the real meaning of America by examining "the meal in the firkin: the milk in the pan; the ballad in the street; the news of the boat; the glance of the eye; the form and gait of the body." Unfortunately, according to Fishwick, seeking a methodology which will be respected academically, we have favored the abstract over the earthy, and we have insisted on explaining our culture from the top down, rather than from the bottom up. Mixing ignorance and bias, many Virginians (whom he knew best) wrote of Democrats, while Negroes were segregated in history books as well as in restaurants. The western counties, Republicans, Negroes, and the twentieth century were isolated and ignored.

It seems that many Americans do not know the meaning of America's motto. E. Pluribus Unum means "Out of Many, One." It is the tension between these two factors that has made our country great. As Fishwick put it, beautifully, one hopes "we can preserve the diversity and flavor which is the material for the Odyssey of the human spirit. People who differ from us are not enemies, they are godsends. In weaving a cultural carpet which is beautiful and strong, we must keep the original fibers so intact that the fineness of each will show through in the finished handwork. It is with the original fibers, the subtle but inescapable differences, that the study of America begins."

Although he'd written on American Studies in transition in the 1950s it was in his 1964 study that he set out to provide "a set of random essays on certain aspects of our pluralistic culture," without making a claim for completeness. The nation described, he affirmed, has created an open one. Men and woman here have tried, in Walt Whitman's words, "to take the hinges off the doors." The essays in *American Studies in Transition* display the honest skepticism that marked the best recent scholarship to that point. Lacking a method, Henry Nash Smith wrote that "the best thing we can do, in my opinion, is to conceive of American Studies as a collaboration among men working from existing academic disciplines but attempting to widen the boundaries imposed by conventional methods of inquiry." In Fishwick's words, "to survive, a movement must be able to adapt to new environments and respond to new challenges. . . . To survive is to change and to compare."

Of course, it is only a small jog from heroes, from antiquity to the moderns—like George Washington, Robert E. Lee, and Teddy Roosevelt—to icons. Icons are images and ideas converted into three dimensions. They're also cultural ciphers, in the sense that they help us decipher or unlock the mystery of our attitudes and assumptions. Pop icons, however, in Marshall Fishwick's words, are new and at the same time old. Icons are invented by all cultures. "We look with our eyes, see with our minds, make with our hands. . . . Icons are symbols and mindmarks. They tie in with myth, legend, values, idols, aspirations." True, millions associate icons with belief, sacred object, veneration. Icons are associated with age and class groups. But, Fishwick ways, "icons, like all artifacts are (among other things) visible and incontrovertible facts. They can be dealt with in space and time. Many can even be broken. Those who break them are iconoclasts."

Coke bottles and soup cans are also icons, that is, anti-icons, because they are omnipresent, not because they're unique. They're accessible, unavoidable. In this sense, they fade even as we venerate them; being new implies obsolescence of form and value.

Where are we heading? According to Fishwick, referring to Benjamin DeMott's *Supergrow,* we may be heading for cultural pollution. On the other hand, going beyond the surface of the pop icon we can see that "pop icons are filling our landscape and forcing channeling of our culture. They are the basis of the new reality. In the Middle Ages all experience found philosophical unity and visual form in a single metaphorical system. Will this be true in the twenty-first century?

In the Introduction to *Heroes of Popular Culture* (1972), Marshall wrote: "In the days of Eisenhower the conqueror, the valley stood so fat with corn that they laughed and sang. Content in one of those havens— the University of Virginia—I wrote of American heroes." In 1972, rereading *American Heroes, Myths and Reality,* which up to 1954, saw everything fit, every hero was linked to the great chain of being, he recognized that his old crop of heroes looked archaic, even irrelevant. There was consternation and chaos when John F. Kennedy was assassinated in 1963. It was the most crucial event in the heroic history of that generation. When Woody Guthrie died in 1967 there was little national mourning, but Woody was a proto-popular hero who would be reincarnated in a talented imitator, Bob Dylan, and in his son Arlo. Guthrie helped to put anti-hero on the center of the stage. So did Norman Mailer, and many others. In their wake came beats and the hippies. Of course, unheroic or anti-heroic characters are deeply rooted in the past. Bob Dylan, "both anti-political and anti-intellectual," was a "three-Minute-Twelve-track-Super-acrylic-Longplay-Hero with an automatic cutoff at the song's end." Is that any way to run Olympics? asked Fishwick.

Clearly, as Fishwick has seen, one field is fluid, dominated by images rather than words. But we know too little about the juxtaposition of public images and the impact of constant media exposure on Americans and those who fascinate us. As Mailer put it, "America is a country which has grown by the leap of one hero past another."

The point is, writes Fishwick, what the newly emerging busy-headed hero stands for is unclear, although he seems "to appear as an expression of Man's quenchless desire to affirm, despite the pressures of our age, the human sense of life." In the early modern period, Washington Irving became a founding father of fakestyle, which eventually overshadowed both oldstyle and folkstyle. Fakestyle impetus came from Europe where people like John Ruskin and William Morris, reacting to early machine civilization, retreated to mythical Camelot. Meanwhile Americans used machines to produce dime novels and give fakestyle an enormous boost. In 1860 *Malaeska: The Indian Wife of the White Hunter,* a "Yellowback" novel written by Ann S. Stephens, pre-figured the deluge of Beadle's Dime Novels, Frank Starr's American Novels, and so on. Folkstyle, in case you haven't guessed, is built on facts and real events—fakestyle on images and pseudo-events.

One result of fakestyle is impermanence. Another key word is interface. Interface is random contact with the life of forms, which, Fishwick notes, gives rise to a new heroic style. "The hero becomes a happening." What can be said is that "When most men lived in the country, folkstyle allowed us to mythologize American culture. By deflating rural values, Fakestyle demythologized our lives." The result is that "tension, not consensus, is the dominating theme." In that context, the key to the heroic personality is not achievement, which used to be a key criterion, but potential. But we are surrounded by the "failure of success," the "malaise of affluence." America is searching for a new ontology. Cultural relocation and heroic transformation are properly the radical interests of a new generation.

Of course, we all know that popular culture is basically subversive. Marshall Fishwick and many of us have been ignored, or shunned, or punished for pursuing popular culture, a movement, although it is not clear if it's a discipline, or a branch of the humanities or social sciences. As Robert Walker put it in 1958, "America has had to explain herself most thoroughly to herself and others." No wonder American Studies, American Culture, and American Civilization flourished. Fluidity was the key. For "Popular Culture is people," Fishwick claimed. "Popular culture is practical and event-oriented—it leans not toward Plato but Aristotle—toward percept, not concept."

What deserves recognition, as I stated earlier, is Marshall Fishwick's knack for invention, reinvention, and articulation. In *Seven Pillars of Popular Culture,* the chapters are titled Demos, Ethnos, Heros, Theos, Logos, Eikons, and Mythos, surely an incredible display of erudition from one who is known for his many books and articles on Popular Culture heroes and icons. But as we learn, "American Pop" is now in Paris, Peking, New York, New Delhi, etc.—all over the world. Popular Culture specialists still can't agree on any method but *it is* all over. To Descartes' conclusion, "Cogito Ergo Sum," we can only reply "Dubito Ergo Sum." We doubt, therefore We are. "The Age of Information increases not only our data but dilemmas. To make it worse—for those in the humanistic tradition—many of our colleagues seem to have given up not only Latin but also English. They speak science, mathematics, and (all too often) jargon."

As we approach the end of this millennium, America's cultural norms have become world standards. Friend and foe alike have adapted and adjusted to America. Near the end of the nineteenth century, it was seen that the real America was found by looking West as Frederick Jackson Turner wrote, not by looking East. Our belief in our Manifest Destiny seemed to be moving inexorably to dominate the Western World. After 1945, via the Marshall Plan, Fulbright grants, and American high tech, the urgent question became how best can we study and understand America?

The pioneering work of Charles Beard, Gilbert Seldes, Vernon P. Parrington, Van Wyck Brooks, Randolph Bourne, Ralph Gabriel, Robert Spiller, and Lewis Mumford appeared in the 1920s and 1930s. But it was World War II, the belief in the "American Century," and our phenomenal material success that forged a keen belief in American distinctiveness. If only we could explain this to the world, we thought, or "persuade" others to be like us, they might become partners in our democratic new world. Scholars like Tremaine McDowell and Arthur Bestor raised new questions: McDowell pointed out the fundamental diversity of human experience, hoping we might find a fundamental unity. Bestor asked: "The Study of American Civilization: Jingoism or Scholarship?" Meanwhile, as they founded the *American Quarterly* in 1949 and the American Studies Association in 1951, the Cold War and increasing tension with the USSR was seen. The implication was that we should not only explore but defend our way of life. At Yale University, Marshall Fishwick heard President Charles Seymour announce that the goal was "To produce a solidified faith in America and devotion to its maintenance."

But early enthusiasts, as Fishwick learned, had a more universal aim: to define a national mind through a new interdisciplinary approach. Another early goal was to move from traditional disciplinary emphasis to holism—to see the forest rather than a single tree. Later on, other subjects surfaced: popular culture, cultural anthropology and the behavioral sciences.

How should this be done? "Method" wars abounded. Who should teach what—and how? Henry Nash Smith suggested in 1957 that he hadn't developed a suitable method. In 1964, in one of Fishwick's first attempts to grapple with these problems, "our aim was to display the honest skepticism that marks the best scholars in our field," more than thirty years later, he's still pursuing this goal.

Ray Browne, Russel Nye, and Marshall Fishwick met in the Detroit airport in 1969 and mapped out plans for the new Popular Culture Association. Faced with the realization that Popular Culture (the operative word is derived from *populus*—of or relating to the people; suitable for the majority; by and for the people) reflected values widely dispersed in and approved by society, they soon found themselves facing a puzzle with many pieces; some are missing, some don't fit, key questions evade the answers. How did we get from the virgin Land, Fishwick asked, to the Raped Environment? Was Marshall McLuhan right when he said if it works, it's obsolete? Is yesterday's technology tomorrow's junk? Has our frontier moved from the West to the Pacific Rim? Will cyberculture make all earlier modes of communication obsolete? Is post-modernism behind us, or ahead of us? We have no choice but to evolve if we are to survive and prosper. None of the old curtains—iron, bamboo, plastic, paper—can block the electronic revolution, the Internet, and the World Wide Web.

Meanwhile, the struggle to define ourselves and our culture continues. As Marshall Fishwick writes in his new book, "We are undergoing a kind of cultural fusion. Method Wars have been joined by Canon Wars, Gender Wars, Race Wars and Culture Wars." How we act, how we see ourselves, in a culture more and more dominated by images rather than words, is crucial. The Electronic Revolution has created new environments of invisible power—new patterns, new space, new style. In that flow there are heroes, and anti-heroes. Ten years ago I asked "Where Have All the Heroes Gone?" Marshall Fishwick has noted that the heroic scene is changing very rapidly, so rapidly that an answer seems beyond us. His article, "The Hero, Lost, Stolen or Strayed?" in his *American Mosaic,* is his way of describing a culture in which C.P. Snow's "Two Cultures" is disappearing. Traditional disciplines are tumbling. New disciplines and interdisciplines are emerging. The anti-hero has had his inning and is waning. The hero and heroine are waxing. This is a fact. But, as Marshall Fishwick has concluded, "we must not think that history is determined by mere facts." In the words of Ralph Waldo Emerson, "who cares what the fact was, when we have made a constellation of it to hand in heaven an immortal sign?"

From 1968 to 1974, Marshall Fishwick was Head of the Art Studies Institute and American Studies Department at Lincoln University. Lincoln, as is well known, is the oldest "predominantly Black" University in the country. In 1968, in an article entitled "What Ever Happened to Regionalism?" he made the point that President Franklin Roosevelt dealt with regions of dust and dissent, men and migrations, convenience and necessity. Surrounding him were James Farley, Harold Ickes, and Harry Hopkins. Flourishing at the same time were John Crowe Ransom, Robert Penn Warren, and Allen Tate (the "Nashville Agrarians"), as well as Robert Frost, Grant Wood, John Lomax, and B. A. Botkin, John Steinbeck, William Faulkner, and Frank Lloyd Wright, to name only the most prominent. "Disillusioned by the Depression, suspicious of technology, international movements, and philosophical abstractions," according to Fishwick, "Americans found in regionalism a home-grown doctrine as real and rewarding as the earth itself."

One of the driving forces of the time, transmitted from Frederick Jackson Turner's words that the United States was to be a "fusion of potential nations and empires, each to be conquered and colonized . . . each to interact with the others," was Turner's disciple Howard W. Odum, a Georgian whose "ism" embraced politics, advocate-propanes, and the struggle against racism. No cloistered scholar, Odum inveighed against lynching, which "blackens the reputation of every state, cripples a race, sets people against people, and retards a wholesome integration of natural culture" (Fishwick, *Parameters* 5-6). In that context, functional regionalism, rooted in the nature of American culture and capable of changing with that culture, was part of the agenda of such luminaries as David Riesman, John Kouwenhoven, John Hague, and Oscar Handlin.

The point, Fishwick continued, is that part of the continued emphasis on regionalism, on regional studies, included Norman Holmes Pearson's statement that we can "speak of Negro writings as a kind of regionalism defined in newer terms. Thus, writing about Jewish characters and themes also takes on certain characteristics of a regionalism." That early, in 1968, Fishwick as he enlarged the scope of American Culture and popular culture, showed the relationship between race and civilization.

As is well known the increasing interest in pluralism in American culture and American popular culture has blossomed since World War II.

In the Introduction to his *American Studies in Transition,* Fishwick repeated Tremaine McDowell's First Law of American Studies: "present the complex design of American life so as to reveal the fundamental diversity of human experience within which students might eventually find a fundamental unity," and then explained that the book was "a set of random essays on certain aspects of our pluralistic culture." As John Hague observed, "as I traveled around the United States between 1971 and 1977, I witnessed accelerating changes in the structure and curricula of many American Studies programs. There were new colleagues—women, Blacks, Hispanics, and Native Americans, among others. Popular Culture and material culture were added. Students were encouraged to live and study abroad . . . there was a sense of mission."

Indicative of this new inspiration were the many books by and on Blacks and Jews, and others in the 1960s and 1970s. Abraham Chapman, Irving Howe, Leslie Fiedler, Daniel Walden, Charles Davis, Saunders Redding, and so many others wrote of the new strands so long hidden or undiscovered in our culture. At long last, as Oscar Handlin wrote, America was made up of immigrants. We were all immigrants. African Americans, Jewish Americans, Native Americans, Hispanic Americans, etc. One no longer had to be ashamed of being an American who was also rooted in a subculture. It was not admitted that America, mainstream America, had borrowed, assimilated, taken words and music, rituals and traditions from many sources. Just as we recognized that "the problem of race" as W. E. B. DuBois put it, "is the problem of the twentieth century," and that a characteristic of Jewish humor is "smiling through the tears," as Saul Bellow explained, so we learned that we were a nation. "From many, One," "E Pluribus, Unum."

A mosaic is a decoration made by inlaying and intertwining small pieces of glass, stone, or jewels to produce a pattern or picture. Certain insects have mosaic vision. They have compound eyes, made up of many independent units, so that objects viewed are not seen in isolation, but as a mosaic. An aerial mosaic is made up of many aerial photographs matched or patched together so as to show a continuous photographic representation of an area. Mosaics have a flow either forward or backward. If they remain static they are in fact dead or dying. Ours, like our civilization, moves forward. Mosaics were the glory of the classical world; they still thrill and inspire us and help us to understand our civilization. Fishwick's book, *An American Mosaic: A New Text for a New Age,* was published in 1997. Like all of his work in the past, it tries to present a series of independent thoughts and insights attempting to show us a view of our nation, now a part of the global village, which no one person or perspective could achieve.

In 1998 Marshall began work on a comprehensive summary of the field he had devoted his life to—*Popular Culture: Cave Space to Cyber Space*. Having read and written numerous monographs, reviews, and articles, he wanted to do his own synthesis. This book, however, would not be yet another monograph. In his own words:

This book is not written primarily for students or scholars, though I hope they will read and enjoy it. I seek a larger audience—the people who make and live our popular culture, as they have done since Homo sapiens stood on two legs and walked.

Today we speak of the "general reader" who buys not monographs but trade books. This book attempts to trade ideas, and make them fresh and exciting to Everyman and Everywoman. I employ the essay style and move quickly from topic to topic, century to century. Most essays end with an Endnote, some few with the more specific footnotes. They are meant to encourage further reading and thinking.

Henry Matrisse said he painted for people who liked to settle back in a red leather chair and enjoy his art. Choosing whatever chair is at hand, I hope my readers feel that way about our quick trip through time and space.

Still hopeful for wider reader response, Marshall had no reason to doubt he already had it from students and colleagues. He has won "Best Teacher Awards" at every American university in which he taught, and both commendations and honorary degrees abroad. Here are four comments from yearly evaluations in recent years:

Summary by Professor Kenneth Rystrom, Head,
Communication Studies (1988)

1. How long and in what capacity have you known the applicant?

Four years as a faculty colleague, three of which I have served as Professor Fishwick's department head.

2. What formal procedures are used at your institution, or within the applicant's department, to evaluate teaching effectiveness?

At the end of each term, students complete formal evaluations of instructors. Results, including students' written comments, are made available to the instructor and to the department head. In addition, faculty members visit colleagues' classes and write peer reviews that go to the instructor, the Personnel Committee, and the department head.

Professor Fishwick consistently ranks among our highest-scoring teachers. His colleagues' regard for his teaching abilities was demonstrated last year when they nominated him for the statewide Outstanding Faculty Award in the area of teaching. The previous year he won one of the Excellence in Teaching awards given by the College of Arts & Sciences.

In terms of student ratings, in a recent (typical) course, Professor Fishwick received a very high 3.7 overall rating out of a possible 4.0. Students rated him especially high in knowledge of subject, success in communicating, subject stimulating, and concern and respect for students. He received a 2.9 rating (out of 3.0) in the category of "effort required in the course." Students regularly describe him as the best professor they have had at Virginia Tech.

3. How would you assess the applicant's effectiveness in small groups, such as advanced seminar?

Professor Fishwick is equally adept at teaching large and small groups. In addition to his regular Popular Culture courses, he frequently teaches advanced new courses in the Honors Program and the Humanities Program. He is an extremely effective speaker in small groups.

4. How would you assess the applicant's effectiveness as a teacher in lecture settings, including large undergraduate classes?

Professor Fishwick's dynamic, outgoing personality (plus knowledge of his subject) largely accounts for his ability to stimulate students in larger classes. But he also has established a campus-wide reputation for his skill in using multiple audio-visual aids to help keep classes lively.

5. Discuss generally any aspect of the applicant's teaching record that you believe should be considered in an evaluation of the applicant's prospective assignment as a Fulbright lecturer abroad. Has the applicant received any special awards or recognitions?

I previously have mentioned some of the recognition Professor Fishwick has received for his teaching. He also has been honored by Yale University as a distinguished alumnus and by the Government of India for his work in that country. On countless occasions he has proved a valuable and effective academic ambassador to countries in every hemisphere.

Summary by Professor Robert Landen, Director,
Humanities Program (1994). ("H" is the highest rating given.)

Teaching (H) Dr. Fishwick's teaching remains effective. He ranks among the most successful of all HUM faculty in terms of his student teaching ratings. Dr. Fishwick is willing to teach a wide variety of courses all of which he handles with great success.

Research/Creative Activity (H) Again, has sustained a truly remarkable level of productivity: Two books published or reissued, 2 scholarly articles, and guest editor of prestigious *Journal of American Culture*'s "Tom Wolfe issue." Too, he continues to publish "op-ed" pieces (particularly in *Roanoke Times-WN*) on a regular basis. Now working on revising a novel into a film or TV production and doing a volume on religion and popular culture.

Service and Colleagueship (H) Dr. Fishwick not only is continuing to coordinate Center's "Humanities and the Arts" subprogram but also is spearheading its effort to establish a long-anticipated concentration in American Studies and Cultures. Both of these activities are very time consuming. He also remains very active in the American Popular Culture Association, a group which awarded him an "Award of Merit" and established a special award that will be bestowed annually in his honor.

Other Comment, Special Notations, or Summary: Statement of goals for '93 indicates that Dr. Fishwick's energetic, effective activities will be sustained in the future. I continue to marvel at his creativity and accomplishment. Another fine year in a long series of fine years contributing to this university's mission and public reputation.

Summary by Professor Robert Comparin, Head,
Mechanical Engineering (1994).
During the Spring Semester of 1993, Marshall Fishwick and I collaborated on a course in *Car Culture*. The course dealt with the influence of the automobile on the development of all aspects of life in our country. We had a very diverse student group with a good balance between students with technical and non-technical majors. We put considerable emphasis on the need for communication between people with diverse backgrounds. For example, our requirement for term papers restricted the topic choice. Students with technical majors had to submit papers with primarily non-technical content and the students with non-technical majors had to include technical content. An additional requirement was that all of their work in the course had to be written so that both Marshall and I could understand it. To insure compliance, Marshall and I both graded all of the student work and arrived at a consensus for a final grade.

The students were responsive and made an honest effort to understand the total picture. The technical students soon realized the need for a better understanding of the impact of technological development on the quality of life. Also the non-technical students now appreciate the need for an understanding of the technology. One example is the need for limiting the pollution of the environment which is caused by automobiles. Any intelligent approach to the problem requires a knowledge of both societal impact and technical feasibility. Dr. Fishwick has brought that knowledge, and his boundless enthusiasm, to this and the other problems of our day.

Summary by Professor Robert Landen (1995):
Key to Notation H = Exceptional; N = Commendable: L = Low Level.
Teaching (H) Student evaluations continue to be well above Center average. Has spent much time developing new American Studies concentration, as well as this concentration's introductory core course "Introduction to American

Studies" which will be offered initially in the Spring 1995 by a group of faculty coordinated by Professor Fishwick. Much student advising. Two teaching awards from outside organizations were presented. Also, continues to try to develop cooperative courses with other colleges, especially Engineering and Architecture.

Research/Creative Activity (H) Professor Fishwick's prodigious scholarly productivity continues yet one more year with two long-term research projects culminating in the publication of two books; one of these, *Go and Catch a Falling Star,* utilized a new publication technology which will allow for continual updating, a technique that attracted much attention including an article in *The Chronicle of Higher Education.* The other book focuses upon religion and popular culture. Also, four journal articles, and numerous newspaper op-ed pieces appeared, he continued his journal and advisory editorships; 14 book reviews.

Service and Colleagueship (H) A large amount of significant service both within this university and outside. Energetically coordinating the development of two Center concentrations, i.e., "Humanities and the Arts," and "American Studies," as well as assisting in planning a new CIS curriculum. Considerable assistance to university's Public Affairs offices re. newspaper, TV, and radio spots. Also consulted with U.S.I.A. in Washington and continues leadership service with national and local Episcopal Church and the Popular Culture Association.

Other Comment, Special Notations, or Summary: Dr. Fishwick continues to be one of this University's and this Center's most energetic, productive, and nationally renown faculty. Next year he will be doing a good deal of international work including a stint in a revived American Studies Center in Austria. Moreover, he is always willing to take on tasks and teach extra courses. He is a person who can be counted upon to help out when things get difficult in the university. In summary. Dr. Fishwick is a fine university citizen, who unfortunately, does not receive the recognition he merits within this university although he is highly respected outside its walls.

A notable student comment came from Tom Wolfe, in his "Preface" to Fishwick's *Go and Catch a Falling Star:*

He was the most magnetic teacher I had ever known, and I headed for the American Studies program at Yale in hopes of acquiring the same dionysian sweep myself. But of course Marshall was, to borrow Huey Long's phrase, *sui generis.* I have followed his career with a growing admiration, through his thirty books, innumerable articles, and newspaper columns. I have also made a point of keeping up with his amazing classroom performances. Lately I have gone to see him in action at Virginia Tech—and I have watched the glittering eye and the glistening smile entrancing another fortunate generation of undergraduates
. . .

Ecce Popular Culture. It has become such a big part of modern life, one can no longer rule it outside the boundaries of scholarly attention. It demands scholars of unprecedented range, powers of synthesis, and, not least of all, energy.

Fellow students, I give you Marshall Fishwick.

Such praise is built on a sturdy platform of pioneering work and tangible achievement by Marshall both individually and in working with others. He is proudest of all with having worked for thirty-five years with Ray Browne. He and Ray founded the Popular Culture Association and through the years they have edited numerous books, all of which they hope have broadened and enriched the study of popular culture and stimulated others to join in their endeavor. Their association seems one to be ended only by the great FINIS to all existences. Their latest endeavor, *The Global Village: Dead or Alive?* comes full-bodied from the Popular Press in 1998. Undoubtedly this academic and personal partnership will generate new ventures and new accomplishments.

The best way to conclude this account of the career of Marshall Fishwick, I think is simply to list his overseas grants.

Fulbright Grants and Overseas Lectures
Eight Fulbright grants (1959 to 1995)—Denmark, Germany, England, India (2), Bangladesh, Korea, South-East Asia. Five additional lecture trips sponsored by the Department of State and the United States Information Agency. Private research trips to England, France, India, and Italy. Salzburg Center in American Studies (1995).

These are the reasons why, in writing about the Marshall Fishwick whom I admire, I have termed him "A Man for All Reasons," as well as a Man for all Seasons.

Works Cited

Browne, Ray, and Marshall Fishwick, eds. *Preview 2000+: Popular Culture Studies in the Future.* Bowling Green, OH: Bowling Green State University Popular Press, 1995. 43-58.

Browne, Ray, Marshall Fishwick, and Michael Marsden, eds. *Heroes of Popular Culture.* Bowling Green, OH: Bowling Green State University Popular Press, 1972.

Fishwick, Marshall. *Parameters of Popular Culture.* Bowling Green, OH: Bowling Green State University Popular Press, 1974. 5-6.

——. Prelude. Postlude. *Seven Pillars of Popular Culture*. Westport, CT: Greenwood, 1985. 3-17, 195-203.

——. "What Ever Happened to Regionalism?" *Southern Humanities Review* 2.4 (Fall 1968).

——. "Where Do American Studies Begin?" *Stetson University Bulletin* LIX (Jameson 1959): 1-13.

Fishwick, Marshall, ed. *Common Culture and the Great Tradition*. Westport, CT: Greenwood, 1982. 4-17.

——. Introduction. *American Studies in Transition*. Boston: Houghton Mifflin, 1964.

——. Introduction, Preface, and "The Hero: Lost, Strayed, or Stolen?" *An American Mosaic: A New Text for a New Age*. New York: American Heritage, 1997.

Fishwick, Marshall, and Ray Browne, eds. *Icons of Popular Culture*. Bowling Green, OH: Bowling Green State University Popular Press, 1972. 1-23.

Odum, Howard. "Lynchings, Fears and Folksongs." *The Nation* 133 (30 Dec. 1931): 720.

Wolfe, Tom. Foreword. *Go and Catch a Falling Star: Pursuing Popular Culture* by Marshall Fishwick. New York: American Heritage, 1994.

M. Thomas Inge

M. THOMAS INGE:
A SMILE ALL AROUND

Michael Dunne

In 1992, M[ilton] Thomas Inge (b. 1936, Newport News, VA) was named Virginia Cultural Laureate in recognition of his long service to the arts and humanities. Significantly, during this same period Inge was also the organizer of the quadrennial "Pogo for President" celebration at the South Atlantic Modern Language Association meeting. In a similar feat of cultural diversity, Inge reviewed the year's work in Faulkner studies for *American Literary Scholarship* during the late 1980s and at the same time began editing the successful series "Studies in Popular Culture" for the University Press of Mississippi. Inge has written extensively about both the Vanderbilt Agrarian Donald Davidson and Richard Outcault, creator of *The Yellow Kid* comic strip. As an internationally renowned scholar of Southern American literature and as editor of the invaluable *Handbook of American Popular Culture,* Tom Inge is assured of a place as one of America's leading academic intellectuals and as a Pioneer in Popular Culture Studies.

Inge's academic development is partly explicable in light of his higher education: a bachelor's degree in English and Spanish from Randolph-Macon College and Master's and Doctoral degrees in English from Vanderbilt University. Inge's subsequent publication—with Vanderbilt Professor T. D. Young—of scholarly books focused on the career of Donald Davidson, as well as Inge's individual scholarship on American authors such as William Byrd, Ellen Glasgow, and James Branch Cabell, testifies to the enduring influence of these educational experiences. Perhaps the same might be said about Inge's annual reviews of scholarship on Nineteenth-Century Fiction (1970-73) and on William Faulkner (1986-88; 1990) for *American Literary Scholarship.* In affirmation of these academic continuities, Inge writes, in the Preface to his *Faulkner, Sut, and Other Southerners* (1992), that the essays collected in the book "represent my continuing concern with the nature of the Southern literary experience and the meaning of being Southern in the United States" (xi). Although one might not have predicted when Inge graduated from Vanderbilt in 1964 that he would forge so prolific and distinguished a scholarly career, on the basis of his academic training one might have assumed that his work would follow along these lines. And yet, as we have already seen, Inge's scholarship and cultural criticism range far more widely.

Elsewhere in the same Preface, Inge provides a clue to his more complex development as a cultural critic and pioneer of popular culture studies. He writes there that growing up in Richmond, "I felt largely excluded from the aristocratic heritage to which many Virginians lay claim. My mother's people had been tobacco share croppers from North Carolina who traveled first to Newport News, my birthplace, and then to Richmond seeking work during the Depression. My father's family had been bakers and laborers from Virginia" (xi). This early proletarian environment hardly seems likely to create an adult content to spend his life discussing polo ponies with Tom and Daisy Buchanan or a professor content to sit on a porch at Monteagle, sipping bourbon and discussing agrarianism with Andrew Lytle. From the beginning, Inge's scholarly career was guided by more demotic forces. As Inge told Charles Slack of the *Richmond Times-Dispatch* in a retrospective interview, a high-school teacher, Hallie Hootman, "convinced me that even a poor boy from Oregon Hill could go to college" (G7). By paying his way through Randolph-Macon College working for the state highway department, Inge embarked on the academic career that would eventually make him feel equally at home with William Faulkner and with Krazy Kat.

Choosing George Washington Harris, author of the Sut Lovingood yarns, as his dissertation topic, rather than a more "respectable" author like Henry Timrod or William Gilmore Simms, gave an early indication that Inge would follow the academic road less traveled. His first teaching appointment after completing his doctoral degree in 1964—in American Thought and Language, at Michigan State University—may also have suggested his disposition toward broader critical enthusiasms than the disciplinary restraints of "English" encouraged in those days. Appointments as Senior Fulbright Lecturer in Spain, South America, and the Soviet Union during the next fifteen years can be seen to confirm the suspicion that Inge was searching for wider disciplinary horizons. That these were the formative years of the national and regional Popular Culture Associations as well should also be noted. The confluence of all these forces most likely brought about Inge's tenure as Resident Scholar in American Studies for the United States Information Service in 1982-84. During those years he toured the world spreading the gospel of American culture as revealed by comic strips and jazz as well as by Twain and Faulkner.

Inge's academic career after Michigan State has involved appointments at Virginia Commonwealth University, Clemson University, and at

Randolph-Macon College, his alma mater, where he is currently the Robert Emory Blackwell Professor of Humanities. In addition to the Fulbright lectureships leading up to his tenure with the USIS, Inge has also filled overseas positions in the Soviet Union, China, and Prague. Awards have also been plentiful. In addition to the Virginia Cultural Laureateship, Inge has been honored by—among others—the American Humor Studies Association, the Mark Twain Circle of America, and the Popular Culture Association. Especially noteworthy is the "M. Thomas Inge Award for Comics Scholarship," annually awarded by PCA. As might be expected, Inge has also held office in numerous national and regional scholarly organizations and has served on the review boards of several scholarly journals, including *American Quarterly, Journal of Popular Culture,* and *INKS: Cartoon and Comic Art Studies.*

Of primary interest and importance to students of American Popular Culture, however, are Inge's three major contributions to that field of research: *Handbook of American Popular Culture* (1978-81; 2nd, revised edition 1989); the *"Studies in Popular Culture"* series for University Press of Mississippi; and, chiefly, Inge's comics scholarship, culminating in *Comics as Culture* (1990).

In its first edition the *Handbook,* published in three segments between 1978 and 1981, contained forty-eight essay-entries, each prepared by what Inge identified as "an authority on the subject" (2nd ed. xxxii). Each of the three volumes was arranged alphabetically with essays ranging from "Animation" to "The Western," "Advertising" to "Women in Popular Culture," and "Almanacs" to "Trains and Railroading." Included in the first volume was "Comic Art" by M. Thomas Inge, a comprehensive study of the often ignored subjects of American comic strips and comic books. The second edition, published in 1989, contained forty-seven entries arranged alphabetically from "Advertising" to "Women" and spread over three volumes and 1580 pages. This edition contained Inge's essay "Comic Strips," characteristically rewritten in large part since the 1978 publication and pruned of all discussion of comic books. Another study, appropriately entitled "Comic Books" and containing a great deal of new material, was published in a companion volume, also edited by Inge, *Handbook of American Popular Literature* (1988), which contained an additional fifteen essay-entries ranging from "Best Sellers" to "Young Adult Fiction." The American Library Association has recognized *Handbook of American Popular Culture* as an "outstanding reference work." Surely, everyone who works in the field of popular culture studies has seconded this judgment of both *Handbooks.*

The "Studies in Popular Culture" series has also made a significant impact in the field. In 1987, University Press of Mississippi decided to initiate a series of books focused on areas of American culture too often "underestimated" in traditional academic scholarship. Because of their very positive past experience working with Tom Inge in the traditional field of Southern literature, the executives at the Press felt confident in turning to Inge to select the works to be published in what might be considered an untraditional field for a university press—popular culture studies. The goal for the project was to publish analytical works by single authors, rather than collections of essays by divers hands, and to include both new scholarship and valuable studies that had fallen out of print. To date, approximately twenty titles have been published in the series, including in the latter category *The Comics* by Coulton Waugh and Arthur Asa Berger's *Li'l Abner: A Study in American Satire.* Inge's own interests as well as his unquestioned authority in the field of comics scholarship are surely evident in the decision to make these important ground-breaking works available to a new academic audience.

Creative new studies, including Inge's own *Comics as Culture* and *Anything Can Happen in a Comic Strip,* probably owe their appearances in the series to the same interests on the editor's part. In addition to Inge's two books, the series has also introduced: a study of British over-reactions to American horror comics, by Martin Baker; *The Art of the Comic Book* and *The Art of the Funnies,* both by Robert C. Harvey; and a study of the "narrative art" of Jack Jackson, Art Spiegelman, and Harvey Pekar, by Joseph Witek. The influence of Inge's long-time involvement in American humor scholarship is probably traceable in two other studies: of Groucho Marx and W. C. Fields, by Wes D. Gehring; and of Garrison Keillor, by Judith Yaross Lee. Less to be expected, perhaps, are three books about American popular music: *Ladies First: Women in Music Videos,* by Robin Roberts; *Country Music Culture: From Hard Times to Heaven,* by Curtis W. Ellison; and *Born in the U.S.A.: The Myth of America in Popular Music from Colonial Times to the Present,* by Timothy E. Scheurer. The last title does, however, echo the editor's old engagement with American Studies, as do two other books about American myths, one about the lasting mythology of *The Last of the Mohicans,* by Martin Barker and Roger Sabin; and the other about the mythology of super heroes, by Richard Reynolds. While evidence of some of Inge's earlier scholarly commitments can be glimpsed in some of these editorial decisions, the catholicity of his intellectual interests is apparent in Inge's support of Lucy Rollin's study of nursery rhymes; Shelley Armitage's book on Rose O'Neill, creator of the Kewpie doll; Neil D. Isaacs on batboys and baseball; David Guest on capital punishment and the novel; Brian Taves on historical adventure films; and Michael Dunne on self-referentiality in contemporary popular culture. It is likely that the individual titles in this series will instruct and delight their readers to different degrees, but it is certain that Inge's advocacy for popular culture scholarship of this sort has contributed mightily to the current good health of the field.

Inge's own popular culture scholarship in the field of the comics extends back to the mid-1970s when he collaborated with cartoonist Bill Blackbeard on a contribution to the bi-centennial history book *A Nation of Nations* (1976) and began his long association with *The Comic Book Price Guide* with "A Chronology of the Development of the American Comic Book." Over the subsequent years, Inge's scholarship and criticism have ranged from *Pogo* to *Krazy Kat,* from Charles Schulz to Walt Disney, from *Comics in the Classroom* to *Comics as Culture.* In the latter volume, Inge brings together new and previously published material to demonstrate that "The comics are well and deservedly loved, but they should be respected for what they have contributed to the visual and narrative arts of the world" (xxi). Wide-ranging analyses of comic style, language, narrative structure, and social influence appear in the chapters that follow, as well as specific discussions of *Little Nemo, Krazy Kat, Snuffy Smith,* and *Peanuts.* Inge also examines relations between comics and William Faulkner, Charley Chaplin, and modern art, as well as institutional comic influences such as *The New Yorker* and *EC Comics.* Here, and in other book-length works including *The American Comic Book* (1985), *Great American Comics: 100 Years of Cartoon Art* (1990), and *Anything Can Happen in a Comic Strip: Centennial Reflections on an American Art Form* (1995), Inge devotes the same scholarly attention and professional integrity to analyses of comic books and comic strips that he elsewhere devotes to the works of American literary giants like Melville and Faulkner. What we can know and say about American culture is thereby broadened and deepened.

Whatever the subject, Inge writes with the same commitment to scholarly integrity. His annual reviews of scholarship on Nineteenth-Century Fiction (1970-73) and William Faulkner (1986-88; 1990) for *American Literary Scholarship* consistently praise careful, thoughtful literary criticism and call to task those critics guilty of cutting corners. In his 1990 assessment of Faulkner criticism, for example, Inge generously praises *The Feminine and Faulkner: Reading (Beyond) Sexual Difference,* by Minrose Gwin, despite the fact that the book's critical methodology differs so radically from Inge's own. Inge concludes, "The result is a disarming and astonishing piece of criticism that cleverly wends its way through the minefields of postmodern theory to challenging conclusions" (157). Readers can feel confident on the basis of Inge's reasoned response that Professor Gwin's work will repay their time and interest.

Inge's negative judgments are equally reasoned. In his 1970 review of criticism on Nineteenth-Century Fiction, Inge writes about a book on Frank Norris that the author's "scholarship is thorough, but textual editors will not approve of his silent correction of errors in the text of the novels, and there is an odd repetition of sentences on pages 18 and 20 (perhaps a typographical error) of the introduction" (201). Readers used to seeing letters to the editor in which wounded authors accuse negative reviewers of superficial reading can only appreciate Inge's scrupulous thoroughness in attending to every single word of the work under review. Twenty years later, in his 1990 review of Faulkner criticism, Inge displays the same attentiveness in discussing "another of [Harold Bloom's] factory-made anthologies devoted to major literary characters, *Caddy Compson.*" Inge writes of this book that "The cover painting strangely depicts a child of about twelve in shorts standing in the branches of a tree rather than Caddy as a seven-year-old child with muddy drawers ascending the tree as in the novel" (159). No detail—whether internal or external to the text—is inconsequential to a true scholar.

According to Inge, many older anthologies of Southern literature fail miserably to maintain such scholarly integrity. As he writes in his "Afterword" to *Faulkner, Sut, and Other Southerners*: "The late nineteenth- and early twentieth-century collections in their introductions and biographical headnotes tended to be more laudatory than critical, and careless in their research" (208). Another essay reprinted in that volume, "The Fugitives and the Agrarians," suggests that some of these problems have continued down to the present day: "Wherever one looks in reference works, literary histories, and anthologies of the past several decades, an error [confusing Agrarians and Fugitives] is likely to be found" (199). The careful scholarship of Inge and the other authors of *The History of Southern Literature,* for which the "Afterword" was originally (1985) written, clearly is committed to redressing such carelessness.

As Inge's attention to cover art on the Bloom collection attests, productive cultural criticism involves more than applying principles of close literary reading. Going the extra scholarly mile must be standard practice. According to *Comics as Culture*, establishing the intellectual roots of Billy De Beck's *Snuffy Smith* comic strip involved a personal inspection of all the books contributed by De Beck to Virginia Commonwealth University (70). Inge's essay "Miguel de Unamuno's *Canciones* on American Literature," reprinted in *Perspectives on American Culture,* is based on his own translations of the poetry. Although his essay "Faulkner and Mo Yan: Influences and Confluences" was originally published in 1992, the bibliography was silently updated for its republication in *Perspectives on American Culture* to include scholarship published in 1993.

Taken together, these cases demonstrate Inge's conviction that the same principles apply to scholarship devoted to major American authors, world literary figures, and popular culture artifacts. For this reason, in *Comics as Culture* Inge criticizes the work of a literary critic who assumed a too-easy correspondence between the character Popeye from Faulkner's *Sanctuary* and the comic strip character of the same name. After identifying several of the critic's serious errors having to do with the history of the *Popeye* strip, Inge concludes: "What the errors do suggest is the cavalier attitude scholars take when they choose to discuss comic art. They tend to bank on vague memories; assume that comic strips do not develop, change, and add characters during the course of their histories; and avoid the truly hard labor of going through newspaper collections on microfilm or locating reprints to check the accuracy of their impressions and assumptions" (89). These are the sorts of errors that Inge's own commitment to the highest standards in pop culture criticism are intended to prevent through good example. In this respect, Inge's work illustrates a principle enunciated by Michael J. Bell in an essay that Inge added to the second edition of *Handbook of American Popular Culture*: "The idea of a discipline of popular culture is relatively new, and the number of active scholars, though growing, is not that large. Students at all levels, therefore, have the opportunity of participating in making the discipline into what it can become. But this can only happen if these beginning contributions try to follow the rules of the scholarship, try to say what they have to say in some coherent and intelligible way, and above all else, try to operate within the consistent universe that a method provides" (1483). The work of the pioneers—perhaps most of all including Inge—point the way.

Because he assumes the same rigorous standards for criticism of canonical authors and pop culture phenomena, Inge frequently and easily passes back and forth over the supposedly great cultural divide in his own criticism. Thus, in "Melville as Popular Culture," a piece reprinted in *Perspectives* but originally written for *A Companion to Melville Studies* (1986), Inge explains to the custodians of that major author's reputation: "Millions of Americans who have never read a line by Melville know the names of Moby Dick, Captain Ahab, or Billy Budd. His works have been repeatedly adapted to film, radio, television, records, comic books, and children's literature. Themes, names, and images are drawn from his fiction in popular literature, games, toys, puzzles, shop and restaurant names, popular songs, riddles, jokes, advertisements, and a variety of commercial products" (67). In another essay reprinted in *Per-*

spectives, Inge adopts a similarly open stance toward another nineteenth-century literary giant, Mark Twain: "If it was Twain's intent to reach the widest possible audience in his own lifetime, and the biographical facts support that idea, then the comic books have helped fulfill that goal in ours. I suspect Twain would have approved and maybe even have published a comic book or two of his own" (126). In *Comics as Culture,* Inge explains a projective fantasy story from *EC Comics* entitled "The Reformers" in terms of Nathaniel Hawthorne's "Earth's Holocaust" (128). These examples go to show, as Inge writes in the Introduction to his *Handbook of American Popular Culture,* that "It would seem to make better sense to describe all of this we have been discussing—high culture, low culture, mass media, popular culture, or whatever—as simply culture. Culture is a creative response to our environment, an effort to make sense out of disorder, a desire to discover beauty and meaning in the ugliness and absurdity of our world. Whether it be simple or complex, elite or democratic, individually crafted or mass produced, we should drop the adjectives 'high' and 'popular' and address ourselves to the total culture of twentieth-century American society without maintaining false distinctions that have no reality in the modern world." Realistically, he adds, "Until that time comes, however, it will continue to be necessary to use the term 'popular culture' as I have in the title of this reference work in the traditional sense" (xxxi).

Therefore, Inge can write in *Perspectives* that during the Great American Depression of the 1930s, "Popular culture said in full what Faulkner said most succinctly in his Nobel Prize address: 'I believe that man will not merely endure: he will prevail'" (134). As is usually the case, Inge writes without apology or explanation for this hieratic/demotic linkage. Unlike the typical English Professor's neighbors, who are always apologetically explaining that their favorite books are "not great literature or anything," Inge allows all cultural commodities to intersect on the same plain. George Herriman, the creator of *Krazy Kat,* thus emerges in *Comics as Culture* as a cultural figure intelligible in terms of high aesthetics: "Like the Dadaists, the Surrealists, and semioticians, then, Herriman instinctively understood that language is not a stable and invariable element in human discourse but instead, more often than not, leads to misunderstanding rather than effective communication" (49). Given Inge's disposition to champion the funny papers against all elitist challengers, it is perhaps unsurprising that he would write this in an essay entitled "*Krazy Kat* as American Dada Art." Nor, perhaps, is it surprising that Inge would make this sort of claim for one of his favorite strips, *Little Nemo in Slumberland* by Winsor McCay: "Freud conceived of art as a middle ground between wish-denying reality and wish-fulfilling fantasy, but McCay appears to have discovered this distinction independently" (*Comics* 33). Least surprising, consequently, is how Inge contextualizes still other comic strips in the same collection: "The three major comic strips set in the South—*Li'l Abner, Snuffy Smith* (without Barney Google), and *Pogo*—all owe allegiance to the lively school of Southern frontier humor in the nineteenth century whose authors used regional dialects, folk humor, and outrageous actions to puncture the pretensions and hypocrisies of polite society" (14). Combining Inge's attractions to comics, Southern culture, and humor in one equation, the statement may be taken as quintessential Inge.

Moving so easily across otherwise insurmountable cultural obstacles allows Inge to develop insights unavailable to less adventurous critics. In *Comics as Culture*, Inge presents this challenging cold-war parallel: "Senator Joseph McCarthy led the charge against alleged traitors in the State Department, while Senator Estes Kefauver investigated what some considered the worse form of subversion—the seduction of the innocent minds by the comic book industry" (117). "I never thought of it that way!" is the reader's most likely response to such an observation. In the same way, we are probably surprised and delighted by Inge's cross-cultural discovery in "Davy, Huck, Clark, and Ollie: 'A Hero in Our Eyes,'" that Colonel Oliver North looked strangely familiar for good reasons: "All of this causes us to recall the wonderful E. W. Kemble illustrations of Huck, round-faced and smiling, in the first edition of Twain's novel, as well as, among many contemporary images, Alfred E. Newman of *Mad* magazine fame and David Letterman of nighttime television comedy" (*Perspectives* 190). On more traditional literary matters, Inge is equally insightful. He characteristically moves from the hero of Robert Penn Warren's highly esteemed novel *All the King's Men,* to popular culture, and back again to the canonical *Great Gatsby*—all in two sentences from *Faulkner, Sut, and Other Southerners*: "Like the great minds of the Enlightenment, Willie [Stark] believed in the goodness and perfectibility of man and attempted to follow the disciplined path to success as outlined by Benjamin Franklin, and later by Horatio Alger, Thomas Edison, and Dale Carnegie. One is reminded of the daily schedule and list of resolutions scribbled as a boy in a copy of *Hopalong Cassidy* by Fitzgerald's Jay Gatsby, another naive dreamer corrupted by the banalities of reality" (140-41). While the topic of Robert Penn Warren recalls Inge's old Vanderbilt allegiance to Southern literature, popular success paradigms demonstrate his comprehension of the broader American culture of which Southern literature is only a small—albeit significant—part. This point is addressed in Inge's 1990 survey of the year's work in Faulkner studies for *American Literary Scholarship:* "[A]nother big topic this year was Faulkner and popular culture. This was true not so much because that was the topic of the proceedings of the annual conference at Mississippi but because many critics are beginning to understand the importance of viewing a major writer within the whole of the culture and not merely the elite aspects of it" (151). The pioneers of popular culture were often among the first critics to reach such an understanding

By means of such cross-cultural analogies, Inge's own critical approach resembles that of an early scholarly hero and predecessor in Southern literary studies, John David Wade, author of *Augustus Baldwin Longstreet: A Study of the Development of Culture in the South* (1924). Inge writes about Wade, "In an age of the first academic specialists he was a refreshing generalist who tried to view his work as teacher and scholar in its broadest cultural context" (*Faulkner, Sut* 122-23). As several previously cited examples attest, the same must be said of Inge the scholar. It is also apparent from a passing remark in the Preface to his *Perspectives* collection that Inge resembles Wade as a teacher as well: "Sharing an excitement of your own with students creates a rewarding environment, and discovering interesting things to research and write about can be the highest kind of pleasure" (xi). This pleasure, which is intended to be shared with his students, is evident throughout Inge's published works.

On the fundamental question of why we find popular culture so engaging, for example, Inge writes in the Introduction to *Handbook of American Popular Culture*: "We want to laugh and forget, not to be reminded of the tragedies and injustices of the world. We also seek in popular culture to have our attitudes and biases confirmed, to know that there are others just like us with the same thoughts, and be encouraged to believe that everything will come out right in the end. By providing a vicarious outlet for our emotional tendencies and a safety valve for our aggressions, the cultural act has a therapeutic effect and makes us feel better physically and psychologically" (xxviii). The evident presence of this pleasure in Inge's cultural criticism helps to make us all "feel better physically and psychologically," as the *linke Melancholie* of the Frankfurt School and the evident snobbery of Jean Baudrillard and Umberto Eco cannot do. For example, this is what Inge says about Henry David Thoreau in an essay reprinted in *Perspectives:* "And like America's greatest humorist, Mark Twain, his humor serves not alone to cause laughter, but also to touch upon the higher verities towards which the independent spirit aspires" (42). Even the vocabulary—*humor, higher verities, independent spirit*—is tonic. Pleasure also results from the insights a free-ranging mind derives from an immersion in the total culture. Thus, in the same essay in *Perspectives* in which Inge observes Ollie North's resemblance to Alfred E. Newman, he observes further, "Certainly most of us responded to the first announcements [about North and Iran/Contra] in the same way we would to an absolutely incredible yarn. In retrospect, it still seems unbelievable" (190). Literature, politics, and popular culture all interact productively to provide a whole greater than the sum of its parts.

At the same time there is an understanding tone here, a recognition that we are all in this together rather than, once again, the arrogance of so much Continental criticism of American culture. In this regard, what Inge says about Iran/Contra illustrates the principle behind his earliest literary enthusiasms. The study of Southern literature, he writes in the Preface to *Faulkner, Sut, and Other Southerners,* "is a way of turning what one already knows to an advantage, but it is also a way of coming to terms with one's self" (xii-xiii). These modest goals are characteristic and consistent, I believe, with the unarguable humanity of Inge's general critical posture. Behind these judgments we detect the presence of a very well informed human being rather than an authoritarian intellectual.

As is evident in Inge's equation of the pleasures of research and the pleasures of teaching, cultural criticism is best performed by those who continue all their lives to be students. This is effectually what Inge says in his essay "Lady Murasaki and the Craft of Fiction." During his term as official cultural ambassador for American Studies, Inge was frequently asked what Americans were doing to make their students better acquainted with the culture outside their shores. Not very much, he conceded, and so, as he writes, "I decided in 1985 to devote a part of my teaching and research time to Asian literature, in an attempt to formulate, at least on a personal level, a response to that frequently asked question" (*Perspectives* 241). The decision is both admirable and characteristic. Tennyson's Ulysses says that it would be "vile . . . to store and hoard myself" instead of "follow[ing] knowledge like a sinking star,/Beyond the utmost bound of human thought." Inge would probably reject a comparison of himself and a literary archetype as grandiose, and yet he could not object to choosing the terms of such a comparison from wide-ranging fields of knowledge. What this all goes to show is that there is so much to read, so much to see, so much to write, so much to teach, we hardly have time to adopt attitudes, to preen ourselves on what we know, to talk down to our fellow inquirers.

The ways in which cultural poles come into contact parallel the ways in which Inge's study of literary humor led to his study of popular humor, especially as revealed in the comics. Inge claims the lines of influence to be quite direct in his Preface to *Perspectives:* "Beginning with my work on the humorists of the Old Southwest and George Washington Harris, I was inevitably led into a study of what makes things funny and more particularly, what makes Americans laugh" (ix). Bill Watterson, the creator of *Calvin and Hobbes,* makes people laugh, but so does Henry David Thoreau. Inge makes the point with due care for literary propriety later in *Perspectives:* "Thoreau is never funny just for the sake of being so. . . . Like the strange, watery world of Walden pond, his humor lies just below the surface, clearly discernible by whoever cares to place his eye to the frozen but transparent surface" (31). Humor is such a paradoxically challenging concept that few can write about it with such ease. In addition to a sure sense of cultural history, the task also requires an elastic sense of humor. Thus, Inge bravely, but persuasively, writes in an essay from *Faulkner, Sut, and Other Southerners,* "That Faulkner may be putting us on much of the time is a suspicion that lurks in the reader's mind throughout his stories and novels" (14). Perhaps Inge should have written, "in the suitably aware reader's mind."

That Inge is himself such a reader can be seen from remarks like the following, from *Comics as Culture:* "Comedy implies an attitude towards life, an attitude that trusts in man's potential for redemption and salvation, as in Dante's *Divine Comedy* or Shakespeare's *Hamlet.* Since comic strips always conclude with resolutions in favor of morality and a trust in the larger scheme of truth and justice, they too affirm a comic view of the social and universal order" (11). We may be psychologically and spiritually renewed by Dante, or Faulkner, but we may also be renewed by George Herriman or Bill Watterson. With such assumptions animating his criticism, Inge himself keeps his mind as open as his eyes. As a result, he can define the comic strip genre with Johnsonian precision in *Handbook to American Popular Culture:* "It may be defined as an open-ended dramatic narrative about a recurring set of characters, told with a balance between narrative text and visual action, often including dialogue in balloons, and published serially in newspapers" (206). With equal aplomb, he can establish the following premise for members of the Herman Melville society: "If scholars have taken Melville too seriously, then American comic artists have compensated by finding inexhaustible uses for him in their humor and satire. It largely is a comedy of appreciation, however, rather than ridicule. The joke is often on the reader unable to come to terms with the magnitude of the writer and his ideas" (*Perspectives* 93). Appropriately, this premise is followed by a long list of Melville jokes that Inge collected from American comic strips

It is somehow reassuring to believe that in a filing cabinet somewhere, Inge has manila folders stuffed with comic strips and jokes about

Melville, Faulkner, Ollie North, and other figures we would not even dream of including in such a list. We can rest assured that, like Holmes, he is on the case. And, he has been on the case for many years. He says in the Preface to *Perspectives* that, despite the warnings issued by Senator Kefauver, "the popular culture of the 1950s turned me into an academic, . . . [r]ather than turning me into a juvenile delinquent or criminal, in accordance with the prevailing opinion of the times (and the present, for that matter)" (*Perspectives* x). Inge says further, in the same collection, that—as was true for so many of us—his first encounter with several canonical texts came via *Classic Comics.* Unlike the genteel schoolteachers of old who expressed shock at the mere prospect of a comic version of *Moby Dick* or *Huckleberry Finn*—and unlike the academic vandals of today who valorize the comic over the literary text for political reasons—Inge recognizes the virtues of each form as an integral part of American culture: "Reading the comic book cannot be the *same* experience as reading the novel, but it can be an altogether delightful experience on its own terms and one that clearly thousands of readers have sought out and found pleasurable. Otherwise publishers would not continue to produce such adaptations of Twain's works as they have for almost fifty years now" (124). On this score, we might recall Inge's similar observation in "Melville as Popular Culture" about the oft-maligned filmed version of *Moby Dick* starring Gregory Peck: "One might add that the film is to be evaluated on its own terms as a cinematic experience: to say that it is not the novel is only to state the obvious but also is finally irrelevant" (*Perspectives* 80). This is how productive cultural criticism gets done—not by means of prohibitions and exclusionary judgments, but by means of common sense analysis of the conditions that actually prevail.

In the case of the comics, this non-ideological, common sense approach has borne great fruit from humble beginnings. Inge apparently decided to begin studying comics in the first place rather as he later decided to study Lady Murasaki. As he explains in the Preface to *Perspectives:* "If the film and the comics were so important to me then, I realized that all aspects of popular culture have had a profound impact on society, and that to study it was another way to understand our national character" (x). In consequence, as Charles Slack writes in a 1992 profile of Inge in the *Richmond-Times Dispatch,* "Dr. Inge has become a leading voice for the artistic and literary importance of one of America's most maligned art forms" (G1). Inge's almost messianic commitment to the project has, unsurprisingly, resulted in a certain amount of academic abuse. Jonathan Yardley, for one, singled Inge out in a 1990 *Washington Post* article as a clear example of what is wrong with today's colleges—they encourage people to study popular culture, including the comics! Inge deflects such criticism with modest pertinacity. In a 1991 interview with Don Oldenburg, Inge typically explains that he assures his colleagues his study of the comics "is not a hobby. . . . My work on comics in the long run will probably be far more important than anything I have to say on William Faulkner" (B5). Since Inge's work on Faulkner is unquestionably first rate, we may easily decide how to estimate his work on the comics.

One indication of Inge's intentions in this work may be inferred from his comfortable mediations between elitist and popular culture. In *Comics as Culture,* for example, Inge writes: "Historians of the comic strip have traced its origin back to a number of sources in western art and culture. . . . Usually the interest in such cultural genealogical research is to dignify and make respectable what is considered a lowbrow form of entertainment." In his own scholarship, on the other hand, Inge assumes that "while it may reflect the influence of all of these antecedents, the comic strip as we know it is a distinct form of artistic expression primarily American in its origin and development" (3). Inge's recuperation of comic studies from the well-intentioned critics who would attempt to graft it onto some more elegant discipline is actually part of a larger commitment. As Inge writes in the Introduction to his *Handbook of American Popular Culture*: "The serious and systematic study of popular culture may be the most significant and potentially useful of the trends in academic research and teaching in the last half of this century in the United States. Scholarly study in this area will help modern society understand itself better and provide new avenues and methods of bringing to bear on contemporary problems the principles and traditions of humanism. It is no longer necessary to justify the study of popular culture by alliance with some other social or cultural purpose" (xxiii). In his own work on *EC Comics,* Inge therefore feels free to proclaim: "Here was creativity of the first order, an inspired blending of the visual and literary media possible only when artists and writers are free to pursue their own standards of excellence" (*Comics* 117). Ringing pronouncements of this sort in favor of an oft-ridiculed form of cultural expression are definitive evidence testifying to Inge's position in the ongoing debate about the appropriateness of cultural levels in America.

In the Introduction to *Handbook of American Popular Culture,* Inge goes beyond even the founding fathers of popular culture studies to establish his own ground of contention. He says there, "I wish to go one step further than both [Herbert J.] Gans and [Ray] Browne. What I wish to argue is that there are *no* distinctions between what we call high culture and popular culture, at least not in this century in the United States, which has witnessed the deep social changes wrought by industrialism, technology, and democracy. What we have is simply American culture. In the mass society in which we have lived, the older cultural distinctions make no sense, and we must seek new ways to understand the forms, functions, and ways of evaluating our arts and creative achievements" (xxix). This is what Inge has been prolifically and effectively doing as scholar, editor, mentor, ambassador, and teacher for over three decades. We may therefore truly say about Inge what has often been said about one of his own cultural heroes, "You're a good man, Tom Inge!"

Works Cited

Thorough bibliographies of Inge's scholarship appear in the two collections of his essays published by Locust Hill Press, *Faulkner, Sut, and Other Southerners: Essays in Literary History* (1992) and *Perspectives on American Culture: Essays on Humor, Literature, and the Popular Arts* (1994). Together with *Comics as Culture* and the second edition of *Handbook of American Popular Culture*, these works have supplied most of the material for this essay.

Bell, Michael J. "Appendix: The Study of Popular Culture." *Handbook of American Popular Culture*. 1459-84.

Inge, M. Thomas. *The American Comic Book*. Columbus: Ohio State U Libraries, 1985.

——. *Anything Can Happen in a Comic Strip: Centennial Reflections on an American Art Form*. Jackson, MS: Ohio State U Libraries, UP of Mississippi, and Randolph-Macon College, 1995.

——. "Comic Books." *Handbook of American Popular Literature*. Ed. M. Thomas Inge. Westport: Greenwood, 1988. 75-99.

——. "Comic Strips." *Handbook of American Popular Culture*. 205-28.

——. *Comics as Culture*. Jackson: UP of Mississippi, 1990.

——. *Comics in the Classroom*. Washington, DC: Smithsonian Institution Traveling Exhibitions Service, 1989.

——. "Faulkner." *American Literary Scholarship, An Annual 1990*. Ed. Louis Owens. Durham and London: Duke UP, 1992. 151-65.

——. *Faulkner, Sut, and Other Southerners: Essays in Literary History*. West Cornwall, CT: Locust Hill P, 1992.

——. *Great American Comics: 100 Years of Cartoon Art*. Washington, DC: Smithsonian Institution Traveling Exhibition Service, 1990.

——. "Nineteenth-Century Fiction." *American Literary Scholarship, An Annual 1970*. Ed. J. Albert Robbins. Durham, NC: Duke UP, 1972. 177-203.

———. *Perspectives on American Culture: Essays on Humor, Literature, and the Popular Arts.* West Cornwall, CT: Locust Hill P, 1994.

Inge, M. Thomas, ed. *Handbook of American Popular Culture.* 2nd ed. revised and enlarged. Westport: Greenwood, 1989.

Inge, M. Thomas, and Bill Blackbeard. "American Comic Art." *A Nation of Nations.* Ed. Peter Marzio. New York: Harper, 1976. 600-09.

Oldenburg, Don. "The Comics-Minded Professor." *Washington Post* 10 Apr. 1991: B5.

Slack, Charles. "Funnies Man." *Richmond Times-Dispatch* 18 Oct. 1992: G1+.

Tennyson, Alfred Lord. "Ulysses." *The New Oxford Book of English Verse.* Ed. Helen Gardner. New York: Oxford, 1972. 644-46.

Yardley, Jonathan. "Funny Business in Academia." *Washington Post* 24 Sept. 1990: B2.

Susan Koppelman
Photo by Lynda Koolish

SUSAN KOPPELMAN:
DIVA OF THE SHORT STORY

Emily Toth and Susan Koppelman

Susan Huddis Koppelman, born on September 22, 1940, into a first generation American-Jewish (Ashkenazi) family in Cleveland, Ohio, set a record in the days after her birth by gaining the most weight the most quickly of any baby yet born in St. Luke's Hospital. From her earliest days, she was committed to outstanding accomplishments.

Koppelman cannot remember a time when her love of books and music was not central to her life. Her favorite haunts were the public libraries of Cleveland and Cleveland Heights, Kay's Magazine and Book Supermarket (where she spent her weekly allowance) and the high branches of an ancient apple tree in the remains of an orchard at the end of her street—perfect for hours of undisturbed reading. She rode her trusty blue and white Schwinn bicycle everywhere.

Her love of knowledge was nurtured by her parents, each the last child of Jewish immigrant families from the Pale of Settlement, on the Russian/Polish border.

The large family of Koppelman's mother, Frances Bollotin (the youngest of eight children), loved to discuss current events and philosophical questions over the dinner table, and were lovers of "high" culture, especially opera and symphonic music. However, lives in Moghilov amid poverty and oppression for Jews, the rigors of immigration with seven young children, and the Great Depression in the United States left them all cautious about financial and health matters, and worrierd about what the future might bring.

While in high school, Frances sang with the Cleveland Symphony Chorus; she read and discussed the classics with on-going Great Books groups all of her adult life. In 1935, her first job was as a legal secretary for a charismatic, energetic, and optimistic attorney brimming with plans for an ever-improving future. They married in 1938 and shared an active social life in Cleveland, dancing to the big bands of the forties, laughing at the local beloved comedian, Mickey Katz, enjoying shows by Sophie Tucker, Eddie Cantor, and Al Jolson, and seeing all the new movies premiered in Cleveland, a practice they shared with their young daughter once she was old enough.

Edward Nathan Koppelman was a cornet-playing, football half-back-become-lawyer who grew up on a small farm as the adored only son and youngest child in the only Jewish family in Creston, Ohio. Between his secular education in the Creston public schools, his participation in the Creston Town Band, and weekends in Cleveland with various relatives while he prepared for his bar mitzvah, "Kop" gained a love for all kinds of music: not only Yiddish klezmer, Hebrew chants, and the songs of the Yiddish theater, but also Protestant hymns, patriotic marches, bawdy vaudeville ballads, and the popular dance music of his time. After an undergraduate career at the College of Wooster, he went on to play football and study law at the Ohio State University. Losing his eligibility to play college football after a professional season with the Canton Bull-dogs, he finished his academic career as a member of the marching band. He opened a private general law practice in Cleveland and remained there for the rest of his life. Although he remained loyal to the Republican Party all his life in deference to his hero, Abraham Lincoln, he had a passionate commitment to justice, fairness, and equal representation of all before the law. His clientele included people of all races, classes, and ethnicities. It was a matter of enduring family pride when he was admitted to practice before the Supreme Courts of both Ohio and the United States.

The Koppelman family of three "jaunted" on weekends, sampling the wonderful variety of ethnic restaurants within two hundred miles of Cleveland: Amish cheese factories, German sausage houses, Scandinavian smorgasbords. They trekked to annual harvest festivals all over Ohio: maple sugar, apple butter, sweet corn. They visited ethnic festivals in Cleveland, watching the Irish clog dancers, the African drummers, and the Spanish flamencos. The family traveled to New York City to see the great musical comedies of the period on Broadway; and to Miami and St. Petersburg, Florida, to experience summer weather in the middle of winter, to collect shells from the shallow waters of the Gulf of Mexico, and to play miniature golf and drink orange juice squeezed from oranges they picked themselves. By exposing Susan to this broad variety of musical, theatrical, ethnic, and agricultural styles and celebrations, her parents nurtured their budding popular culture scholar. At the same time, they stimulated her political sensibilities. They boldly strolled through the lobby of Miami's Eden Roc hotel, closed to Jews.

One time in St. Petersburg, young Susan, on a shopping trip with her mother at Webb City, which advertised itself as the biggest drug store in the world, was thirsty. She saw a line of people at one drinking fountain and no one at the other, which she had no reason to recognize as the "Colored" fountain. She stepped up to the fountain with no long line before it, but, as she described it later:

"Suddenly my braids were yanked from behind in a brutal way that both hurt and terrified me. And then my head was thrust forward and my lower right front tooth hit the head of the fountain and my tooth was chipped." Her attacker was an "ugly red-faced man, really big, screaming about 'Yankees and Jews and Nigger Lovers.'"

She still recalls the terror of that encounter, and her mother's courageous reaction. Frances Koppelman showed no fear at all—only disgust that anyone would treat another human being that way. The chipped front tooth, a baby tooth, fell out later that year, and the incident was apparently forgotten—but never by Susan.

Her dawning awareness of social injustice was fed by that incident, the knowledge that hotels excluded people because of their religion or race, revelations about the anti-Semitism of Arthur Godfrey—the popular, folksy radio host, stories about Henry Ford's anti-Semitism, and the discovery that some of her classmates lived in "restricted" areas.

However, the defining event of her early years was her 1948 viewing of the films of the liberation of the concentration camps. Subsequent revelations about the ruthless enslavement of Africans, the Spanish Inquisition, the Crusades, the Salem witchcraft trials, and the Trail of Tears, confirmed her lifelong commitment to social justice activism.

Like her parents before her, Susan had the benefit of a "binocular" education: a secular education in exemplary public schools and a rigorous education in the history, sociology, and various theological philosophies of Judaism at one of the largest Conservative synagogues in the country: Park Synagogue. She learned about Solomon Schechter's American Revolution as well as George Washington's, about Ellis Island as well as the Massachusetts Bay Colony, and about Peter Stuyvesant's attempt to exclude Spanish Jews fleeing the Inquisition from New Amsterdam as well as the New World's promise of religious freedom. This binocular education prefigured and prepared her for work as a feminist popular culture scholar who understood from her earliest years that what is "high" culture for one group may be "low," "folk," or "popular" culture from the perspective of another, that the elements underlying the categories are dominated not by aesthetic principles, but by socio-political factors and power inequities, and that there are only "histories" and never "history."

Susan's first twelve years were mostly idyllic. Her mother was devoted to her and made it possible for her to study art at the Cleveland Museum of Art, theater at the Cleveland Playhouse, and music in public school and with members of the Cleveland Symphony Orchestra.

She shared "high" culture with her mother, attending the symphony, light and grand opera, new music concerts at the Cleveland Institute of

Music, and the annual May Show at the art museum. With her father, she learned to "root, root, root" for the home team, and saw the last World Series won by the Cleveland Indians (1948) and practiced ballroom dancing by standing on his feet as he whirled them both around the kitchen. Her father sang "Summertime" to her: "Your daddy's rich (an optimistic and unfulfilled prediction) and your mama's good looking (the truth)" and Susan felt safe and happy.

When she was small, one of her favorite haunts was the small space under the table in the kitchen, where she could eavesdrop on her mother's friends in their daily kaffee klatches. (Later, she would say that she was learning the methodology for oral history, but did not yet know the name of the field. Her introduction to *Women's Friendships: A Collection of Stories,* recalls the interesting and often heroic and community oriented lives of those women.) From those overheard conversations, and through long and intense phone chats during her youth and adolescence, she learned about women's friendships, mothers and daughters, interpersonal relationships, and social clues—all the knowledge that is unique and highly developed among most girls and women. Many of her mother's friends, especially Ruth Benjamin, who took the unusual course for a woman of her time, after her husband's sudden and early death, of continuing to operate, and expand, their construction business, served as models for Susan of independent women.

Meanwhile, her mother both modeled and emphasized being popular, well-liked, and attractive: it was the cultural message overwhelmingly given to young girls in the early 1950s. So Susan took modeling and makeup classes at a local department store, and went to Arthur Murray for ballroom dancing lessons. Once Brownies and Girl Scouts were over, she was persuaded by her mother to join Young Judea and B'Nai B'rith Girls' social clubs to develop and practice her social skills. Always eager to please her mother, Susan did as was suggested, offered her parents' home for their meetings, managed to get herself elected treasurer of both groups, gave her treasurer's report at the beginning of the meetings and then disappeared to the basement, where she read until it was time for refreshments. Her mother's gracious welcome and endless supply of delicious homemade brownies made up for Susan's apparent peculiarities.

At the end of sixth grade, Susan's scores on city-wide achievement and aptitude tests, among the highest in Cleveland, garnered scholarship offers to private girls' schools. After family discussion, these were declined. Her father said, "We came to this country to participate in the democracy. Private schools aren't part of that!" Besides, private schools didn't match the opportunities for musicians in the Cleveland Heights public schools.

The principal of her first junior high told her parents that Susan was "abnormally smart for a girl" and that if some sort of intervention wasn't devised to distract her from intellectual accomplishments, she might never achieve "normal happiness." He wanted her parents' cooperation in a project to "dumb her down" and a promise that she would never learn of her "dangerous" intelligence. Her parents decided Susan had every right to know about her abilities.

When the principal, in her mother's presence, delivered the dire news: "There are no limits to what you can learn," Susan, who was notorious in her family for her inability to carry a tune, asked, "Does that mean I can be a singer?"

For the first two years of junior high, Susan was among a small group of Jewish students bussed daily to a neighborhood in which Jews had never lived, and where they were seen at best as oddities, at worst as scourges. Although some of her teachers were academically inspiring, especially her English teacher, Nettie Morris, one of the two teachers to whom she dedicated her first short story anthology, *Old Maids: Short Stories by 19th Century U.S. Women,* none noticed that the boys on those busses tormented the girls, and abandoned them to similar torments by neighborhood boys. During this period Susan first experienced sexual molestation.

In seventh grade she discovered a brochure entitled "One Hundred World's Best Novels" published by the librarians at the Cleveland Public Library. That list of books constituted her private curriculum for the next six years: she was determined to read every one of them before she was graduated from high school. However, she finished high school having been too bored to get even half way through *Moby Dick, Ulysses,* or *War and Peace,* which were on the list, and having read in a single sitting *Peyton Place,* which was not. Instead of reading the listed novels, she read the listed authors. If she discovered one she liked, as she did Jane Austen, Sherwood Anderson, the Brontë sisters, and Dostoyevsky, she read all the novels and then sought out biographies of the writer. During her raids on the shelves devoted to the authors she loved at the open-stacked Cleveland Public Library, she first encountered literary criticism. She thought it was very boring, and quickly returned to reading what she always thought of as "real books."

But during that same seventh grade year in junior high, her life was changed forever when Kop suffered the first of a series of strokes that turned him into a deeply depressed, easily angered, increasingly irrational shell of his former self. He ceased to be her adoring protector and cheerleader, while her mother suddenly had to assume the role of family breadwinner, caretaker, and medical advocate. Her mother assumed these new roles with courage, managing to maintain the family home and a minimally reduced lifestyle, but she was no longer available to Susan in the way she had always been. She was now working full time, running her husband's law office, out of the house early, home late. Susan also had to assume new responsibilities. She felt abandoned, at the same time that (in her words) "puberty attacked her like a science fiction virus, turning her sturdy and familiar little girl body into a caricature of a sex kitten." Once she developed earlier and more prominently than most of the other girls in her class, she was not only sexually harassed on the bus, but also molested by a teacher. Ashamed and embarrassed, Susan told no one. Later, in her 1960s consciousness raising group, she learned how common sexual abuse is. Once she noted that popular culture produces and promotes images of women as dependent and victimized, she began collecting advertisements and song lyrics.

Meanwhile, Frances managed to send Susan to Interlochen music camp in Traverse City, Michigan, for the summer between junior and senior high school. The extra musical training that summer (including eight weeks of intense harp lessons and a college-level course in the physics of sound) enabled her not only to qualify for the Cleveland Heights High School Concert Band in her first high school semester, but to win the first-chair position. Her accomplishment was celebrated in the 1956 *First Chair of America National Yearbook for Outstanding Bands, Orchestras, and Choruses.* The volume was dedicated to her high school music director, John Francis Farinacci. He further prepared her for her work in popular culture by celebrating all types of music. While rock and roll was still vigorously denounced in some quarters as "The Devil's Music," he shocked adults and thrilled students by opening the 1956 football season with a rousing performance of "Rock around the Clock."

Susan's literary achievements were honored in that same year with one of the coveted appointments to *The Crest,* the prize-winning literary magazine at the high school. When she was not selected editor by the faculty advisors in her senior year, and the positions went to young men, they explained to her that although she deserved the honor, she didn't need the office on her college applications. "After all," they told her, "you'll just get married, anyway."

Although musical activities were the dominant activity of her social life, her private life was consumed with literary delights, endless reading, and non-stop dedication to writing stories as she had been doing since first grade. Protracted reading of the author blurbs on the backs of book covers convinced her that New York City was the literary center of the world. So after her 1958 high school graduation, and with the financial support of her mother, Susan headed for New York.

That fall, she was a first-year student at Barnard College, where her sister students included Twyla Tharp, Erica Jong, Rosellen Brown, Louise Bernikow, and dozens of other young women who would eventually have a great impact on the popular culture of the United States. Barnard advertised that "New York Is Barnard's Laboratory," and Susan took full advantage of access to that laboratory. She attended at least one off-campus lecture and one Broadway play each week: she saw the original production of *West Side Story* more than a dozen times, explored the off-off Broadway theaters and movie revival houses, and listened to readings and lectures at the YMHA. She attended the last U.S. public reading by T. S. Eliot and listened with shock and horror as the SRO audience grew increasingly hostile and demanding when he declined to read "The Love Song of Alfred J. Prufrock," a poem he said had bored him for half a century. She delighted in being one of only seven audience members at a lecture by Thornton Wilder about his dear and quirky friend, Gertrude Stein, and alternately wept as Allen Ginsberg gave the first public reading of his great poem "Kaddish" and laughed as his friend Jack Kerouac meandered back and forth across the stage, too drunk to read his work, but perfectly audible as he grumbled about how little they were paying him.

She loved New York, was fascinated by the cosmopolitan and international population of Barnard, and, in her second year, met a Columbia boy who eventually became her first husband. John Cornillon, born in France during World War II, had most of the same intellectual interests, artistic ambitions, sense of culinary adventure, and political passions she did. Together they spent Saturdays at Times Square, arriving at 10 a.m. when the quadruple feature movies opened, sitting through four films, crossing to the $1.19 steakhouse that had just opened on 42nd Street for a quick dinner, and then heading back to another theater for four more films. They took classes together in mythology and Chinese poetry in translation, and wandered the art museums together with a sense of claiming their inheritance. They read the "Beats," those Columbia boys and their friends who had created a new American literary movement. Susan noticed that both the "Beats" and the business majors expected "their" women to wash their clothes, but poets thought she should do it in the waters of a cold, rushing creek, while the business majors thought it reasonable to buy a washing machine. They listened to Ray Charles, danced to Elvis, read French poetry and philosophy, and wrote stories which they read aloud to each other.

When Susan's father died in May of 1961, she moved back to Cleveland to live with her mother. She finished her undergraduate work at (now Case-) Western Reserve University, where her high school friend, Phyllis Sutton (Andersen), was finishing her degree, too. The two young women had exciting years, taking many courses together. Because each was engaged to someone far away, the two had a wonderful time free of the social pressures to date that had figured so prominently and time-wastingly in their adolescent years. While at Reserve, Susan completed undergraduate majors in literature, comparative literature, psychology, and sociology, with a minor in economics.

Susan and John married September 1, 1962, after her graduation, and they returned to New York for his last year at Columbia. She worked in the Columbia University Library, then did substitute teaching in Spanish Harlem, until John's graduation—whereupon they headed west to San Francisco for several unhappy months, with a short stop for their first look at Bowling Green, Ohio.

On their return east, on a whim, they applied for admission and graduate teaching assistantships at the Ohio State University. Susan was offered both; John got neither; but they moved to Columbus anyway. Susan was astonished to learn that by marrying a resident of another state, she lost her life-long Ohio residency. A woman was, in those days, subsumed under her husband's residency, regardless of her own. Susan's outraged protest and exposure of this injustice led to a change in the policy—either member of a couple could thereafter choose to assume the residency of the spouse, or retain the residency of origin. The success of her protest thrilled her.

In September 1963, Susan began to teach freshman composition, John accepted a job at the University library, and they took courses together in creative writing and 19th-century U.S. literature (and not a single woman was included in any of their course syllabi). They gathered a group of other writers and artists around them (Susan, a superb cook, was known for her hospitality as well as her witty and learned conversation) and started an underground literary magazine called *Gooseberry.*

One of Susan's professors (the first of several) told her that she was brilliant, but that her husband was crazy, and that John would drag her down. The marriage was difficult: romance vied with violence and betrayal in patterns that have since become well known via the short-story tradition Koppelman has recovered and included in *The Other Woman: Stories about Two Women and a Man* and *"Women in the Trees:" U.S. Women's Short Stories of Battering and Resistance, 1839-1994.* After a year in Columbus marked by the assassination of President Kennedy, they moved to Cleveland. While John tried to "find himself," Susan tried, with limited success, to market his writing while substitute teaching. When she sold her own first short story, their relationship became more strained.

They joined the alternative poetry scene in Cleveland and published more work in *Gooseberry* and other underground magazines and newsletters. D. A. Levy's regionally famous Renegade Press published several chapbooks of Koppelman's work. Very active in the local civil rights movement, they also developed interest in the growing ecology and natural foods movements.

At one point they took jobs with an auto delivery agency, driving back and forth across the country in their own version of *On the Road.* They delivered cars up and down the West Coast, and explored all the romantic sounding places they had only read about: Hollywood, Carmel, Big Sur, Venice. During this time Susan wrote her first novel.

But the Vietnam War was escalating and, with John at risk for being drafted immediately, despite his repeated appeals for conscientious objector status, the couple became increasingly involved in the anti-war movement. John applied and was accepted at Crane Theological School (Tufts) in Boston, where they moved in 1966. John studied for the Unitarian ministry while Susan founded an adult education program for women and began to create and teach women's studies courses through the facilities of the Unitarian Universalist churches. Throughout the Boston area, she taught about "The Problems and Potential of Women" and "The Art and Practice of the Journal."

Separating from John in 1967, she finished her course work for a master's degree at Ohio State—and then encountered a major academic roadblock.

Of the half dozen thesis proposals Koppelman submitted, including one on the female Bildungsroman, one on nineteenth-century U.S. women novelists, and another on journals as a legitimate literary genre, not one was accepted. One professor told her there was no such thing as a female Bildungsroman, nor were there any women novelists worth writing about. Moreover, the journal was an undisciplined and useless form. Although she submitted a list of one hundred female Bildungsromane, from *Mill on the Floss* to *Peyton Place,* she was pushed into writing on Shakespeare instead.

But the opposition to women would-be scholars in the mid-1960s was often more than academic. It was quite personal, as Susan found when one of her professors told her that "You are very smart and very pretty, but much, much too delicate for the demanding and competitive life of academia. You should teach in high school."

Susan and John reconciled, and, more determined than ever to teach, to write, and to concentrate on what has since come to be called Women's Studies and popular culture, Susan returned to Boston. On November 1, 1968, the couple's only child, Edward Nathan Koppelman

Cornillon, was born. The following summer she defended her thesis and received the M.A. degree in literature from Ohio State in August of 1969. In the fall of 1969 she began teaching in the English Department at Bradford Junior College.

In early 1971, all three Cornillons arrived in Bowling Green, Ohio. Susan, with her usual tenacity, had researched all the possibilities for graduate study in areas she loved, and found the one program in the country that seemed perfect: at Bowling Green State University, she was able to pursue her own scholarly interests, to study U.S. women's writing and history, and women's roles and portrayals in all the genres of popular culture. She affiliated as a doctoral candidate and taught as a graduate fellow in the English Department, and introduced women's studies to the campus as an instructor in the Experimental College; she did her scholarly work with the Center for the Study of Popular Culture, just recently founded by Ray and Pat Browne.

Between the spring quarter of 1971 when she introduced "The Problems and Potential of Women" to the campus to spring of 1974 when she became ABD, Koppelman continued to collect popular culture images of women. She pioneered in developing multi-media programs (often with the help of audio librarian Bill Schurk) for teaching and conference and community programs. Koppelman prepared audio tapes tracing images of women in popular music lyrics from her father's pre-World War I adolescence to the 1970s adolesence of her students. Using old TV commercials, she prepared videos tracing images of women in TV advertising. Multi-screen slide shows—juxtaposing advertising images of women's breasts with before and after photographs of women's breasts in plastic surgery journals (1950-1970)—shocked audiences with the evidence that female beauty is a cultural invention. A multi-screen slide show accompanied with audio tapes explored the social and emotional torment of women judged to be too fat in a culture determined to minimize women in all ways.

At Bowling Green, Susan was older than the average graduate student. Jews were rare and thought by some of her students to have been extinct for almost two millennia, and John began to behave more and more peculiarly. She persisted with energy and drive to educate herself and the world about women's accomplishments and trials. Her dissertation director, Ray Browne, an unusual academic, encouraged virtually all pursuits of knowledge. As Susan Koppelman wrote in the dedication to her first book, Ray Browne says, "about tentative dreams, 'Why not?' "

Susan Koppelman Cornillon inaugurated another aspect of her popular culture work at Bowling Green: her ability to bring together diverse and interesting scholars, and get them and their texts to speak to one another. She created, and published in 1972, the first anthology of feminist criticism for the Second Wave of the Women's Liberation Movement. Her *Images of Women in Fiction: Feminist Perspectives* was also one of the earliest books published by the Popular Press at Bowling Green State University. *Images of Women* is still considered the benchmark book for feminist criticism. It is so recognized in Toril Moi's *Sexual/Textual Criticism* and Jane Gallop's *Around 1981,* as well as other histories of feminist criticism.

Unlike the books that would follow in the field, *Images of Women* was not narrowly focused on elite or literary texts. Its contributors discuss sex, race, and class long before those topics were fashionable among jargon mongers; Joanna Russ, Lillian Robinson, Tillie Olsen, and other writers dissect, with wit, a wide variety of literary pretensions and expectations. Contributors write about science fiction, romances, detective stories, best sellers, and lesser-known writers. Several mention such authors as Kate Chopin, who in the early 1970s was barely known, but is now part of the U.S. literary canon.

In the engaging spirit that was also characteristic of Popular Culture at Bowling Green, *Images of Women* did not pit popular against elite writers. It welcomed them all, and suggested new and vitally important questions to be asked of any work of literature or culture. With sections on "The Woman as Heroine," "The Invisible Woman," "The Woman as Hero," and "Feminist Aesthetics," the book's contributors discuss not only what is, but what might be. Further, the essays are written in an accessible style, in accord with the assumption among popular culturists that scholars' discoveries should be knowledge that can be communicated to everyone with vigor and imagination.

Images of Women was launched at the annual Midwest Modern Language Association meeting in St. Louis in November of 1972, where Susan Koppelman also met her lifelong friend and ally, Emily Toth (then a graduate student at Johns Hopkins University). Over the next twenty-five years, they would devote endless and delightful hours to analyzing patriarchal pretensions, celebrating women's achievements, trumpeting each other's greatness, laughing, and eating a lot.

At the April 1972 Toledo conference of the Popular Culture Association, Susan had organized, moderated, and presented her own work along with that of several others at a session called "Images of Women in Fiction," the first Women's Studies session at PCA, which was celebrating its second annual conference. The following spring, 1973, in Indianapolis, she organized over a dozen panels, bringing scholars from all over the country to participate in the first national gathering of Women's Studies scholars, and inaugurating the study of women's popular culture as an official part of the deliberately anarchical convention. She created panels on such subjects as women in advertising, popular music, movies, and much more: she brought to PCA the political excitement that the women's movement was engendering outside academia. Because of her efforts, PCA has always been open to panels on women and women's perspectives.

Starting in late 1972, she served on the English Department's Textbook committee, and began to study literary anthologies—which proved to be the beginning of her life's work in recovering the history of U.S. women's short stories. She found that virtually every anthology contained the same short stories by the same few white, apparently heterosexual, men, plus a few women who were either contemporaries of the compiler(s) or from the period 1880-1910. This pattern of (mis)representation fostered the conventional wisdom that women had no literary tradition, and that their writing deserved little recognition or space. The average anthology devoted one-seventh of its space to white women. She began trying to recreate the "real" history of women's accomplishments in the genre of the short story.

But practical realities were surfacing in her life. Her husband seemed only marginally employable and increasingly troubled: she would have to continue in her role as major breadwinner and primary parent. She completed her doctoral work in 1974, got a Ph.D. from Bowling Green in 1975, and entered the job market when it had already begun its long slump. She accepted a job at Washington University in St. Louis as Associate Director for the Office of Campus Programming (the job that used to be called Dean of Women—before the campus radicalism of the 1960s), and was responsible for developing and implementing programs for women on campus and for working with the heads of campus housing, medical services, the bookstore, and buildings and grounds to respond to the needs of women on campus. She also represented Washington University with the Inter-Institutional Higher Education Coordinating Council where she created programs for women administrators, faculty, and students to share resources on seventeen campuses. Much of the work she proposed and accomplished brought to elitist educational institutions in the area their first campus programs using popular culture materials and performers. For instance, she sponsored the first appearances on the campus of Washington University of feminist singer Holly Near, science-fiction writer Joanna Russ, menstruation scholar Emily Toth, and writer Tillie Olsen.

When the Cornillon family moved to St. Louis in 1974, they bought the house at 6301 Washington Avenue where Susan would live for the next twenty years. The eleven-room house became a popular gathering place for potlucks honoring visiting campus speakers, such as Alix Kates Shulman, as well as students and community women. Susan's son Nathan grew up in a world of houses whose rooms were lined with books; his favorite, familiar playgrounds were college campuses; and the weekly midnight showing of *Rocky Horror Picture Show* was right around the corner.

However, the Cornillon marriage continued to disintegrate, and took its toll on Susan's scholarly and literary work. Although she continued to read short stories and develop her vision for the project that would engage her life—the history of U.S. women's short stories—the increasing tensions with John prevented her from finishing many of her projects. She was also in conflict with some of her bosses at Washington University, who wanted a less activist set of programs. She began interviewing for other jobs.

But her health suddenly deteriorated with the onset of ulcerative colitis in July 1976. Her illness was chronic and severe: she was forced to retire on disability. She and John separated in 1979. When their divorce was final in 1980, she took back her name, Susan Koppelman.

Many scholars have long periods of latency—of thinking about their major projects. Like most authors and most achievers, Koppelman had known her vocation from the beginning. But relationships—including the pull of popular culture to be the heroine in her own romance—had derailed her from completing and writing what she knew.

Divorce, and even disability, freed her to decide what she really wanted to do (within her physical limits) and what she could manage (with always limited funds). She became adept at finding friends (her mother's training); she created huge networks of women scholars, who came to know each other at conferences and through her letters. Through voluminous "Dear Friends" letters to her correspondents, she engaged them in the ongoing work of recovering and studying women's writing and popular culture from the past. The "Dear Friends" letters also helped free her own voice as a writer. She stopped trying to communicate with a pompous professor in her head, and started writing as a lively, wry correspondent, a woman speaking to women with wisdom and humor, gossip and vision.

Meanwhile, her mother nudged her, as always, to "practice her social skills." So Susan attended a singles event in St. Louis where—to her astonishment—she met and came to love and marry Dennis Mills. Coming from a completely different world, practical and talented with his hands, Dennis, an auto mechanic and restorer of Studebakers and Ducatis, enhanced her work by fixing up her huge house, creating several rooms of her own in which she could write and complete her research projects. He has never failed to champion and support her work, and he became Nathan's father.

Eight years after her first book appeared and within five years of her 1980 marriage to Mills, Koppelman published three books: *Old Maids: Short Stories by Nineteenth Century U.S. Women Writers; The Other Woman: Stories of Two Women and a Man;* and *Between Mothers and Daughters: Stories across a Generation.*

The three collections of U.S. women's short stories written between 1835 and 1982 cluster about different themes fraught with importance in women's lives. All include stories from the popular fiction genres as well as "literary" and "experimental" fiction, and portray the ways in which women teach each other through stories, presenting characters and plots that are both role models and cautionary tales. Koppelman's collections, which she refers to as "literary archaeology," are part of the international intellectual project engaged in by Dale Spender (*Women of Ideas*), Cathy Davidson (*Revolution and the Word*), and other researchers. The purpose is to recover and re-view women's writings to see what they truly say to and about women—not to men's preconceptions of women.

Old Maids, for instance, is about single women—but not the dried-up spinsters of patriarchal myth. The central figures in Koppelman's collection are not portrayed as life's losers, but as women who've chosen—or been given the opportunity to choose—to create their own lives. These strong and independent women's lives are linked to changes in the law and economic possibilities for women as the Women's Suffrage movement gained strength and accrued successes.

Among the authors showcased in *Old Maids* are women unknown in the mid-1980s but now entrenched in the U.S. women's literary canon: Catharine Maria Sedgwick, Elizabeth Stuart Phelps, Rebecca Harding Davis, Mary E. Wilkins (Freeman), and Frances Ellen Watkins Harper, author of the first-known short story by an African American writer.

For each story in *Old Maids,* Susan Koppelman also pioneered in creating a new kind of headnote, now known as the "Koppelnote." Koppelnotes are intricate, accessibly written, and extremely well-researched story introductions. They provide not only an overview of each author's education and literary career, but also an intimate peek into her private life as a woman. Koppelnotes tell us about each writer's relationships with her mother, sisters, women friends, and literary colleagues, as well as any marriages or romances with men. Koppelnotes discuss each author's opinions about the theme of the collection, sometimes quoting her, and they analyze her relationship to class and money. Koppelnotes clarify each writer's unique contributions to women's lives and letters, and they provide what audiences want in all writing that is worth reading: gossip, humor, and new information.

The Other Woman, stories about love triangles, is also a book of rethinkings. U.S. women writers, Koppelman found, neither glamorize the third party, the outsider woman, who is often younger, more conventionally beautiful, and freer than the wife, nor do they demonize her. Women authors commonly support the wife, but far more radically, they often show the wife and the other woman forming an alliance rather than vying for the man's favor.

Many of the stories, from the earliest "The Quadroons" (1842) by Lydia Maria Child, explore multiple dimensions and intersections of the vulnerability of women who love men whose power over them is reinforced by racism, anti-Semitism, classism, and other forms of social inequity, in addition to sexism. Another rediscovered writer is Charlotte Perkins Gilman, now known for her classic "The Yellow Wallpaper" as well as *Herland:* in "Turned," her *Other Woman* story, the wife and other woman form an unbreakable partnership. *The Other Woman* includes stories about African Americans, Native Americans, and Asian Americans, and explorations of verbal and physical violence and pornography. But the greatest richness of the stories comes from the relationships between the women, their shared understandings and bondings. In the last story, Jane Rule's "A Perfectly Nice Man," a man's first and second wives fall in love with each other.

In *Between Mothers and Daughters,* Koppelman continues to show that what a woman thinks of as a personal problem—the disdain for "old maids," the infidelity of a husband, or the bittersweet connection between mothers and daughters—is actually a common social situation, which women have long been describing, analyzing, and often solving in stories. Koppelman shares her discovery that most women writers' first publication is a mother/daughter story portraying the relationship that is the closest, most enduring, and sometimes most painful as well as most joyous in women's lives. Besides showcasing stories by Phelps and Wilkins, *Between Mothers and Daughters* also includes classics by Tillie Olsen ("I Stand Here Ironing") and Alice Walker ("Everyday Use").

The stories in *Between Mothers and Daughters* are about joys and regrets, losses and unexpected triumphs, the coping with too few and too terrible choices, as well as the absence of choice, personal quests, and triumphant collaborations. *Belles Lettres* called the book "a testament to the transformative power of fiction."

It is also the first Koppelman collection to include Fannie Hurst, who later became a separate research interest: intermittently in the 1990s, Koppelman edited *The Fannie Hurst Newsletter,* arranged conference sessions about the author, convened several meetings of Hurst scholars, and worked to interest others in doing Hurst research. Hurst, as the Koppelnote to "Oats for the Woman" points out, is often disparaged as a "sob sister:" elite critics assume that because she was popular, she must have been no good. But what made her popular was her ability to describe the lives of "common people," especially the dreams of impoverished working women.

After *Between Mothers and Daughters,* the first collection with Koppelnotes written on a computer (Nathan demonstrated his support for her work by teaching her how to use a computer), Koppelman continued her research into women's writings of the past and her development of new methods and resources for this research, and she continued to share her discoveries at conferences and via her "Dear Friends" letters. She continued to read at least three short stories by women every day, and took notes on recurring themes. But starting in the mid 1980s, she also became responsible for ailing and dying elderly relatives, which meant constant trips from St. Louis to New York, Cleveland, and Arkansas, and constant battles with lawyers, landlords, and doctors. Her health suffered.

Still, she managed to put out a short story collection in 1988 especially suitable for families. *"May Your Days Be Merry and Bright:"* *Christmas Stories for Women* includes stories from Louisa May Alcott to Ntozake Shange. This collection focuses on the history of occasional literature in general as well as the history of the Christmas story in particular. And in addition to its scholarly importance, *"May Your Days be Merry and Bright"* continues to be reprinted annually and has achieved the status of classic Christmas traditional reading. The fifteen stories include works by Wilkins, Jewett, Cather, Hurst, and Alice Childress, with whom Koppelman developed a deep friendship. Childress joined the Advisory Board of the Hurst Society and wrote the Introduction to a reprint of Hurst's favorite of her own novels, *Lummox.*

Meanwhile, despite her caregiving responsibilities, Susan Koppelman in the 1980s continued to carve out space for herself not only as an independent researcher and writer, but also as a scholar and mentor in Women's Studies and Popular Culture. Unlike academics whose titles are given to them, often for years in rank, Koppelman worked for and earned every distinction she got. And there were many.

For ten years, off and on, she was President of the Midwest Popular Culture Association, keeping that organization alive with her energies. In 1985, the Women's Caucus for the Popular/American Culture Associations created four awards named after women who had pioneered in the field, and the annual prize for the best feminist anthology, multi-authored, or edited work was named the Susan Koppelman Award. Her work was supported with grants from the American Council of Learned Societies and the National Endowment for the Humanities.

Meanwhile, at meetings of the National Women's Studies Association, Susan Koppelman created a new convention presentation format, the fishbowl, in which seven or eight women constitute an informal-looking panel, often seated around a makeshift dining table, to chat about a topic of great general interest. While noshing, they share ideas with each other and the audience about such themes as "Trashing," "Getting Published," "Jewish Feminism," "Gossip," and "Feminists Raising Sons." Her fishbowls have been widely acclaimed as highlights of the NWSA conferences.

From the conference circuit in the 1980s, and through her correspondence, Susan Koppelman continued to build a network of scholars and potential collaborators. Her only full-length collaboration, *The Signet Classic Book of Southern Short Stories* (1991), with the writer Dorothy Abbott, is a departure. It includes writers of both genders; it is not based on a theme, but on a region; and its headnotes are short, not Koppelnotes. Although the book has sold well and become a standard text in the newly emerging field of Southern Literary Studies, and Koppelman is delighted with the ample and historically accurate representation of African Americans and white women, she was dissatisfied with the work as a whole and returned to her own methodology for her future collections.

For *Women's Friendships,* she tried another innovative form. She chose the twenty-one stories, carefully balanced by time period, style, race, ethnicity, and tone, and then sought out a different woman to write each headnote. In some cases, the headnote writer is the leading authority on the story's creator, as with Carol Farley Kessler on Elizabeth Stuart Phelps. In others, the headnote writer is a biographer of the writer, as with Judith Arcana on Grace Paley. Two are by professors introducing stories by women who were once their students: Linda Wagner-Martin on Maria Bruno, and Joanna Russ on Madelyn Arnold. And some are long-time friends of the writers, such as Patricia Clark Smith on Paula Gunn Allen.

The net effect is to show the richness not only of women's perspectives on friendship, but also to show the vivid variety of women's writing, both in fiction (the stories) and nonfiction (the headnotes). In her Introduction, Koppelman puts together the theories that have animated her work: that women have written about everything; that every kind of woman has written and told her story; that those stories can be found; and that once they are found, stories can change women's lives and enable them to ignore and transcend patriarchal judgments—and decide what's important for themselves.

After *Women's Friendships* appeared, Koppelman acquired another title, first in *Belles Lettres* and then generally across her network. She became known as The Diva of the Short Story.

Meanwhile, there were other changes in her life. Her husband's health and her own began to deteriorate, and the market for his special skills began to dry up in St. Louis. Nathan was grown up and living his own adult life. Susan and Dennis needed a warm, dry climate. A 1992 taxi accident in Washington, D.C., where she was attending the National Women's Studies Association conference, also caused her to need considerable physical therapy and a long recovery period. In 1994, the Koppelman-Mills household, which typically included at least six cats, moved to Tucson. In addition to the weather, the city also met Susan's need for a benign cultural and literary climate, with such long-time friends as Annette Kolodny, Sheila Tobias, Joanna Russ, and Betty Burnett already living there. And it complied with Dennis's wish for a rust-free environment for his growing collection of Studebakers and motorcycles.

Also in 1994, Susan Koppelman published *"Two Friends" and Other Nineteenth-Century Lesbian Stories by American Women Writers* —a book widely hailed (erroneously) as her "coming-out book." (Koppelman has commented that when she wrote about dead authors, African American authors, or Christian authors, no one ever assumed she was dead, black, or Christian.) For the collection, she recovered an exciting mystery, "The Long Arm" by Mary W. Wilkins (Freeman), and a remarkable "coded" story by Octave Thanet called "Max—Or His Picture." The title story, an extraordinary one by Wilkins, was heretofore unknown to scholars. Koppelman completed her research for this collection while at the April, 1993 PCA/ACA meeting in New Orleans, asking antique shop owners and jewelers in the French Quarter for help decoding the mysteries of "Max."

In 1996, Koppelman brought together her lifelong emphasis on the major themes in women's lives as they appear in U.S. women's short stories, and created her most activist collection, *"Women in the Trees"*: *U.S. Women's Short Stories about Battering and Resistance, 1839-1994.* Her passion to promote knowledge, safety, and justice for battered women was fueled not only by her own past, but also by her son's response to the murders of Nicole Brown Simpson and Ron Goldman. Koppelman views *Women in the Trees* as "a kind of intervention," and her long book tour helped give voice to women silenced by years of violence and abuse.

Her 1996-97 tour included stops and talks in, among other places, Minnesota, Nebraska, Ohio, California, Texas, Missouri, and Louisiana. She met audiences in bookstores, churches, synagogues, university and high school classrooms, battered women's shelters, community centers, and a women's prison. Everywhere she heard similar stories: of men who are charming in public, but who isolate the women in their lives and then torment them, physically and verbally, often for years. She arranged for local counselors from local battered women's shelters to attend all of her talks and many women in her audiences left not only with a book, but with hope for a changed life and new connections to safety.

In the stories in *Women in the Trees,* some women characters lose hope, lose strength, sometimes lose everything. Sometimes their batterers murder them. But not all the stories are sad: often they are empowering. Kate Chopin's "In Sabine," for instance, appears to be the only nineteenth-century story in which a woman escapes her batterer—but it may not be alone. Zora Neale Hurston's "Sweat" and Estela Portillo Trambley's "If It Weren't for the Honeysuckle" describe sweet revenge. The stories provide testimony of the long history of men battering women in every social class, region, and ethnic group. But in the 1984 "I Don't Believe This" by Merrill Joan Gerber, readers are treated to evidence of important social change with the appearance of the first battered women's shelter in a short story. The last stories, Beth Brant's "Wild Turkeys" and Barbara Harman's "Happy Ending," are hymns to justice and right thinking, and celebrations of women's warmth and generosity toward each other.

Although it includes an Introduction and Afterword analyzing the stories' significances, and describing the ways in which battering is imbedded in U.S. popular culture, *Women in the Trees* does not have Koppelnotes—and for a profound reason: several of the story authors didn't want information about themselves to appear in print, because they did not want readers to think of them as battered women.

Throughout her collections and in her friendships and mentorships and in her life's work, Susan Koppelman has struggled to listen to, and respond to, the voices of women. The patterns of women's lives, she knows, are the patterns reflected in and reinforced by all levels and dimensions of culture, from popular to elite to marginal to folk. Women create culture, through food and gossip and the retelling of stories of the past, through giving advice, healing hurts, pushing others to transcend their limits, and tending their gardens. Women's lives *are* the stuff of culture.

In 1998, Susan Koppelman received the American Culture Association Governing Board Award for Outstanding Contributions to American

Culture Studies. She was the first woman to receive the award, and she was honored not only as the Diva of the Short Story, but also as a mentor, role model, and an early prophet.

In the early 1970s, Susan Koppelman joined the struggling Popular Culture movement, and made sure it was open to women. In the mid 1970s, Koppelman introduced feminist considerations of popular culture to the Midwest Modern Language Association. In the late 1970s, as one of the founders of the National Women's Studies Association, Koppelman and Emily Toth made certain that this new academic field included popular culture studies. By the 1990s, thanks to her efforts, Popular Culture was famous as a conference and a movement in which women are welcome to share in the feast.

Susan Koppelman's Books

Images of Women in Fiction: Feminist Perspectives. Bowling Green State University Popular Press, 1972.
Old Maids: Short Stories by Nineteenth Century U.S. Women Writers. Routledge and Kegan Paul, 1984. Translated as *Alte Jungfern* (German), 1988.
The Other Woman: Stories of Two Women and a Man. Feminist P, 1984.
Between Mothers and Daughters: Stories across a Generation. Feminist P, 1985.
The Signet Classic Book of Southern Short Stories (with Dorothy Abbott). Signet, 1991.
Women's Friendships. U of Oklahoma P, 1992.
May Your Days Be Merry and Bright: U.S. Women's Christmas Stories. Wayne State UP, 1993; Mentor, 1994, 1995, 1996, 1997.
Two Friends and Other Nineteenth Century Lesbian Stories. Plume, 1995.
Women in the Trees: U.S. Women's Short Stories of Battering and Resistance, 1839-1994. Beacon P, 1996.

Russel B. Nye

RUSSEL B. NYE:
MAKING A CAREER OUT OF CURIOSITY[1]

Maurice Hungiville

We think of pioneers as stubborn, brave souls who venture deep into uncharted territory in search of the new. They face unpredictable dangers, a hostile environment, attacks by unfriendly natives and innumerable hardships. The scholarly pioneer who ventures beyond the respectable established disciplines also endures hardships and takes risks. The natives encountered on the frontiers of popular culture might be friendly, even flattered by the unexpected scholarly attention, but those left behind in the well-settled areas often feel the special hostility of the rejected. To them the pursuit of the new seems like a repudiation of the old, the respected, and the established.

The virtues of the pioneer—courage and confidence, curiosity and endurance—were certainly needed in the 1960s when Russel Nye began his studies of popular culture. His long journey into this new frontier of knowledge took him over a formidable mountain of criticism, a fully developed, deeply entrenched tradition of disdain for the popular, the common and the ordinary.

Hostility to popular culture was especially strong in the universities where the "new criticism," popularized by conservative southerners, dominated most English departments. Promoting a method of close, intense reading, the new critics valued complicated elitist literature. The more obscure, the more complicated, the more teachable and, therefore, more valuable text. Accessible and obvious popular literature was understandably scorned, devalued, or simply ignored.

English departments were, above all, concerned with modernism, the complex elitist literature of James Joyce, T. S. Eliot, Ezra Pound, and Wallace Stevens. "The mind of literary modernism," Richard Hofstadter observed in *The Progressive Historians,* "is convinced beyond doubt or hesitation of the utter speciousness of bourgeois value, and it is altogether without hope, usually without interest, in the proletariat."

Popular culture, from this perspective, was an enemy of modernism. By offering pleasant, undemanding diversions, popular culture prevented readers from sharing the challenging, deeply religious and intensely therapeutic experiences of "real" literature. If literature, as Kafka insisted, "must break up the frozen ocean within," popular culture could only drain off readers whose deepest needs were trivialized by shallow satisfactions.[2]

Modernism, combined with Marxism, created additional obstacles on the path to popular culture. To the Marxist, popular culture was, like religion, another opiate of the people. While such transparently manipulative propaganda might be used to brainwash the proletariate, it held no intrinsic interest.

In addition to the "new criticism," modernism and Marxism, there was McCarthyism. The senator from Wisconsin and his movement were primarily political, but the defensive responses of the anti-McCarthy intellectuals were cultural. Thus the McCarthyism which disrupted American political life in the 1950s would distort American intellectual life in the 1960s. Intellectuals in explaining McCarthy would also explain away a vital American populist tradition. This new obstacle to popular culture studies began with Richard Hofstadter's observation in *The Age of Reform* (1955). "Somewhere along the way," he wrote, "a large part of the populist-progressive tradition turned sour, became illiberal and ill-tempered." McCarthyism, Hofstadter suggested, might have had its origins in "certain tendencies that had existed all along, particularly in the Midwest and the south."

In reviewing Michael O'Brien's *McCarthy and McCarthyism in Wisconsin,* Russel Nye would point out that Hofstadter's suggestion had become in other hands a general indictment of the Midwest. To Peter Viereck, for example, McCarthyism was "the same old isolationist, Anglophobic, Germanophile revolt of the populist-radical lunatic fringers against the eastern, educated, Anglicized elite." It wasn't long, Nye noted with a Jimmy Durante quote, until "everybody got into the act." Soon political-cultural suspicions about the Midwest had been expressed by such leading American intellectuals as Edward Shils, Talcott Parsons, Daniel Bell, and Nathan Glazer.

Such attempts to explain or "exorcise" McCarthyism added yet another impediment to popular culture. If political populism was a disturbing, anti-intellectual, possibly anti-Semitic rejection of the eastern elite's political leadership, then popular culture could only be a rejection of the cultural leadership of the eastern elite.[3]

In 1960, the eastern elite found an ideal spokesman in Dwight Macdonald, whose famous attack on ordinary popular taste, "Mass Cult and Mid Cult," appeared in *The Partisan Review*. An admitted snob, Macdonald believed that "all great cultures had been elitist affairs, centering in small upper-class communities."[4] Thus he valued James Joyce because he resisted mass culture and wrote for the educated, disciplined reader who expected culture to be challenging. For the same reasons, Macdonald criticized Hemingway and Twain. They had made artistically dishonest and damaging concessions to the popular audiences of their time. Popularity, in Macdonald's aesthetic, was convincing evidence of inferiority.

"Mass Cult and Mid Cult," reprinted in *Against the American Grain* (1962), became yet another obstacle to discourage any intellectual interest in ordinary people and their diversions. The 1950s had already generated a large library of cultural criticism, a formidable literature of contempt directed at mass man, the culture which produced him and the culture which amused him.

David Riesman's *The Lonely Crowd* (1950), an enormously influential study, had questioned the authenticity of popular culture by identifying the "other directed Americans" whose tastes and values were so easily manipulated by advertisers. C. Wright Mill's *White Collar: The American Middle Class* (1951) and W. H. Whyte's *The Organization Man* (1956) added sociological and psychological dimensions to the diagnosis of the middle class. Edgar Z. Friedenburg's *The Coming of Age in America* (1954) and Jules Henry's *Culture Against Man* (1963) accepted the diagnosis and extended the symptoms to a new generation of unfortunate Americans.

Creative writers also contributed to the shelf of Jerimiads lamenting the bleakness of life in America. Sloan Wilson's *The Man in the Gray Flannel Suit* (1944), John Updike's *Rabbit Run* (1960), and Richard Yate's *Revolutionary Road* (1961) all captured something of the age. The sociology and the fiction of the period suggests, then, that the major American enemy was conformity rather than communism. The 1950s, in the collective memory of the sixties, was seen as an age of conformity presided over by that perfect product of a bland popular culture, President Dwight D. Eisenhower. Elected and reelected with overwhelming landslides, Eisenhower was, nevertheless, regarded with scorn and contempt by the intellectuals of the day. Paul Goodman, writing in *Growing Up Absurd* (1956), described the president as "an unusually uncultivated man. It is said that he has invited no real writer, no artist, no philosopher to the White House. Presumably he has no intellectual friends; that is his privilege. But recently he invited the chief of the Russian government to a banquet and the musicale. And the formal music of that musicale was provided by a Fred Waring band playing 'Oh, What a Beautiful Morning,' and such other numbers. This is a disgrace."

American intellectual life at the time when the pioneers of popular culture were first advancing into this unclaimed and generally scorned area was usually hostile to the average, the ordinary, the popular. High culture was dominated by an elitist cultural establishment whose elitism was intensified by insecurity. The New York intellectuals were an extremely gifted, closely connected, paradoxically provincial family. This family of writers, some poets, some novelists, but mostly writers of intellectual journalism, was largely urban, largely but not exclusively Jewish. Most of them, like Dwight Macdonald and Paul Goodman, were associated with the *Partisan Review*. Some like Lionel Trilling and Irving Howe were professors, but others like William Phillips and William Barrett and Philip Rahv were combative, free-lance critics.

Literature and politics to these intellectuals were arenas where ideas, especially those of Freud and Marx, were debated, attacked and defended with a ferocity rarely seen in the Midwest. The intensity originated in their insecurity and alienation. Many of these writers were, of course, first-generation Americans whose families had fled the fascism of their native lands where ideas had erupted into armies and concentration camps. Above all, they were unassimilated Americans who "did not feel that they belonged to America or that America belonged to them."

In 1967, Norman Podhoretz chronicled the vulnerabilities of this uncertain elite in his candid memoir *Making It*. Podhoretz, a second generation member of the *Partisan Review* family, was sensitive to their vulnerabilities because he shared them. For Podhoretz education and the assimilation of American culture in general was a process of betrayal, of rejecting an unacceptable part of one's past. After a year commuting to his studies at Columbia University, Podhoretz felt a sense of shame when he discovered that in acquiring new tastes he had lost his old Brownsville accent. Education for the first-generation American had, it appears, some unforeseen and disturbing consequences. It insured, Podhoretz wrote, "that I would no longer be comfortable in the world from which I came."

These, then, were the formidable impediments to any acceptance of popular culture which confronted some restless young scholars in the middle of the twentieth century. Their ability to master and then go beyond and beneath the elitist culture needs to be studied as well as celebrated. Russel Nye was one of these young scholars. His contributions to the history of popular culture were unique, indispensable and deeply rooted in his own family history.

Russel Nye always felt at home in America. His family, originally from England and Denmark, had been here since 1635. The first American Nye, Benjamin, came to America on the ship "Abigail" and settled with Freeman's company of colonists in Lynn, Massachusetts. Benjamin Nye's great-grandson, Joseph Nye (1723-1790), lived through the

Revolutionary War and his son Bartlet Nye served in the Revolutionary army.

The son of this Revolutionary War veteran, Wendall Nye, was Russel Nye's great-grandfather. Wendall's six sons fought in the Civil War. Two were killed in that war and a third died in the Western Indian wars. Charles H. Nye, Russel Nye's grandfather, served as Quartermaster with the 43rd Wisconsin Regiment. Assigned to Tennessee along with a regiment of Black troops, the 43rd helped protect Nashville from Confederate General Nathan B. Forrest's cavalry raids. Sergeant Nye's regiment saw little action, although they did capture and hang a Confederate sniper. In the final days of the war they began construction for the National Cemetery in Nashville. The 43rd regiment lost two men in battle, and 71 died from disease, usually dysentery.

After being mustered out on June 24, 1864, Sergeant Nye settled in Platteville, Wisconsin, where he taught at the State Normal school. In 1892 he was elected superintendent of schools for Grant county. Russel Nye's father, Charles H. Nye, Jr., continued the family military tradition by serving in the Spanish American War before settling down in Viola, Wisconsin, to practice dentistry.

Russel Blaine Nye was born in Viola in 1913. When his father died in 1922, young Blaine, as he was originally called, came into a rich heritage of memories, values, and traditions that his family had amassed in over two centuries of American life. An orphan with an extraordinary sense of family, Nye would always be fascinated by his own history. He would one day write a Nye family genealogy and a brief history of his grandfather's Civil War regiment for circulation among his relatives. His earliest publications were products of the family archives he read in Aunt Lanie's attic.[5]

Conor Cruise O'Brien, the Irish historian, critic, and man of letters, has defined the historical inheritance which we all, to some extent, experience. There is, O'Brien writes:

a twilight zone of time, stretching back for a generation or two before we were born, which never quite belongs to the rest of history. Our elders have talked their memories into our memories until we come to possess some sense of a continuity, and the form it takes—national, religious, racial or social— depends on our own imagination and on the personality, opinions and garrulity of our elder relatives. Children of small and vocal communities are likely to possess it to a high degree, and if they are imaginative, have the power of incorporating into their own lives a significant span of time before their individual births.[6]

Nye's "twilight zone" gave him an extraordinary sense of history. Raised by the old soldier's daughter, Mrs. Lonair Chase, young Nye learned to revere—and emulate—his grandfather. The family patriarch had been a soldier and a scholar, a teacher and an administrator. He was, above all, an educator. When he died in 1923, his obituary noted "his wonderful influence over the young people with whom he came in contact. He understood the problems of youth, and possessed a sympathetic nature, always striving to make better men and women of those who were students at the Normal."

His grandfather was Russel Nye's first and most influential history teacher. The old man's stories and songs of the Civil War recreated the past with an immediacy no textbook could equal. His lessons even included some visual aids from the Tennessee skirmish, a dagger and a rifle taken from a Confederate sniper in the final days of the war. A cousin, Robert Nye, remembers how "the bearded figure of Grandfather Nye stands over all of us in spirit. His high standards and scholarly excellence influenced us all." Motivated by his grandfather's standards, young Nye became a successful and popular student. At Viola High School he played football, participated in debate and "oratory." When he graduated in 1930 he was given an award as "the best all-around student."

By this time Nye had shed the name "Blaine" and began to call himself "Bill" Nye. His model "Bill Nye, a. k. a. Edgar Wilson," was a frontier humorist in the tradition of Artemus Ward and Josh Billings. Noted for his dead pan humor ("Wagner's music is better than it sounds"), "Bill Nye" would provide his young namesake with a gentle, understated comic style which reverberates in some acclaimed scholarship, particularly *The Unembarrassed Muse: The Popular Arts in America*.

In 1930 Nye left Viola, Wisconsin, to study at Oberlin College in Ohio. There he found a familiar intellectual atmosphere consistent with his family's values and history. Like an Afro-American student who attends a historic Black college, Nye sought to reinforce rather than challenge the values he had formed. Education was meant to extend his identity, to claim rather than repudiate his uniquely American past.

Created out of an Abolitionist controversy, Oberlin College was a living tribute to the constitutional rights and academic freedoms Nye would write about in his second book, *Fettered Freedom*. Originally established in Cincinnati as the Lane Theological Seminary, the school was intended to train preachers in the Evangelical faith. In 1834 when Lyman Beecher was president, an Abolitionist student, Theodore Weld, organized a series of debates on the topic Abolitionism versus Colonization. After the discussions the students voted overwhelmingly in favor of immediate emancipation. The debates led, moreover, to action—students began to organize the Negroes of Cincinnati into clubs for the promotion of Abolitionism.

The Lane Board of Trustees feared both racial and financial unrest. Business relations with slave territory across the Ohio River were a concern and so too were the editorial attacks from newspapers. Finally, the Board of Trustees dissolved all student societies and forbad all debate and discussion which would distract students from their legitimate theological studies. The students, led by Theodore Weld, saw this assault on their constitutional rights as a sin, a crime, and a mutilation. Their manifesto proclaimed that "proscription of free discussion is a sacrilege! It is boring out the eyes of our soul. It is robbery of the mind! It is the burial of the truth!"

Although President Beecher tried to resolve the dispute, the outraged students and two professors started up their own college in Oberlin, Ohio. The new college remained a center of Abolitionist ferment. In 1858, a year after the Dred Scott decision, students rescued an escaped Negro from federal agents. After their arrest, they were cheered as martyrs by the huge crowd which gathered outside their jail in Cleveland. Their actions, as Nye argued in *Fettered Freedom,* helped clarify and popularize the idea that assaults on slave rights would inevitably jeopardize the constitutional rights of white men.

By the time Russel Nye arrived at Oberlin College in 1934 the school had evolved into a first rate liberal arts college. The nature of the school's change is suggested by the title of a 1969 history, *From Evangelicalism to Progressivism at Oberlin College, 1866-1917.* There was a continuity of commitment in Oberlin's identity. The issues might change, but the identity of the college retained something of its original spirit of service, even though the passionate capacity for moral outrage faded.

Oberlin's tradition of liberalism, particularly in regard to African Americans, continued well into the next century. In 1918, for example, a black student punched a white student who had suggested that the black's impressive academic achievement might have been the result of cheating. The white student, Robert Maynard Hutchins, went on to become the president of the University of Chicago. The black who decked him, Vern Johns, went on to become pastor of the Dexter Avenue Baptist Church in Montgomery, Alabama, where he set a standard of militancy for his successor, Martin Luther King, Jr. Hutchins and Johns ultimately became friends at Oberlin and both delighted in telling the story.[7]

At Oberlin Nye continued his high school interests in football and debate. He took part in debates on such questions as "Limitations on

Income and Inheritance" and "Socialism and Capitalism." At one of these events the future historian of progressivism assumed the role of Norman Thomas to debate another student who served as spokesman for President Roosevelt. Nye, it is said, won the debate but lost a friend. The Roosevelt impersonator went on to become a powerful official in Oberlin's alumni organization. Consequently, Nye's collection of honorary degrees never included any recognition from Oberlin College.

Undergraduate experience at Oberlin College was not all solemn study and earnest debate of urgent issues. There was nothing monastic about Oberlin in the 1930s. The depression imposed economic restraints, but it was still possible to raise small funds from some of the more gullible and prosperous students. With another student acting as his "shil," Nye would boast that he could tear a deck of cards in two. Farm work back in Viola had made him unusually—and visibly—strong, but most students after trying it themselves would place their bets. "Bill" Nye's hands were quicker than their eyes and the torn deck helped finance some extracurricular trips to Elyria.

The nearby town of Elyria had a number of speakeasies. John Shaw, a classmate of Nye's, recalls some undergraduate drinking in a working-class section of town where one could get "a murky home brew from rather unsanitary bottles."[8] When prohibition ended Shaw and Nye were astonished by legal beer they could see through.

Studying, drinking, and debating were not enough for "Bill" Nye's energies. He played football and excelled as a punter. Shaw recalls a photo of Nye in *The Cleveland Plain Dealer.* The photo included a caption with a typo identifying the kicker as "Jumping Bill Eye." (The next time Nye's photograph would appear in *The Plain Dealer* would be in 1945, the year he won the Pulitzer Prize).

After studying his past at Oberlin Nye went on to fashion his future at the University of Wisconsin. In Madison, Nye found a Midwestern model for the unique combination of academic activism, scholarship, and service his grandfather had exemplified. The University of Wisconsin, as Nye would recall in *Midwestern Progressive Politics,* was founded in 1848, just a few years before Wisconsin was admitted to the Union. The university and the state would grow up together. John Bascom, who became president in 1874, would encourage experimentation, new ideas, and, above all, "new ways of building binding relationships between university and state." The "Wisconsin Idea," first promoted by Bascom, was carried on by his successors, who took advantage of the close proximity of the campus and the capitol in Madison. By 1912, thirty-seven University of Wisconsin faculty members were serving in state government. Others served unofficially as consultants to

Senator Robert La Follette's regular "lunch club" where state and university problems were regularly discussed.

The University of Wisconsin was an exciting institution when Russel Nye began his graduate studies in 1939. Leslie Fiedler, S. I. Hiakawa, and Walter Rideout were graduate students and the faculty included the prolific Harry Hayden Clark. Clark, one of the first academicians to see American literature as something more than a thin and inferior outgrowth of English studies, had studied at Harvard in the 1920s under Irving Babbitt. Babbitt's essentially ethical view of literature gave his student—and his student's student—a feeling for the moral significance of literature. After earning his M. A. at Harvard in 1924 Clark had come to Wisconsin where he would remain until his death in 1971. Although he wrote or edited fifteen books and directed over three hundred dissertations, Harry Hayden Clark never received a Ph.D. and this, it is said, accounts for Nye's never using any title more exalted than mister.

As a professor and leader of an emerging, if uncertain, profession, Clark urged a compromise between the new critics who demanded a close reading of the text and the intellectual historians who insisted on attention to the larger ideas which formed the context. For Professor Clark it was not a choice between either close reading of particular texts or concentration of grand general ideas. Ideally and practically, both were required. The scholar, he argued in 1934, "must be willing to follow the trail of an author's thought, regardless of whether it leads into politics, religion, philosophy, economics, social relations, education or literary theory." Only after these disciplines had been explored would the scholar be prepared "to recreate the contemporary climate of opinion."[9]

The relationship between graduate school professors and their students sometimes reenacts psychologically the dynamics of family relationships. Certainly there are negative aspects to any originally unequal relationship, but methods, interests, and above all, values do get passed along as part of a family heritage. Nye's former student, Dale Herder, has written about this intellectual fatherhood, the process by which one scholar recreates part of himself in a student's mind so that the transfer of talents comes to resemble a genetic inheritance.[9] Nye suggested something of this eerily accurate analogy when he referred to one of his most productive former students, David Anderson, as "Harry Hayden Clark's grandson."[10]

Professor Clark directed Nye's dissertation, an ambitious biography of the historian George Bancroft, but Grandfather Nye back in Viola had first suggested the topic. The old man, Russel Nye remembered, often remarked that all questions could be answered by one of three books—

the *Bible, Webster's Dictionary,* and George Bancroft's *The History of the United States.* If his grandfather took Bancroft so seriously, Nye reasoned, there must be a reason for the historian's widespread popularity.

Once he had plunged into his research Nye found Bancroft to be a fascinating and, no doubt, familiar figure. Bancroft had been a scholar and a teacher, but his life had not been limited to libraries. He was an energetic participant in, as well as an observer of his time who combined study with public service. He had been a democratic party activist, a speech writer for president Andrew Johnson, and an ambassador to England.

Harry Hayden Clark encouraged young Nye to apply for a Knopf publishing company grant designed to help young scholars with a $1,200 award. Nye's application for the award mentioned that he had "read 575 volumes of biographies, memoirs, diaries and journals of every man of prominence with whom Bancroft had come in contact."

The anonymous Knopf award judges were enthusiastic about Nye's manuscript. Professor Clark's letter of recommendation had characterized Nye as a brilliant young scholar who was destined to become another Allen Nevins. The Knopf reader, H. S., remarked that Clark's prediction was "an understatement." He also insisted that Nye's biography would find a popular market. "I am willing to concede," H. S. wrote, "that a book which is almost a history of a century of American life, a book so full of color and motion and drama, and a book so well written must necessarily have a poor market." A second Knopf reader, known only as S. M., also agreed with Clark's prescient statement about Nye becoming another Nevins. Indeed, he compared Nye to Nevins and Bancroft. "Brilliant," S. M. wrote, "is not quite the word for either Bancroft or Nye, as it is not the word for Nevins. The minds of these men incandesce; they burn with a strong steady glow characterized not by brilliance but by sustained power."

Thanks to the enthusiasm of his anonymous readers Nye won the grant. The $1,200 enabled him to travel and examine original Bancroft documents in the New York Public Library, the Massachusetts Historical Society of Boston, and the American Antiquarian Society of Worcester, Massachusetts.

When Knopf published *George Bancroft; Brahmin Rebel* in 1944 the reviewers were nearly as ecstatic as the anonymous readers. Edmund Wilson, reviewing for the *New Yorker,* wrote that it was "as good a life as we are likely to get." Odell Shepard, who had been Harry Hayden Clark's professor at Trinity College, recommended the book to readers of *The Nation* as "a thoroughly interesting and important story which is neither diminished in the telling nor unduly magnified." Henry Steele Commager recommended the book to readers of *The Herald Tribune* as "the definitive biography of the great historian" and Howard Mumford Jones praised the biography for *New York Times* readers as a "solid historical contribution." Alan Nevins described the Bancroft biography as "thoughtful, scholarly, shrewd and well written" to readers of *The Saturday Review.*

Russel Nye's biography achieved, then, the kind of popularity and professional respect that Bancroft's own books once enjoyed. Distinguished professional historians recommending his biography to readers of newspapers and general interest magazines must have confirmed some of the convictions Nye had inherited from his grandfather and later found in George Bancroft. In spite of the impressive reviews, Nye was genuinely surprised when he learned that his biography had won the Pulitzer Prize. By this time, May of 1945, the young scholar, his wife Kay, and three-year-old son Pete were living in Cleveland. He was already at work on his second book, *Fettered Freedom.*

"This is all new to me," Nye told a *Cleveland Plain Dealer* reporter who sought him out in the stacks of Cleveland's Public library. When asked what gave him the idea for a biography of George Bancroft, Nye spoke of the book's beginnings back in Viola, Wisconsin. "Why, it seemed the most obvious book to do. I recalled my grandfather's devotion to the venerable historian. Bancroft's ten-volume American history occupied the most prominent spot in the house, and it was to Bancroft my grandfather turned as a final authority on any controversial point. So I began looking around."

Once he began looking around Nye found a wealth of primary materials. "Bancroft," he explained, "left a profusion of original documents. His motto seemed to be 'Save everything!' There were diplomatic reports, notes from his days at the Court of St. James, and even personal memos."[11]

Nye's research in Cleveland concerned Theodore Weld the abolitionist agitator who played a crucial role in the transformation of Cincinnati's Lane Theological Seminary into Oberlin College. Nye originally planned a biography of Weld, but his interests went beyond Weld's colorful personality; in fact, the prevailing ideas of his time were Nye's primary concern. The age was more attractive than the individual. Nye had acknowledged this wider interest in his application for a Rockefeller Grant. In an October 1943 letter to John Marshall, a Rockefeller executive, Nye noted that his "aim is actually not so much the narrative of Weld's life as a study of the rise of Abolitionist sentiment in the West as seen through Weld's career."

The shift in focus from an individual to his age had worked in the Bancroft biography and Nye was understandably reluctant to give up successful strategy. The same approach to Weld, however, made for an abstract, diffuse discussion of ideas and their relationships. Nye recognized the somewhat arid, academic nature of his study. "It is," he wrote Alfred Knopf, "a historical, purely academic study heavily footnoted."

Because his first book had been assisted by a Knopf grant Nye had a contractual obligation to offer the firm his next two manuscripts. By 1946, however, when Nye's *Fettered Freedom* manuscript arrived at the office, Knopf's enthusiasm for the Pulitzer Prize winning scholar had faded. *George Bancroft; Brahmin Rebel,* for all the honors and reviews, proved to be a commercial failure. It sold a mere 4,205 copies and earned only $1,259. Knopf's readers recognized *Fettered Freedom* as a book that would be "useful for reference, but one that is hardly good reading." Slavery and Civil rights issues were not yet the nation's agenda and the Knopf reader sensed that "the subject itself is unpopular, and a popular book about the Abolition controversy would be a different book."

Knopf's rejection of *Fettered Freedom* identified two significant problems. First, Nye's reliance on secondary sources denied his scholarship originality. For the next twenty years his books would be distinguished by graceful prose, a gift for synthesis, and enthusiasm, but reviewers would consistently note a lack of originality. The second problem was the publisher's, or more generally, the problem of commercial publishers who had to make a profit. Knopf was a distinguished firm, but it could not afford to subsidize unprofitable scholarly research.

Scholarship, even for Pulitzer Prize winners, is an enormous risk. The scholar, like the wildcatting oil producer, can hit some dry holes. Fortunately, at the very time Knopf was rejecting Nye's second book, *Fettered Freedom,* Michigan State College established a college press. This modest little press had, characteristically, evolved from the college print shop. Initially it published course materials, lab manuals and syllabi. With a small income from these instructional services and a modest subsidy from the college, the press was able to publish scholarly books which had no commercial potential.

The Michigan College press, in spite of its humble beginning in the print shop, had high hopes and high standards. The Pulitzer Prize winner's manuscript was sent out to independent readers, Clement Eaton of the University of Kentucky and Arthur Schlessinger, Jr., of Harvard. After favorable evaluations from the outside readers (Schlessinger judged the Nye manuscript to be "a valuable scholarly contribution both to the history of the anti-slavery movement and to the history of our tradition of civil liberties"), *Fettered Freedom* was published in 1949. The first edition was dedicated to the Civil War service of his grandfather and great uncle.

In Memory of
Charles Henry Nye
45th Wisconsin Vol. Regt.
1862-1865

Loring James Nye
7th Wisconsin Vol. Regt.
1861-1865

The dust jacket of the first edition explained how the book had begun back in Viola. *Fettered Freedom,* according to the author, was conceived some twenty years ago in a conversation with his grandfather who served as a sergeant of Wisconsin Volunteers in the Civil War. When asked why he joined the Union Army, the old gentlemen replied, "To guarantee freedom for everybody, for the slave, for myself, and for you." To find out what his grandfather meant, Dr. Nye in later years resolved to go back into slavery controversy. This book is the result.

Fettered Freedom earned some positive reviews in scholarly journals, but as Knopf had expected the book went unnoticed in the popular journals of opinion and the newspapers which had featured such enthusiastic reviews of the Bancroft biography. Nye's second book succeeded as a university press book. It enjoyed a moderate, steady sales over the years and brought both income and prestige to the small academic press. The presence of the college press, by offering Nye and other faculty members a means of sharing their research, helped build a community of scholars in the isolated East Lansing community. Nye's friends and colleagues at the time included Richard Dorson, the pioneer folklorist, Herbert Weisinger, the author of the classic study, *The Paradox of the Fortunate Fall,* and A. J. M. Smith, the distinguished Canadian poet.

At Michigan State College Nye's Pulitzer Prize was both an honor and a liberation. The prize, combined with his innate stubbornness, freed Nye's research and writing from careerist motives. His omnivorous curiosity and tireless energy were combined with what might be called a promiscuous or at least unselective generosity. Nye would write for anyone who asked for an article or a book, whether they were ambitious young instructors cranking out a shabby mimeographed publication or Henry Steele Commager and Richard B. Morris organizing a multivolume *New American Nation* series. Consequently, his articles might appear in obscure, eccentric newsletters like *The Baum Bugle,* published by Wizard of Oz fans in Michigan's Upper Peninsula or in a Michigan State College house organ called the *Key Reporter.*

For Russel Nye, far more than most professors, teaching, research, and public service were closely related. One reinforced the others until all three activities blended into a unified life of the mind. The tasks which often pull professors in different directions seemed to pull together for Nye. The unusually close relationship between teaching and research can be seen in Nye's 1949 application for a Rockefeller grant. Nye and two Michigan State colleagues proposed to study "regional aspects of folklore, art, music, literature, language, and history." Their purpose, in addition to preserving archival materials, was to train graduate students who could also merge scholarship with teaching. The graduate students would be "equipped in the traditional sense" but they would also "recognize in teaching and research the connections between them and the social, historical, and cultural backgrounds of the students they teach and the traditions they live within."

Public service at most universities can, like charity, cover a multitude of sins. As evidence of merit in this murky area, some professors might lead boy scout troops while others enriched themselves with lucrative consultantships. In this area, Russel Nye did what he was uniquely qualified to do—he fought for the constitutional freedoms he had studied in *Fettered Freedom*. Nye was chairman of the English department in 1952 when two colleagues were accused of being fellow travelers. Nye defended the professors both publicly and privately. An article in the Lansing State Journal entitled *MSU Backs ex-Red* included a statement by Nye testifying to his colleagues' loyalty. Privately, he wrote a memo warning Dean Lloyd Emmons that the anonymous accuser was "a man of definite instability who could cause real trouble." The potential for trouble was greatly increased by the fact that John Hannah, the Michigan State president, had taken a leave of absence to serve as President Eisenhower's Assistant Secretary of Defense.

For this risky public service Nye was the right man in the right place. His national reputation, his local popularity and, above all, his mobility increased his influence. Nye always had job offers and when principles were involved he was prepared to leave. Once his recommendation for a faculty member's raise was ignored he told the administration to find another chairman whose judgment they could respect. The professor got his raise and Nye stayed on as chairman of the English Department.

In spite of special circumstances, a president who was an assistant secretary of defense and a state Capitol just down the street from the campus, Michigan State came through the McCarthy years without violating professors' constitutional freedoms, and without imposing the loyalty oaths which disrupted and demoralized other professors at other institutions.[12] William Gorham Davis, a prominent member of the University of Wisconsin's Law School, once explained how Wisconsin avoided loyalty oaths. "If a respected faculty member," Davis noted, "privately informs the right regent at the right time that he will . . . resign if the regents impose a loyalty oath on the faculty, the proposal will never see the light of day." At Michigan State, a respected faculty member performed the same kind of public service.

Russel Nye's public service, defending on campus the values he professed in the classroom and analyzed in his books, gave his career a unity and scope that was not unlike George Bancroft's or Grandfather Nye's. There was, however, a price to be paid for fulfilling all three faculty commitments. Nye's teaching and administrative duties kept him in East Lansing, limiting his research to the library and keeping him from the primary materials which had distinguished his award winning biography of Bancroft.

Russel Nye's third book, *Midwestern Progressive Politics,* reflects this limitation. Like his first two books, *Midwestern Progressive Politics* originally began as a biography, a life of Senator Robert La Follette. Senator La Follette's daughter, Flo, however, was writing her own biography of the senator, a continuation of her mother's biographical efforts. With control of the La Follette papers, the primary documents needed for the biography, she was proceeding at a leisurely, amateur pace. Without access to the La Follette family papers, Nye redirected and expanded his study into a sweeping survey of Midwestern intellectual history.

The manuscript from his publisher's perspective was disappointing. One Knopf reader found the book exasperating, even "hopeless." "The whole thing," he wrote, "has been written from secondary sources." The result was "a boiled down version of certain aspects of American history in the last half of the nineteenth century," and "a slick-quick capsule over-all history of the period." The second Knopf reader made the same judgment. Nye's reliance on secondary sources made the book derivative and "basically unoriginal."

The reviewers, for the most part, agreed with the Knopf reader, but Richard Hofstadter had many positive things to say about *Midwestern Progressive Politics* when he reviewed it for the *New York Times* on July 15, 1951. He recognized, for example, the book's relevance to the contemporary political atmosphere in which fear of foreign ideologies contributed to what he would in 1965 call "the paranoid style" in American politics. *Midwestern Progressive Politics* was, Hofstadter wrote, an obituary recording "the history of the slow death of laissez-faire in the United States and the origins of the welfare state idea. Mr. Nye's materials make it clear that the use of the state for economic reform is not an importation but an outgrowth of native progressivism and a response to American needs." Hofstadter was aware of the book's lack of originality, but in his review this minor flaw was noted with sympathy. "Because of the breadth of the task, few aspects are explored in detail and neither his research nor his interpretation is remarkable for originality."

Other reviewers, with varying degrees of impatience, reiterated Hofstadter's complaint about originality. William Hesseltine, Nye's former professor at The University of Wisconsin, reviewed the book for *The Progressive* in 1951. Hesseltine recognized Nye's gift for "superb synthesis" and "contagious enthusiasm," but he lamented the lack of originality. "Russel Nye's story of Midwestern politics," he wrote, "has little new in it. It tells a familiar tale of political disturbance from the Grangers in the 1870s and the Populists in the 80s to the election of Truman in 1948."

Robert S. Maxwell, a University of Kentucky professor, had similar complaints when he reviewed *Midwestern Progressive Politics* for the *Indiana Magazine of History* in 1952. "This account," he noted, "contributes little new information and apparently is in no part based on original research or manuscript materials." Maxwell also found the central theme, the uniqueness of the Midwest "strained" and unconvincing. Nye's exclusive concern with the Midwest ignored the fact that "the heritage of progressivism had passed to Hyde park and the New Deal." Nye's study, he concluded, might be of interest to the general reader, but "the historian will regret that Nye did not 'dig deeper and broader' into the problem."

Professor George E. Mowry had similar complaints when he reviewed the book for *The American Academy of Political and Social Science Annals* in 1953. "The lack of primary materials," Mowry concluded, "accounts for the fact that there are so few new ideas in the volume." The reviewer for *American Quarterly* (Summer 1951) recorded a variety of complaints—he wanted fuller use of novelists' insights and more comment on the psychological origins of protest. Professor Wallace Evan Davies also voiced the familiar complaint that the book was not "startlingly original or profound." Even a reviewer from Oberlin College, Robert Gray Gunderson, noted the lack of primary sources. In an otherwise positive review in *The Quarterly Journal of Speech,* Gungerson noted that although Nye's study was "written largely from secondary sources, this volume is distinguished for its astute analysis rather than for its new information." Thomas Ross, the reviewer for *Indiana Magazine of History* (March 1952), recognized that the book might be "useful survey for undergraduates," but he complained that, "Professor Nye seems to have given little attention to manuscript collection and other published material."

Nye must have been disappointed with the reviews because his intention, to write scholarship for a popular audience, was so generally misunderstood. But if the reviewers disappointed, the readers, or at least one reader, did not. Nye, who had once argued the views of Norman Thomas in an Oberlin College debate, must have been pleased by a letter from the old socialist to Eugene Balsley, an editor of the Michigan State Press who had sent him a copy of *Midwestern Progressive Politics.* Thomas had both high praise and an immediate use for the book. "I intend to recommend it to my class in the New School of Social Research when I come to an appropriate place which will probably be my next lecture" (MSU Press Archives, November 30, 1951).

Nye's fourth book, *A Baker's Dozen* (1956), represented a major innovation in both content and form. For the first time Nye would devote an entire book to minor characters who were neglected, underestimated, or ignored. They were, in short, ideal popular culture topics. He would present them, moreover, in essays rather than chapters of traditional, narrative history.

In *A Baker's Dozen* Nye turned away from the great thinkers and theorizers, the leading actors and decision makers who dominated traditional histories. Instead he wrote of the intrinsically interesting, if insignificant, characters who had stumbled briefly onto the national stage to enjoy what Andy Warhol would later call their obligatory fifteen minutes of fame. Nye's previous books, as we have seen, began as biographies, but soon drifted into larger intellectual histories. The life was overshadowed by ideas and the subject was absorbed into his age.

Nye's fascination with these thirteen eccentric individuals kept the focus firmly on his subjects. The comprehensive view of an entire age was never attempted here. There is, instead, a series of sharply defined close-ups, small mini-biographies which never fade into anything larger. The author does connect these characters with the prevailing themes of American history, but they remain individuals and never become merely examples of something else.

Some of these characters had turned up in Nye's books before. Nat Turner, for example, had been mentioned but not really discussed four times in *Fettered Freedom*. In *A Baker's Dozen* Nye deftly integrates him with Elijah Lovejoy, the Abolitionist editor, in a chapter called "Road to Freedom." Turner, as a result, seems to emerge from his footnote in intellectual history. He steps from the background to the foreground and becomes the strange, haunting character who would later inspire William Styron to recreate him in his masterful "meditation on history," *The Confessions of Nat Turner.*

In *A Baker's Dozen* the historian has taken up a new genre, the essay. Now Nye has room to dramatize and analyze. He employs novelistic techniques, sets the scene, and orchestrates quotations until they seem like dialogue. Above all, he selects and controls his material with greater freedom. There is in the essay no ground to cover, no required topics which must be discussed. There is room to describe, develop, and dramatize.

The reviewers seemed to share Nye's fascination with these footnotes to history. All of Nye's thirteen characters were recreated from biographies, and Nye's notes on sources consist of four tightly packed pages of works he consulted. Other scholars supplied the facts for these biographical essays, but Nye supplied the artistry which satisfied his reviewers. There were no complaints about the lack of originality because the originality was in the artistry.

For the first time since the George Bancroft biography he was able to satisfy both the scholarly and the popular audience. On March 17 *The New Yorker's* anonymous reviewer thanked Nye for "a most enjoyable book" whose exhumations were "well worth an acquaintance." Karl Meyer, writing in *The Washington Post,* judged the book "among the years' most entertaining." Nye's thirteen "crisp profiles of Americans who are as interesting as they are unknown," were recommended as "caviar for the curious."

William O. Clough, *The Progressive*'s reviewer, enjoyed the book and recognized, as Nye did, that "minor figures may illuminate the pages of history, public sentiment or popular behavior more than profound generalizations." Both the popular and scholarly reviewers agreed on the merits of the book, but sometimes disagreed about the obscurity of Nye's subjects. Hal Bridges, reviewing for *The Saturday Review,* asserted that "Mr. Nye's minor mavericks, villains and heroes are truly the stuff that footnotes are made of." A more scholarly reviewer, Eugene H. Roseboom, writing in *The Ohio Historical Quarterly* (October 1957), disagreed with the depth of oblivion "to which history had consigned some of these thirteen unusual Americans." Roseboom, after examining five recent college textbooks, found that only Simon Girty was omitted from all five texts.

Edward Everett Dale recommended the book to readers of *The American Historical Review* as "beautifully written by a master craftsman." Wood Gray, the reviewer for *The Mississippi Valley Historical Review* (June 1957), acknowledged that the book was "directed at the general reader and non-specialist" and designed to rescue "thirteen interesting, even bizarre, personalities from varying degrees of oblivion." The scholarship "is impeccable," the author has "unusual insight into character and the significance of events and a flair for the apt phrase." Richard N. Current, in the *Wisconsin Magazine of History* (1957), wrote that Nye had "succeeded brilliantly in bringing each of them to life in a balanced, honest portrait with well chosen details." Current also recognized that each portrait was "a telling illustration of some eddy or main current in the blood stream of American history."

The popular and scholarly acclaim for *A Baker's Dozen* may have inspired another collection of essays about characteristic American ideas rather than American characters. *This Almost Chosen People: Essays in the History of American Ideas* was an abstract discussion of familiar ideas decidedly less appealing than *A Baker's Dozen*. By 1966 certain American ideas had brought the nation to the tragedy of Vietnam. Ideas about free enterprise, equality, or progress could no longer be contemplated with scholarly detachment. That Nye quoted President Lyndon Johnson on the American sense of mission might in those days have been a provocation.

Whether it was the book's intrinsic imperfections or the era's discontents, *This Almost Chosen People* received some disturbingly negative reviews. Vague complaints about Nye's lack of originality had been muted in past reviews, small qualifications in otherwise positive evaluations. These complaints now found devastating documentation in reviews that were worse than negative. They were hostile, almost abusive attacks on the book and the author. The uncivilized spirit of the time may have contributed something to the roughness of the review. Established reputations in those days were frequently assumed to be inflated. American ideas, moreover, were regarded with deep distrust.

Professor David Brion Davis of Cornell University struck the first blow at Nye's book. In his two-fisted attack in the September 3 *Saturday Review* (1966), Davis assailed the collection of essays as "oversimplified," "stale and platitudinous," and above all, insufficiently multi-disciplinary. Nye, Davis continued, "fails to confront the baffling, theoretical, methodological problem of intellectual history." His book, as a result, lacked "quantitative analysis" and "a firm theoretic framework."

The book's organization was weak and its quotations were repetitious and unselective. "One tires," Davis wrote, "of the same witnesses being recalled to say virtually the same thing." The content, moreover, was so elementary and basic that Davis questioned the book's intended audience. "So much space is devoted to summarizing basic American history that one almost has the impression of a series of lectures designed for a foreign audience." To Davis, *This Almost Chosen People* was not just a bad book, not just a failure, but a disgrace and, to judge by Davis's language, a crime. Because of Nye's prestige these essays could bring an entire discipline into disrepute. "Such a bad book," Davis concluded, "would not implicate an entire field of study if the author was not a highly knowledgeable and versatile historian."

Professor Davis's criticisms were devastating and enormously influential. The influence of these criticisms increased dramatically when Lyle Blair, Michigan State University's feisty press director, launched an ill-advised advertising counter-attack on the review. The unintended consequence of this bizarre public reply to the reviewer was to publicize the negative review. On October 6, 1966, *The New York Review of Books* featured a full page ad: "If you don't like intellectual history read the Saturday Review, September 3, p. 26, a Review of *This Almost Chosen People.*" A footnote, printed up-side down, added "We don't really like an up-side down point of view. We simply think this is a very good book." Blair's counter-attack on the review continued in the October 20 issue of *The New York Review of Books* with another full-page ad recommending a positive review of *This Almost Chosen People* which had appeared in the *Library Journal* on September 15, 1966.

As usual, there was a scholarly time lag in reviewing. By the time the quarterly or annual scholarly journals were published Davis's review had been widely publicized. The subsequent reviews in the scholarly journals reflected the Davis review and sometimes specifically referred to it. Thus David W. Levy reviewing for the *Wisconsin Magazine of History* in the spring of 1966 expanded on Davis's criticisms. This joint review of Nye's essays and Perry Miller's *Nature's Nation* left Levy "standing in awe of the power of Perry Miller's mind," and ready to make some invidious comparisons. Nye's book, he wrote after praising Miller's, "suffers by comparison." He acknowledged that Nye wrote "fluently and clearly," presenting his material "understandably, even too simply, to the layman." In addition to oversimplification and excessive quotation, Levy observed that the seven essays "are identical in form. They each begin with a broad introduction of a page or two in which the idea is defined." These initial pages, Levy acknowledged, were both valuable and interesting They were followed, however, by "a string of loosely-held-together quotations designed to prove or demonstrate something about the development of the idea through time. The first quote might be from Bradford of Winthrop or John Smith; the last, inevitably, is from Adlai Stevenson, John Kennedy or Lyndon Johnson." Levy noted that Nye was "weak in discriminating betyween his sources, too often content to equate an opinion of Henry George with one of Andrew Carnegie." For all these reasons, Levy concluded, "the book fails to come off."

Other academic reviewers came to Nye's defense, but not very quickly and not very forcefully. George W. Anderson, reviewing for *Indiana Magazine of History* (1967), described the dilemma of the scholar who seeks a popular audience. Nye, he noted, "was confronted with a monumental task of compression, synthesis, and generalization. Inevitably, he exposes himself to the criticism of the specialist."

Merle Curti's review in the *Journal of American History* (March 1967) was a superficially diplomatic, obviously evasive, possibly snide defense of Nye's essays. Curti recognized that "one" concerned with details could take exception to a few matters in *This Almost Chosen People*. These matters included "the somewhat oversimplified presentation of the complex and changing thought of John Stuart Mill." There were also some additional criticisms that "others" might make. Nye, for example, often "does not adequately distinguish between illustration and evidence; he hardly does justice to the problem of intellectual leadership; and in the essay on free enterprise he omits the recent role of the so-called industrial-military complex." Curti continued this masterful orchestration of criticism. "Still others," he continued, "might regard the author as 'old fashioned' in downgrading such currently fashionable ideas as neo-Freudian assumptions." "They" might also think "that many of his quotations are very familiar" and there is little that is new or original.

Curti's own views were not much more positive than those of the anonymous critics he summarized so deftly in such disturbing detail. His praise, after such criticism, was mild and familiar. Nye, he observed, is a tolerant summarizer; he lets everyone have their say. He writes with "clarity and grace" and he gives "generous recognition to his predecessors." Curti, in conclusion, found that he could recommend the book to the general reader and "novices in American intellectual history."

John William Ward of Amherst College put the entire matter, a not very edifying skirmish of scholars, in the proper perspective when he came to review *This Almost Chosen People* for *The American Historical Review* in April of 1967. "Professor Russel B. Nye," he began, "has written a book for the general reader of American history, which is not to say the professional should not read it." After a brief summary of the essays, Ward referred to the "rather coy up-side down advertisements in *The New Your Review of Books*." "What," he asks, "is one to say to readers of *The American Historical Review*?" His answer was a rebuke to both Nye's critics and his publisher. "It is hard to believe that any general historian of the history of the United States, let alone a specialist in American intellectual history, will find much new here; it is still harder to believe that any American historian will not welcome the work of a professional who has chosen to turn to a greater audience."

The reviews of *This Almost Chosen People* must have been disturbing and distasteful. Lyle Blair's curious advertising campaign may have been unwise and counterproductive, but it was nonetheless satisfying. On July 22 Blair wrote to Bruce Miller, a *Saturday Review* editor: "I can attest to the selling power of the *Saturday Review*. Largely due to the devastating attack on *This Almost Chosen People,* we have sold out the first edition and have just ordered a rush reprint. No book on our list has ever sold better." On the carbon of this triumphant note Russel Nye wrote, "This is one of the funniest letters in years."

Nye could afford to smile at his critics. His ego never began to equal his gifts and by 1966 he was happily at work on his masterpiece, *The Unembarrassed Muse.* If his books were sometimes without originality, they were without pretension too. Nye always sought the widest possible audience. Historians, he had learned back in Viola, did not write only for other historians. Nye never lapsed into a specialized, professional vocabulary. He had a gift for lucid, unpretentious prose because he was an unpretentious person, a scholar who would sometimes satirize the heavy language of criticism.

After the publication of *The Unembarrassed Muse,* Nye exchanged some lively letters with his old undergraduate friend from Oberlin, John Shaw. He wrote of the fun he had experienced while researching popular culture, getting to know "personally or by letter a large number of interesting and sometimes crazy people." One letter to Shaw included a Xerox of a cartoon he had found in an old textbook and a scholarly commentary:

I am enclosing herein an original Shaw, which I found drawn on the inside cover of a French text, Le Voyage de M. Perrichon, owned by me. The date of the sketch is believed to be circa 1932-1933, thus placing it in the early phases of Shaw's artistic development, or, as Von Schmorgas has called it in his monumental study of the eccentric Ohio genius, his "Puce Period," pre-dating the unhappy era to which we shall make no reference here. Despite the youthful lack of discipline evident here in Shaw's early work, there is apparent also the energy and zest that characterized his later work in his chemistry text, his advanced Spanish composition text and his more mature work on restaurant menus. It is thought by some critics (notably the Austrians Freud and Jung) that this sketch is part of a larger work planned for the men's lavatory of the gymnasium, never completed because of Shaw's withdrawal or "weltschmertz" period. Since this is one of the few Shaws that has not been searched out and burned by angry art-lovers, guard it well.

Nye's letter to his old friend from Oberlin College communicates the sense of fun, the irreverent spirit of play which enlivens the happy scholarship of *The Unembarrassed Muse.* Because he exploits the freedom of the essay while avoiding the solemn requirement of academic history, Nye achieves some of the "genial humor" and "hidden laughter" that Thomas Carlye once detected in George Bancroft.

The Unembarrassed Muse would be Nye's best book. It was a personal and professional triumph which swept away all criticism concerning originality. The lack of original materials or primary sources and documents had limited Nye's scholarship since he had traveled to George Bancroft's papers a quarter of a century earlier. *The Unembarrassed Muse* solved the perennial problem of primary sources and access to original documents. By turning to popular culture, Nye had transformed the neglected world of mass culture into a readily accessible archive of original materials. It had always been there, but it took a certain kind of pioneer to perceive and then exploit it.

The Unembarrassed Muse made popular culture a respected—and expected—addition to standard histories. Nye's next book, *Society and Culture in America, 1830-1860,* published in 1974, was a masterful wedding of popular culture and intellectual history. The marriage was a happy and equal union of once incompatible disciplines, which signaled the arrival of popular culture in two traditionally conservative domains—the history profession and the university curriculum. Nye's scholarship and public service were, as we have seen, closely related. He wrote about constitutional rights as a scholar and defended those same rights as an administrator. With the development of popular culture Nye's scholarship and teaching would help shape a movement. The making of a movement required both political and entrepreneurial skills. Nowadays we might call such activities "networking" or "mentoring." In the 1960s scholars in the more rigidly traditional disciplines might have called it conspiring. The two chief conspirators, Russel Nye and Ray Browne, began their conversations when Browne, a newly minted Ph.D. from UCLA, joined the faculty of Purdue University in 1960. What began as conversation soon grew into conferences and associations, papers and publications. The first 1962 conference at Purdue featured a Nye paper with the provocative title "A Juvenile Approach to American Culture." This essay, which traditionalists might have regarded as descriptive of the new enterprise, would be published in *New Voice in American Studies* (1966). The second conference in 1964 would also result in a volume of essays, *Frontiers of American Culture* in 1968.

When Ray Browne left Purdue for Bowling Green University in 1967 the dream of a new discipline became a reality. Popular culture flourished in Ohio. The *Journal of Popular Culture* was founded in 1967; in 1969 the Popular Culture Association was established within the American Studies Association. Russel Nye, was, appropriately, the first president of the association. In 1978 the American Culture Association was established.

The appeal of popular culture resided in its accessability, its fresh, unexamined newness, its promise of originality. The classics of American literature had been explained and explicated; every technique had been analyzed, every theme traced, every influence identified. The canon seemed so encrusted with commentaries that nothing remained to be said. Young scholars seeking new topics and new publications were soon drawn into the dream of a new discipline.

The new scholarly organizations became for Nye an extension of the classroom, an opportunity to teach students how to be colleagues. Nye's interest in his students did not end when they left MSU with Ph.D.s in hand. He continued to guide their research and promote their careers. He helped them get grants, publishers, and jobs. At popular culture conferences Nye roamed from session to session, recommending new sources to be quoted, suggesting new publications in need of articles, and departments in need of young scholars.

At Michigan State, Nye had begun his popular culture courses in a modest, tentative fashion. At first an extra class was assigned to popular culture materials. Attendance at this extra session was optional and the lectures were supplementals to the main business of the syllabus. By 1970 Nye had developed specific sources on popular culture. In 1972 he had the pleasure of editing *New Dimensions in Popular Culture,* a volume of scholarly essays written by the students of his English 983, Literature and Popular Culture.

Some distinguished books had their beginning in Russel Nye's seminars where students learned to value "the common and the ordinary." In a letter to the author, Bob Steuding recalls Nye commenting on the essential, often overlooked, technology of barbed wire and water pumps in the development of the frontier. Steuding went on to write regional history with curiosity and compassion for ordinary people whose homes and histories were swept away by the overwhelming force of progress. Steuding's *The Last of the Homemade Dams,* a study of New York state's Ashoken reservoir, reflects Nye's "attention to the value and importance of the ordinary."

Other books by former Nye students suggest the scope of popular culture studies. *The Lost Tradition of Mothers and Daughters in Literature* (1980) by Cathy N. Davidson, *Creating Rosie the Riveter: Class, Gender, and Propaganda during World War II* by Maureen Honey, *Reading the Romance: Women, Patriarchy, and Popular Literature* (1984) by Janice A. Radway. These books, along with Michael Steele's *Knute Rockne: A Bio-Bibliography* (1983) and *Christianity, Tragedy and the Holocaust Literature* (1995) remind us that popular culture once served to incubate some new disciplines which now stand unchallenged on their own.

In the evening of his life Russel Nye could see that the frontier of popular culture had been extended. Vast new areas were safely settled and new resources were exploited. These materials, thanks to the pioneers of popular culture, have enriched the traditional disciplines with new subjects, new methods, and a new kind of originality.

As he observed his students' contributions to scholarship, Nye must have had a very personal experience of Henry Adam's insight, "a teacher affects eternity. He can never tell where his influence stops." Russel Nye knew how far his grandfather's influence had reached. He could have no doubt of his own enduring contribution to American intellectual life.

Notes

1. I am indebted to Janice Radway for my title, a fine phrase which appears in her memorial remarks on Nye delivered at the American Studies Association convention on Nov. 4, 1993. This is also a good place to thank Russel Nye's wife, Kay Nye, his nephew Monte Nye, and his cousins Richard and Robert Nye for generously sharing memories and family documents. I am also indebted to Professor Maurice Crane, Director of the MSU Voice Library, the Harry Ransom Humanities Center at the University of Texas which houses the Knopf publishing records, and the Rockefeller Foundation archives which retains copies of Nye grant applications. The Michigan State University Press Archives and the Michigan State University Libraries Archives and Special Collections have also been helpful. My letters from former Nye students and associates will eventually be deposited in the Russel B. Nye Popular Culture Collection in the MSU library.

2. Franz Kafka, letter dated Jan. 27, 1904, as quoted in Ernst Pawel, *The Nightmare of Reason: A Life of Franz Kafka* (New York: Farrar, Strauss, Giraux, 1984) 158.

3. Russel Nye, "Myths after McCarthy," *Progressive,* Oct. 1967: 45-47.

4. Michael Wreszin, *A Rebel in Defense of Tradition: The Life and Politics of Dwight Macdonald* (New York: Basic, 1994) 353.

5. R. B. Nye, "The Lure of the West a Century Ago," *Michigan History* 29 (Apr.-June 1945): 204-08.

6. Conor Cruise O'Brien, "The Parnellism of Sean O'Faolain," *Irish Writing,* July 1948: 59.

7. Taylor Branch, *Parting the Waters: America in the King Years 1954-1963* (New York: Simon and Schuster, 1988) 9.

8. Milton Stern, letter to the author, Nov. 10, 1994, and John Shaw, letter to the author, Aug. 14, 1994.

9. Robert Falk, ed., *Literature and Ideas in America: Essays in Honor of Harry Hayden Clark* (Athens, OH: Ohio UP, 1975) x.

10. Dale Herder, "A Tribute to Russel B. Nye (1913-1993)," *MSU Alumni Magazine*, Winter 1994: 28-29.

11. J. A. Wadovick, "Pulitzer Author Digs Up Data Here," *Cleveland Plain Dealer,* 16 May 1945.

12. Michael O'Brien, *McCarthy and McCarthyism in Wisconsin* (Columbia, MO: U of Missouri P, 1990). A student's first amendment rights were violated during this period. David Murley's unpublished 1991 thesis, "Un-American Activities at Michigan State College: John Hannah and the Red Scare 1946-1954." Nye's public service as a journalist and administrator and speech writer is discussed more fully in my "Russel Nye: The Professor in Public Life," *Academe: The Bulletin of the American Association of University Professors,* 81.3 (May/June 1995): 24-27.

Peter C. Rollins

PETER C. ROLLINS:
TIRELESS WORKER AND MENTOR

Michael K. Schoenecke

One day in late August 1974, when I was a second-year Ph.D. student at Oklahoma State University, I discovered a "purple flash" in my mailbox from Assistant Professor Peter C. Rollins; the mimeographed memo stated that graduate students should talk with him if they were interested in presenting at the 1975 National Popular Culture Association meeting in St. Louis. Like most graduate students, I did not think that we would be allowed to appear before national forums; furthermore, I wondered what popular culture studies actually involved, particularly since I was an aficionado of popular music, film, and sports. Prior to introducing myself to Dr. Rollins, I spoke with other graduate students on the fourth floor in Morrill Hall who shared their vague notions about popular culture studies—a very new area of academic study at the time. I then decided to introduce myself to Dr. Rollins. Little did I know at that time that my academic goals, which seemed destined to a life-long study of John Keats, were going to change dramatically. Dr. Rollins told me that I could write and present a paper on singer Harry Chapin's music, and he provided me with some valuable insights on how to begin.

To my joy and surprise, he suggested that I call Chapin directly. About two weeks later, I conducted a ninety-minute telephone interview (which Dr. Rollins requested the English Department to fund) with Chapin who talked candidly about his music, his life, and his lyrics. He also asked me to send him a copy of the finished paper, which I later did, and he sent written comments back to me. The research project took on special excitement when Chapin called me at home to ask about how the paper was progressing and to see if I had any follow-up questions. Since my introduction to popular culture, Peter C. Rollins has served as one of the discipline's most energetic, enthusiastic, and supportive mentors.

Peter began his undergraduate career at Dartmouth College; however, because its literature faculty emphasized the "New Criticism" and forgot history, he transferred to Harvard University's History and Literature honors program begun by Barrett Wendell in 1909. Upon completion of his undergraduate degree with high honors in 1963, Peter was commissioned a lieutenant in the United States Marines. (His father administered the oath.) As part of his three years of military service he was assigned a tour in Vietnam. His experiences as a weapons, mortar, and rifle platoon commander taught him much about the perils, rewards, and trials of leadership. With his tour of duty behind him, he returned to Harvard to earn his Ph.D., with an emphasis in American Studies. At the age of twenty-five, as an enthusiastic graduate student, Peter attended the PCA's 1967 Toledo meeting, and he notes that he, unlike many territorialistic scholars, was immediately comfortable with the Popular Culture approach; PCA's academic thrust was a logical extension of his History/Literature and American Studies schooling in Cambridge where Perry Miller and Henry Nash Smith were both respected.

When one thinks about "advancing the study" of a particular discipline, one often thinks primarily of scholarly writings and offices held within national and/or regional organizations. Although Peter has successfully fulfilled these roles, he has advanced the study of popular culture through a multitude of additional efforts. Since 1994, he has served as Co-editor of the *Journal of Popular Culture* and the *Journal of American Culture* and as PCA/ACA's Director of Development. In partial fulfillment of these duties, he attends regional and national meetings as well as PCA international conferences so that he can stimulate the exchange of ideas; however, his primary task, which he works on rigorously, is to establish connections with other professional organizations such as the American Historical Association and the Organization of Historians as well as promoting and guiding PCA/ACA members with grant writing. Gary Edgerton notes that Peter "has worked tirelessly to enhance PCA/ACA's visibility and to lay the groundwork for the associations' members' grants." While Gary served as President of ACA, he described Peter as "helpful and friendly"; "as Director of Development, Peter provided the associations' officers with the continuity to bring things to fruition." Peter's approach to improving the Popular Culture Association and its program is simple: involvement leads to greater understanding and enthusiasm, inspiring old members and attracting new ones.

Mike Zalampas, Jefferson City College, worked closely with the Brownes and Peter when the national meeting was first held in Louisville. Mike and his equipment crew provided the associations with audiovisual materials, but, as too often is the case, their work is underappreciated. Peter, as Mike recalls, would often stop by the audiovisual room to "sit down and chat" with Mike and his crew and to "find out how things were going." Once, when Mike was quite ill, Peter asked Mike to go to his room to rest, and Peter supervised the delivery and retrieval of audiovisual equipment. The young, college helpers were quite surprised that one of the associations' leaders was so vocally supportive of their efforts and provided upbeat, positive enthusiasm for their work. Peter took the time to stop by and tell the crew thank you for the work they did. Although the gesture might seem insignificant, the time and the words meant a lot to the tired crew.

In my opinion, Peter's greatest academic achievements have been his work on Will Rogers, a popular culture icon who was attuned to and "related to the ideas and events of his time." The Will Rogers project included editing and publishing 22 volumes of Will Rogers's writings along with a comprehensive index. In 1983, Greenwood Press published Peter's *Will Rogers: A Bio-Bibliography;* this thorough study examines Rogers as humorist, as performer, and as symbolic representative of his time; as a result of Peter's extensive research and insightful readings of Will Rogers, the book was nominated for three national awards. *Will Rogers: A Cowboy's Guide to the Times* (1976), a superb compilation film, has been broadcast on the Discovery Channel, and has been awarded the following prizes: the Governor's Award (1st place) at the Oklahoma Film Festival; the Bronze Medallion at the Himisfilm International Film Festival; the Bronze Hugo at the Chicago Film Festival; the Chris Award at the Columbus Film Festival; the CINE Golden Eagle, the highest award for a documentary. (Because *Will Rogers: A Cowboy's Guide to His Times* has been a cinematic and financial success, Peter has repaid NEH the money he received from the initial grant—a rare achievement.) Such recognition clearly shows that Peter's scholarly work is relevant and accessible not only to the academic community, but to a general audience. Peter, like Will Rogers, has combined a mastery of regional style with a vision of our country's popular culture.

Since August 1972, Peter has taught in the English Department at Oklahoma State University, and his energy and enthusiasm for his teaching and scholarship have earned him a Regents Professorship which he has held with distinction since 1989. (In fact, he is the only Regents Professor the Department of English has ever had.) Unlike many university professors, he continues to teach not only his graduate classes in film and American culture, but undergraduate service classes in order to help develop the students' writing and intellectual skills. As a result of Peter's notoriously close supervision of theses and dissertations, his graduate students have published their work as articles and books. Peter is actively involved with his graduate students. I remember going to his home one Saturday morning at 8:00 a.m. so that he could help me with a conference paper; more importantly, I recall phoning Peter at his office one day and telling him that I was having difficulty with my dissertation.

He told me that he could come to my house, a thirty-minute drive, to work with me, and he asked if my wife, Debby, could bake one of her famous pecan pies. That night he worked with me from 7:00 p.m. until 3:00 a.m. When we emerged from the study, we found our wives asleep on the couch and floor. What has always impressed me is Peter's willingness to help, although he expects and deserves an honest effort from the student. In Paul Walters' Introduction to his thesis, he lovingly wrote, "I want to thank Dr. Rollins for persevering with this project, and I want to thank myself for putting up with Dr. Rollins' persevering." Peter rightly expected and demanded quality work from his students, and his editorial comments were always positive in tone while encouraging the author/student to produce concise, precise research. As Zia Hasan, one of Peter's former students and now a Vice President for Academic Affairs at Claflin University, fondly recalls, "Peter's positive influence as a teacher included driving me hard; he had high expectations for me and for all of us [his graduate students], but then he had high expectations of himself, too. He let us be creative; he had a magic touch, and I could count on him to give me an honest apprasial of my work." Peter's graduate students truly appreciate his academic expertise which covers so many diverse areas, but most importantly, they thank him for his honesty, his friendship, and his trust.

Perhaps Peter's most significant and popular accomplishment at OSU was the creation of the OSU Filmathon, which has been his principal extension activity since 1973. Approximately 58 local people attended the initial regional meeting, which was designed to enhance film literacy on campus and within the region; however, by 1981, better than 600 people, some traveling long distances by car and airplane, attended the cinematic screenings and workshop programs. Scholars, representing as many as seventeen different institutions from across the nation, delivered forty-five-to-ninety-minute presentations on various aspects of film before audiences of 300 or more. Participants viewed feature films, documentaries, and experimental films that were shown from Friday through Sunday evenings. If one had the tenacity, one could preview better than 100 films in one weekend, and many of the region's cineastes, who were visually thirsty for quality films in those days before video, took full advantage of this cinematic waterhole. However, OSU students were encouraged to view the films for their particular area of study and then to attend the panelists' presentations. Whereas many programs only allow the attendees to be passive listeners, OSU's Filmathon encouraged all participants to discuss the presentations as well as other thoughts on cinema. In other words, the participants worked in an atmosphere of collegiality, promoting the exchange of ideas and cinematic literacy. Many of my former students appreciated the opportunity to discuss filmmaking with such film notables as Alvah Bessie, David Raksin, Edward Dmytryk, and Oklahoma's own Ned Hockman. Every participant benefited from the formal and the casual presentations and exchanges.

Working with OSU cultural geographer Steve Tweedie, Peter has produced a series of nationally syndicated radio programs dealing with the history, sport, music, fine arts, and economics of the Southwest. He is also a popular speaker at various regional civic programs in Oklahoma, where he has delivered presentations on such diverse topics as Oliver Stone as historian; pioneer women in literature and film; the Holocaust as history and literature; Will Rogers; John James Audubon; the influence of the media on the criminal justice system; and images of men and women in *Playboy*. This civic involvement, which generally includes a luncheon and a minimal honorarium, has taken the study of American and popular culture to the public. As we know, much of the American public has become suspect about the relevance of humanities research on our campuses. Much of the public believes that a professor, which to them entails life-long employment, teaches three classes a week and spends the remainder of each week at home resting or golfing. However, Peter's active participation with local, regional, and national civic organizations provides them with the opportunity to see and to hear how the study of popular culture and American culture affects their lives; his civic work has truly kindled the interest of the non-academic community. For 1996 alone, he has held the following offices in civic groups: Department of Oklahoma Commander, Military Order of the World Wars; President, The Retired Officers Association, Cimarron Chapter; Chairman, Veterans Task Force, 1st Congressional District. Ted Bardwell, Commander of Eastern Oklahoma Chapter of the Military Order of the World Wars, praises Peter for his willingness to "preserve military history." The 1997 Memorial Day activities in Tulsa, OK, honored Sgt. Ruben Rivers; to celebrate and to pay tribute to Sgt. Rivers' patriotism, Peter coordinated the ROTC troops and worked as a liaison between Floral Haven Cemetery and the veterans' groups. Bardwell enthusiastically noted that Peter works diligently with veterans' organizations in Oklahoma and Washington, D.C. to make sure that the veterans receive the benefits they deserve for their military service. Commander Bardwell enthusiastically noted that Peter maintains contact with the regional veterans while working with U.S. Representative Steve Largent on issues that affect veterans and their benefits.

In Peter's "Introduction" to the first issue of the *Journal of Regional Culture,* he wrote that the "gift" of regional studies provides "challenging work . . . for scholars of American regions." In 1979, Peter along with Texas Christian University's Fred Erisman organized the initial meeting of the Southwest/Texas Popular Culture and American Culture Associations, which attracted 129 participants and which met concurrently with the OSU Filmathon. This organization has continued to grow and to prosper under Peter's leadership because he encourages its members to build foundations for an authentic sense of place. Peter initially took the reins and served as President of the Southwest Chapter from 1977-82. He has been the Program Chair and Host for six meetings which have been held at Oklahoma State University and at Tulsa, and America's War Eras Chair from 1989-1994. He served as guest editor for the first issue of the *Journal of Regional Culture* in 1981 and an issue of the *Journal of American Cultures* in 1991 which contained interdisciplinary approaches to the study of the West. Beginning with the 1996 meeting, the Southwest/Texas Popular Culture Association now publishes its presentations on CD-ROM, an innovative format which he once again edits and produces. Peter's foresight and energy have enhanced the visibility and scholarly endeavors of our regional associations. Even when Peter did not host a regional meeting, all of the other Program Chairs contacted him regularly to seek advice and comfort. Without a doubt, Peter not only answers questions, but smoothes ruffled feathers and quiets anxieties for those new at organizing programs; it is important to note that Peter has always made himself and his expertise available. This generosity is infectious; the Southwest/Texas PCA/ACA's success reflects his concern for people and for the association. Beginning with the 1996 program, Peter has posted a preliminary program on the internet so that all interested participants can learn early when they are scheduled to present; this year's notice also shares our work with the world. Indeed, the web site program received over 3,000 "hits."

Although many graduate students could not afford to attend and present papers at the national meetings, Peter helped defray their travel costs to the regional meetings; more importantly, Peter encouraged graduate students to assume positions of responsibility. Graduate students have served as Program Chairs, Area Chairs, and Panel Chairs with the regional program; by placing them so early in key positions, the students learn what is expected from professionals.

Because of his leadership, the Southwest/Texas Popular Culture Association unanimously voted in 1992 to establish a Peter C. Rollins Award, to be given annually for the best graduate paper on popular culture. As he stated in a telephone interview, Peter has tried to keep "the spirit of democracy alive, a spirit which distinguishes the regional and the national associations from other scholarly organizations." He often says of graduate students, "You are our future," and he means it; bringing them into the operations of the regional groups makes them want to stay with our movement. Rather than being reluctant to accept new ideas, Peter's positive energy and his support emerge when he helps to put new ideas into action.

Peter has provided a means by which the students can earn credit by attending the regional meetings. He conducts early sessions with the students and reads/grades their papers. But one should note that Peter does more than simply read a paper and assign a grade to it; he provides the students with his now famous "Bouncing Footnotes" that explain not only why the paper received the grade it did, but thoroughly details what the student can do to improve the content and style of future efforts.

At the national level, Peter has also been a tireless worker. He has attended and presented papers at the national level since 1971. He has also served as President of the Popular Culture Association (1982-84), as Vice-President (1979-82), as Executive Council Member (1976-77), as Program Chair (1980-82), as well as—at different times—area chair for Film, Vietnam Studies, Korean Conflict, Operation Storm, and Media Bias. The last four areas were originated by Peter, but, since he believes that no single person should take a proprietary attitude toward an area, he has passed the torch to others so that they can bring in fresh ideas. As President, Peter brought the national meeting to the Southwest when we met in Wichita, Kansas. Although many members feared that going "West" might disastrously impact attendance, the meeting was a great success; in fact, the Wichita meeting attracted more participants than any previous national meeting. While he promoted collegiality and visibility of the Southwest's popular culture sites, Peter lead the PCA/ACA members on a tour of the Wichita Art Museum and the Mid-American Indian Center. A 10-K run was held for want-a-be runners in the organization, as well as an unforgettable program entitled "Wargames II: Extended Percussion and Professional Wrestling." I'll never forget having a "Cow-boy Koolaid" (beer) with Ray Browne and Peter on Wednesday evening before the meeting; later, when Ray and I decided to return to our rooms, we were both memorably surprised when the elevator door opened and we faced four sets of identical twins who were attending a twins convention being held concurrently with our meeting at Wichita's Hotel Broadview.

Whereas J. Fred MacDonald established the Area Chairs concept for the national and regional meetings, Peter, who followed Fred as PCA President, expanded the roles and responsibilities of Area Chairs; he created and wrote specific guidelines, which are still used today. By diversifying the leadership at both the national and the regional level, Peter freed the people who work at Bowling Green's Popular Press from many tasks and got more people participating in the direction the PCA would take, including the Open Forums. To honor the founders of the Popular Culture Association and to reward them for their excellence in popular culture studies, Peter introduced the Ray and Pat Browne Award.

While the world as well as academia was making a move toward computers and technology, the Popular Culture Association lagged behind for a while until Peter convinced some of its members to integrate technology with its programs. Peter helped create H-PCAACA so that members can exchange course syllabi, read book reviews, and "Brother" Paul's reports as well as other information related to the study of popular and American culture. Peter, with my help, created *Reviews in Popular Culture* which initially broadcasts its reviews on the internet and then publishes a hard copy in either the *Journal of Popular Culture* or the *Journal of American Culture*. The National Web Site, which began in 1995, provides popular culture scholars with easy access to program information, area chairs, the Chorba and King Reports, current book reviews, a history of the popular culture and American culture movements, and links to other popular culture sites (http:h-net.msu.edu/2pcaaca/). The creation of the Web Site has been highly successful because it has increased the PCA/ACA's visibility on an international level: better than 70,000 people have "visited" the web site since its creation. From August to November 1996, there were better than 2,500 "hits" on the web site; it is important to note that our Web Site has been "visited" by representatives of both town and gown.

Although many people know that Peter served as an Infantry Officer in the Vietnam War, few of them realize that Peter was decorated for his service with the United States Marine Corps. In fact, he received four medals including the National Defense Service Medal and the Vietnam Service Medal. Peter's continued participation with Vietnam and other war eras reflects his love and admiration for America, for her veterans, and for all Americans. Although many veterans and non-veterans still harbor a cynical view of America and her involvement in Vietnam, Peter has remained optimistic and supportive of America and her military. His approach to military studies is quite simple and honorable: he borrows from his understanding of military values and culture, and he celebrates those individuals who have defended America and served in her armed forces. As a result, he continues to produce scholarly materials such as cinematic, television, and radio programs and journals that address America's involvement in Vietnam. His documentaries include *Television's Vietnam: The Battle of Khe Sanh* (1992), *Television's Vietnam: The Impact of Media* (1986), and *The Westmoreland Trial: Insights and*

Implications, which is in pre-production. Peter also edits the *Journal of the Vietnam Veterans Institute,* whose mission is to develop and foster legislative, public policy, and educational initiatives that positively address issues of importance to veterans. The journal has addressed such issues as The Westmoreland Trial, Neil Sheehan's *Bright and Shining Lie*, Discrimination Against Vietnam Veterans, Vietnam in Academe, The MacNamara Book and Legacy, and The POW/MIA Experience as History, Literature, and Film. Peter was a dedicated Marine officer who wants to preserve military history and patriotic education.

When Peter attended the 1972 AHA meeting in New Orleans, he introduced himself to John O'Connor and Martin Jackson who had recently begun publishing *Film and History* as a newsletter. During their conversations O'Connor was impressed with Peter's "academic and personal support, breadth of interest, training in American History, and his work as a filmmaker and scholar." Early issues of the journal contain articles written by Peter; so impressed were O'Connor and Jackson that they asked Peter to serve as one of the journal's first advisors and to assist them with editorial policy; in 1995, after John O'Connor suffered a stroke, Peter became Editor of *Film and History;* the journal reflects Peter's and John's shared academic values and friendship; the journal continually acknowledges O'Connor's accomplishments within the interdisciplinary study of history and film. O'Connor notes that Peter brings a "unique constellation of talents, understanding, and personal experience to the journal; as an editor, he is intelligent, and he doesn't shy away from a stand. As a result, Peter has broadened the scope, involved more scholars and contributors during his tenure as editor." Because of Peter's hard work and vision, the first 20 years of *Film and History* are now available on CD-ROM, and Peter and the journal are responsible for bringing Oliver Stone, Gary Wills, and Michael Medvid to speak at AHA meetings.

Since Peter holds that the cultural historian is compelled always to work within the framework of truth, having no license to fabricate, he is eternally conscious of the matter of validation, although it is not to be carried to the point of absurdity. Like his advice to graduate students, his writing convinces his readers by clarity and vividness. As a result, Peter does not pack so many trivialities into his writing as to obscure the meaning of his work. Peter's scholarly work about the Vietnam War is written with the personal touch because it is not enough for the cultural historian to concern himself alone with cold abstractions. He must also keep the subject timely, vital, and human.

Peter was accompanied to the 1992 Southwest/Texas PCA meeting in Amarillo by a lovely, gentle, kind woman whom he later married.

Since then, all of us have been blessed by Susan Rollins' warmth and tact, and she continues to be a touchstone not only for Peter, but for many of his friends and colleagues. Susan has also delivered presentations on musicals at national and regional PCA/ACA meetings, and she has co-edited with Peter a book on images of popular culture; Peter and Susan have even founded their own press. Susan holds a special place with me because she has become my "gaming" mentor. With her guidance, patience, and expertise, I managed to leave Las Vegas with a lot more money than I took with me.

Peter's scholarship, his leadership, and his organizational abilities have strengthened the Popular Culture and American Culture Associations. He willingly serves as a mentor for not only his graduate students, but for many regional and national scholars who owe many of their publications to Peter's hard work, encouragement, and critical eye. The Popular Culture Association's evolution has been an upward trajectory because Peter has been such a selfless, tireless worker and mentor. Perhaps, as Gary Edgerton pointed out, "the PCA/ACA membership doesn't know how much Peter has done for the associations since he helps lay the groundwork behind the scenes. Peter clearly plants seeds and cultivates them; in my sense, he has moved the associations forward." Peter has served as a filter through which individuals and associations have poured their thoughts and ideas; he has enthusiastically mediated upon those perspectives and generally turns the vinegar into wine.

Fred E. H. Schroeder

FRED E. H. SCHROEDER:
PIONEER IN THE FIELD

Michael T. Marsden

It would be fair to say that Fred Schroeder has had several careers. He was trained as a rural school teacher at a normal school near his hometown of Manitowoc, Wisconsin. From 1952 to 1960, he taught elementary and junior high school grades in several Wisconsin communities, while finishing his Bachelor's degree in English from the University of Wisconsin during summers and by extension and correspondence courses. In 1960, he was a Woodrow Wilson Fellow at the University of Minnesota, where he received both his Master's degree and doctorate in American Studies. He was a most productive faculty member at the University of Minnesota, Duluth from 1963 until his retirement in 1996.

His early days in the public school classroom set the stage for his contributions to pedagogical research. A review of his list of scholarly publications will reveal many articles on pedagogy, several on rural schoolhouse design, and a thoughtful volume on the art and science of teaching the humanities entitled, *Joining the Human Race: How to Teach the Humanities,* which was published in 1972. In the Preface to that volume, he wrote:

The most dynamic force in American public education today is the "humanities" movement, which initially grew out of various kinds of "Great Books" courses, but which has had influxes from a number of other contemporary movements in education. These boil down to two key words of the seventies, *relevance* and *interdisciplinary,* but they include such current enthusiasms as team teaching, modular scheduling, the inductive method, popular culture, the lively arts, minority studies, and nondirective teaching. There is great energy and excitement in these approaches to education, but they are too frequently marked by faddishness, superficiality, and lack of discipline. (xii)

It would seem that he was setting the agenda not only for the academic world in the 1970s, but his own scholarly agenda for the next quarter-century as well.

While Fred Schroeder continued to publish some dozen scholarly articles on pedagogical issues from the teaching of interdisciplinary humanities to curricular reform, the publication of his book, *Outlaw Aes-*

thetics: Arts and the Public Mind, in 1977 presented his agenda for Popular Culture Studies as a second thread in his life's work. His dedication of the volume sets the tone: "Dedicated to those I love, the quick and the dead." And the book's thesis is clearly stated:

To be somewhat more precise, this is a book about aesthetics—the philosophy of taste—; and about American studies—the investigation of our national character—; and about popular culture—the social, psychological and material environment of the majority of the people. At times, this book will be about a combination of all three subjects which might be called American popular aesthetics, but it would be unfair to label the whole book, because to do so would tend too much toward narrowing the scope of my intent. (1-2)

Later in the Introduction, Fred Schroeder notes that one perspective he has developed about America and popular culture is that is all there is —popular culture or the wilderness, take your choice.

This volume was begun in 1970 and completed in 1976, well before Roland Barthes was trying to come to terms with American popular culture and well before Herbert Gans was struggling with the popular taste and developing his concept of "taste culture." Fred Schroeder's book on *Outlaw Aesthetics* not only established the issue of popular aesthetics as an appropriate and important field of inquiry, but it helped guide his own research into Popular Culture Studies which would include such specific research topics as video aesthetics, the wish book, popular culture before printing, popular radio, popular photographs, museums, taboos and tabooism, electrical plugs and receptacles, front yard landscaping, decorative arts as social history, and the archeology of American culture.

In his book, *5000 Years of Popular Culture: Popular Culture Before Printing,* which was published in 1980, Fred Schroeder assembled a collection of essays which served as a powerful corrective to those who would equate popular culture with the modern. While not abandoning the notion of mass production and distribution of cultural forms, Fred Schroeder is able in this volume to demonstrate that popular culture is not tied to a time period. The relationship is much more complex and involves the interactions of historical, social, and economic forces. It is in the introduction to this collection of essays that Fred Schroeder boldly suggests a clear connection between popular culture and taxation. He writes:

Popular culture emerges with taxes, most of all. Taxation implies a political structure, an economic system and an ideology that transcends the natural units of family, tribe, and clan. It also implies extended lines of communication (and with them, non-local authority, maintenance and policing.) And it implies the metropolis. This does not mean that popular culture is itself an urban culture. (8)

He was thus able to help open vast new areas of research for future scholars. Fred Schroeder collected another remarkable series of essays in 1981 in a volume entitled, *Twentieth-Century Popular Culture in Museums and Libraries.* By decrying the lack of attention to popular culture materials which have existed through time, he is able to establish the need and significance for expanded and respectful collecting and preserving of our collective culture. In the Introduction, after acknowledging the significant efforts of the Smithsonian and the City of Oakland, California to collect, preserve and display everyday American life, Fred Schroeder succinctly notes: "we cannot help but wonder what substance there could be to American life if we were to remove mass-produced commercial artifacts [from a collection]" (5).

In 1993, Fred Schroeder published his delightfully informative volume, *Front Yard America: The Evolution and Meanings of a Vernacular Domestic Landscape.* As he notes in the Acknowledgments to this volume, his interest in the topic dates back a quarter-century to when he first began to photograph homemade yard ornaments. This volume is a significant contribution to the literature of the American vernacular and effectively illustrates the lifetime of careful thought and attention Fred Schroeder has given to the ordinary things of everyday life which in many cases turns out to be extraordinary.

Fred Schroeder has also found time in his career to be an administrator, serving variously as Director of the Humanities Program, Director of the Center for American Studies, Director of the Institute for Interdisciplinary Studies, Head of the Department of Humanities and Classics, Director of the Interdisciplinary B.A. Program and as Director of Graduate Studies for the Master of Liberal Studies Program. During his various administrative assignments at the University of Minnesota-Duluth, he also served as President of the National Association for Humanities Education, which met jointly with the Popular Culture Association/American Culture Association for several years to explore areas of mutual interest, as well as President of the American Culture Association. Fred Schroeder was the founder and President of the Superior Chapter of the American Culture Association where he helped to focus on quality research at the regional level.

A man of considerable charm and wit, he turned the disappointment he experienced as a young scholar denied the opportunity to do the kind of cultural research he wished to do, into a life-long support for the work of countless other young academics whom he helped to shape and mold into productive scholars of culture writ broad and deep. The real impact he has had on the professional scholarship of many others who have been inspired by his work and encouraged by his support is effectively exemplified by Andrew Gulliford's award-winning book on the rural one-room schoolhouse, *American Country Schools,* the success of which was due in no small part to Fred Schroeder's considerable encouragement.

As a teacher, a scholar and a mentor, Fred Schroeder demonstrated that the academic self is not divided, but rather multifaceted and integrated. He has been a champion of interdisciplinary study in general, and Popular Culture Studies in particular. As his life's work clearly demonstrates, he has been a true pioneer in the field of Popular Culture Studies.

Selected Bibliography of Fred E. H. Schroeder

Publications: Books

1993   *Front Yard America: The Evolution and Meanings of a Domestic Vernacular Landscape.* Bowling Green State University Popular Press.

1981   *20th-Century Popular Culture in Museums and Libraries.* Bowling Green State University Popular Press.

1980   *5000 Years of Popular Culture: Popular Culture before Printing.* Bowling Green State University Popular Press.

1977   *Outlaw Aesthetics: Arts and the Public Mind.* Bowling Green State University Popular Press.

1972   *Joining the Human Race: How to Teach the Humanities.* Everett/ Edwards, Deland.

Publications: Essays on Cultural and Historical Topics

1993   "Interpreting the Archaeology of American Culture: A Proposal for an ACA National Conference on Material Culture." *An American Culture Association "Dream Conference."* Ed. Fred E. H. Schroeder. 18-24.

1992   "Lifestyles: Interpreting Social History through Decorative Arts." *Proceedings* of the 1989 Conference of the Association for Living Historical Farms and Agricultural Museums. 63-69.

1991   "*Homo Sum: Humani Nihil a Me Alienum* Puto: Popular Material Culture and the Humanities." *Rejuvenating the Humanities.* Ed. Ray B. Browne and Marshall M. Fishwick. Bowling Green State University Popular Press. 35-47.

1990   "Landscapes of Fear in English Mysteries." *Clues, A Journal of Detection* 11.2 (Fall/Winter 1990): 65-84.

1989 "Extra-Academic Agents for Cultural Literacy in America." *Journal of American Culture* (Spring): 17-24.

1987 "Vernacular Front Yards as Landscapes of Meaning." *Proceedings of Meanings of the Garden Conference.* University of California, Davis.

1986 "More Small Things Forgotten in Domestic Electrical Plugs and Receptacles, 1881-1931." *Technology and Culture* 27.3 (July): 525-43.

1986 "Interpreting and Reinterpreting Associative Historic Sites and Artifacts." *Technical Report 6.* American Association for State and Local History, Nashville.

1985 "Local History and Newcomers." *History News* 40.7 (July): 18-21.

1985 "Schoolhouses." *Built in U.S.A. American Buildings from Airports to Zoos.* Preservation Press. 150-53.

1984 "SHH! Don't Touch! Thoughts on the Tabus of Cultural Institutions." *Taboos and Tabooism in Culture.* Ed. Ray B. Browne. Bowling Green State University Popular Press. 7-18

1983 "Food for Thought. A Dialogue about Museums." *Museum News* 61.4 (Apr.): 34-37.

1982 "Exploring the Fourth Dimension: Helping Newcomers Understand Community History" (with ten photographic illustrations by author). *Small Town* 12.5 (Mar., Apr.): 8-15.

1982 "*National Enquirer* Is National Fetish! The Untold Story." *Objects of Special Devotion, Fetishes, and Fetishism in Popular Culture.* Ed. Ray B. Browne. Bowling Green State University Popular Press. 168-81.

1981 "Schoolhouse Reading. What You Can Learn from Your Rural School." *History News* 36.4 (Apr.): 15-16.

1980 "Collecting and Using Popular Photographs." *Drexel Library Quarterly* 16.3 (July): 73-88.

1980 "Accountability: A Covenant with the People." *Midwest Museums Quarterly* 40.3/40.4 (Summer/Fall): 4-11.

1980 "Types of American Small Towns and How to Read Them." *Southern Quarterly* 19.1: 104-35.

1980 "Unsolved and Insoluble Problems of Popular Culture." *The Sphinx: A Magazine of Literature and Society* 111.3: 38-41.

1978 "Radio's Home Folks, Vic and Sade: A Study in Aural Artistry." *Journal of Popular Culture* 12.2 (Fall): 253-64.

1978 'The Little Red Schoolhouse." *Icons of America.* Ed. Ray B. Browne and Marshall M. Fishwick. Bowling Green State University Popular Press. 139-60.

1977 "Introduction: The Discovery of Popular Culture Before Printing." *In-Depth: Popular Culture Before Printing.* Ed. Fred Schroeder. *Journal of Popular Culture* 11.3 (Winter): 627-40.

1977 "Educational Legacy" Rural One-Room Schoolhouses." *Historic Preservation* 29.3 (July-Sept.): 4-9.

1976 "Feminine Hygiene, Fashion and the Emancipation of American Women." *American Studies* 17.2 (Fall): 101-10.

1976 *Designing Your Exhibits: Seven Ways to Look at an Artifact.* American Association for State and Local History, Technical Leaflet 91, *History News* 31.11 (Nov.).

1974 'The Development of the Super Ego on the American Frontier." *Soundings: An Interdisciplinary Journal* LVII.2 (Summer): 189-205.

1973 "Video Aesthetics and Serial Art." *Western Humanities Review* 27.4 (Autumn): 329-41.

1970 "Semi-Annual Installment on the American Dream: The Wish Book as Popular Icon." *Icons of Popular Culture.* Ed. Marshall M. Fishwick and Ray B. Browne. Bowling Green State University Popular Press. 73-86.

1969 "A Bellyful of Coffee: The Truckdrivin' Man as Folk Hero." *Journal of Popular Culture* 2 (Spring): 679-86.

1969 "And Now, a Word from the Silent Generation." *Western Humanities Review* 23 (Winter): 23-28.

1968 "The Plaine Plain Plane School of American Painting." *Dalhousie Review* 48 (Summer): 231-36.

1966 "Enter Ahab, The All: Theatrical Elements in Melville's Fiction." *Dalhousie Review* 46 (Summer): 223-32.

1965 "Andrew Wyeth and the Transcendental Tradition." *American Quarterly* 17 (Fall): 559-67.

1965 "Obscenity and Its Function in the Poetry of E. E. Cummings." *Sewanee Review* 7 (Summer): 469-78.

1964 "Horatio Alger, Jr.: America's First Literary Realist." *Western Humanities Review* 47 (Spring): 129-37.

Publications: Teaching Methods and Curricula

1991 "Globalizing the European Renaissance: Problems and Answers." *Humanities Education* 8.3 (Summer): 33-38.

1991 "Plain Talk about Institutional Survival." *Curricular Reform.* Ed. Mark Clark and Roger Johnson. Southern Humanities Press, 1991. 53-56.

1987 "Ten Humanities Views of Cities." *Humanities Education* 4.2 (Spring).

1985 "The House of Life: Planning a Classroom for Interdisciplinary Humanities." *Humanities Education* 11.3 (Sept.): 31-36.

1983 "Over 60 Inches and Under 30 Years: Finding and Serving New Audiences." *Roundtable Reports: The Journal of Museum Education* 8.3 (Spring): 3-6.

1982 (with James G. Boulger). "Advocating Small Town Practice in the Medical School Curriculum: A Model for Success." *Small Town* 12.6 (May-June): 15-19.

1981 "Trends for the Future in Humanities for the Gifted Student." *Roeper Review: A Journal for Gifted Education* 4.2 (Nov.): 12-15.

1979 (with Christene M. Levenduski). Humanities Education: 1979, The State of the Profession as Reflected in the Results of a Survey of Teacher Certification Policies in Fifty State Departments of Education." *Humanities Journal* 11.1 (Spring/Summer): 4-13.

1974 "Writing Themes about Popular Literature: Definitions, Classifications, and Applications." *Minnesota English Journal* 10.1 (Winter): 3-13.

1970 "The Use of Popular Arts in a Course in Popular Culture." *Popular Culture and Curricula.* Ed. Ray B. Browne and Ronald J. Ambrosetti. Bowling Green State University Popular Press. 47-58.

1968 "Where Angels Fear to Tread: Humanities Program in the Secondary Schools." *Minnesota English Journal* 4 (Apr.): 24-28.

1968 "How Not to Assign "What-Did-You-Do-Last-Summer"": A Cumulative Course in Writing Personal Narratives." *English Journal* 57 (Jan.): 79-84.

1966 "How to Teach a Research Theme in Four Not-So-Easy Lessons." *English Journal* 55 (Oct.): 898-902.

Emily Toth

Photo by Prather Warren

EMILY TOTH:
MS. MENTOR MEETS KATE CHOPIN

Susan Koppelman and Emily Toth

Emily Toth—biographer, novelist, and dispenser of advice to people whether they want it or not—has contributed humor and gossip and a strong feminist slant to popular culture studies. For twenty-five years, she has been a gadfly and a paper presenter at the American/Popular Culture Association meetings, while teaching successively at six different universities, publishing nine books, and making trouble for the sexist, the lazy, and the pretentious.

Unlike many academics, Emily Toth (rhymes with both) actually comes from working-class roots—although they were concealed by her upwardly mobile parents.

Dorothy Ginsberg, the daughter of Polish Jewish immigrants, and John Fitzgibbons, an Irish-born immigrant, had met at a "party for the Party" (the Communist Party) in New York City in the late 1930s. Dorothy, a committed member of the Young Communist League, loved to trek up to Harlem and dance at the Cotton Club. John found Party fund-raising parties to be good places to "meet girls," but he really preferred sentimental Irish songs to American pop. Dorothy was a high school dropout and a Depression-era baby who worried about money all her life; John was a high school graduate who claimed later that he was a graduate of Union College in Schenectady—and was never caught. "Feckless Irish," Dorothy used to say. (She was an expert at satirical and hilarious discussions of ethnic stereotypes.)

They were married in March of 1941, nine months before Pearl Harbor. But John, although he had become an American citizen, did not serve in World War II. He was deferred once for athlete's foot and later for being too old, when his daughter's birth was impending. (His deferment for athlete's foot made him a neighborhood hero and role model during the Vietnam era.)

Their daughter Emily Jane Fitzgibbons was born in New York City on March 17, 1944. Dorothy resisted pressure to name their child "Patricia," because of St. Patrick's Day, and opted instead to name the baby for Emily Jane Brontë, her favorite author.

With a secular Jewish mother and an ex-Catholic father, Emily grew up with no religion and an anthropological curiosity about organized religion and its believers. She did like to hear Old Testament stories, especially ones with sex and violence and peculiar popular customs, but she much preferred the MGM Hedy Lamarr Victor Mature version of "Samson and Delilah" to the one in the Bible.

Before she began kindergarten at age five, Emily had taught herself to read. With her best friend and neighbor, Frederica Liss, she delighted in making up stories. They were just learning to write down those stories when John Fitzgibbons was offered an excellent job in Cleveland, Ohio, in 1952. With many trepidations ("Do they have electricity out there?" friends asked, and "What about hostile Indians?"), Dorothy packed up the family to move to the Midwest.

At first they lived on the East Side, where Emily, a pupil in the gifted children's program, learned French and music and was encouraged to follow her intellectual curiosity: she did reports on pyramids, pepper, and much more. Her brother Dennis was born when Emily was eleven, and a year later, they all moved to Lakewood, the first suburb west of Cleveland.

There Emily came of age with a mother who felt totally alien. There were few Jews in Lakewood, and there was no one to chatter with in Dorothy's first language (Yiddish). Lakewood was a wholesome Midwestern environment that—for a New York Jew—seemed like something from another planet. Everyone was nice and well-mannered and earnest, and Dorothy's ironic sense of humor was often taken as nasty instead of sparklingly clever. The natives also had, in her eyes, strange food tastes: they preferred bland jello salads and macaroni and cheese and knew nothing about real food, such as pastrami, salami, and knishes.

Of course Emily was embarrassed by her mother (all teenaged girls are), and Dorothy was also an eccentric character with an enthusiastic interest in things wildly inappropriate for her own age. She loved to dance (jitterbug and swing); later, enthusiastically off-key, she sang along with Elvis and the Beatles on her car radio. (When, in the 1980s, she went with Emily to see Cheech and Chong's latest movie, she enjoyed being half a century older than anyone else in the theater when all the heads were humming and singing together: "Up in Smoke . . . Up in Smoke . . .")

As early as the 1950s, Emily's parents had allowed her to read anything she wanted, and she was twelve when *Peyton Place* was published. She had already tried, and failed, to read Alfred Kinsey's *Sexual Behavior in the Human Female* (too many Latin and Greek words). But *Peyton*

Place was not only accessible—it was also the first contemporary novel she'd ever read in which a girl grows up to be a writer.

Emily had known her vocation early: she wrote her first novel, a popular-style historical romance with lovers named Charles and Diana, when she was just nine. But Grace Metalious, in *Peyton Place,* not only created a portrait of the artist as a young woman (Allison McKenzie), but also introduced topics that were unknown to a girl growing up in Lakewood, Ohio in a close and loving family. Metalious covered rape and incest; wife beating; abortion; and a mysterious backyard sexual act in which a man's head disappeared between his very pregnant wife's legs, while several teens watched. (It was years before Emily learned what that act was called.)

Being a teenager in Lakewood, Ohio, in the 1950s meant being cleancut, wholesome, and (in retrospect) rather dull. But Emily Fitzgibbons livened up her early teen years by being a major fan of the Cleveland Indians. For several years she ran the Rocky Colavito Fan Club, honoring Cleveland's most beloved player, until he was traded to Detroit in 1959. After that, the Indians' baseball fortunes disintegrated for decades. As late as 1995, a sportswriter about the Indians' long-term malaise called it *The Curse of Rocky Colavito:* they were still paying.

Emily Fitzgibbons, meanwhile, was seizing opportunities to learn her craft as a writer and to observe teenaged culture. She was editor-in-chief of the Harding Junior High School newspaper, and feature editor of the Lakewood High *Times,* for which she wrote two columns of gossip and jokes: "M & Ms" and "Fitzbits." She was an honor roll student who did props and makeup for school drama productions, and envied the popular students who starred in the plays (but she got better grades). She was also a perpetual finalist in the Cleveland *Press* Spelling Contest and once won a trip to Greenfield Village, an old timey recreation of a rural village, with lots of tools: she thought it was very boring. When she won a prize for a Lakewood parody of the *Canterbury Tales,* she received a congratulatory fan letter from the coroner.

With her best friend Max (Madelon Van Deusen), Emily created satirical songs to make fun of the students in the most popular crowd: "There go the Senior Speakers—rah rah, corn on the cob" was one of their favorite ditties. Emily and Max collaborated on song books and lampoons, and have remained lifelong friends, despite their separation after graduation in 1961.

"You're going to an Eastern snob school," neighbors said when Emily was accepted at Swarthmore College; Max would go to populist Ohio University. At Swarthmore, Emily continued her practice of falling in with a nerd crowd, and was dimly aware of class differences. She knew *La Bohéme,* for instance, because her father loved it, but the rest of classical music, like most of elite culture, was unknown territory. Among wealthy students who had grown up with Bach, Beethoven, and Brahms, she was a secretly defiant lover of Elvis, the Ronettes, and Connie Francis at her most soulful. (In high school, with her steady beau, Francis's "Lipstick on Your Collar" had been Their Song.)

At Swarthmore, Emily did get involved in activism, in civil rights protests on the Eastern Shore of Maryland. Once, after a harrowing day in which the black and white groups were thrown out of bowling alleys and movie theaters and shot at, they all got together for a dance and Emily learned to do the "Funky Chicken."

At Swarthmore, she was not yet involved in feminism. It was too early.

She majored in English, but her great love was Classics: not for the philology, but for the gossip. She would hunker down in the library stacks and read obsessively about the gods and goddesses and their schemes and peccadilloes—and how mortals were forever getting sucked into them. When she found an error in a book by an Oxford don, C. M. Bowra, she wrote him a mildly chiding letter—to which he responded with a vituperative fulmination. Emily's Classics professor was delighted, even awestruck that she'd heard from the Great Man. From that point, she decided that fulminating academics were good; that it was great fun to correct people; and that she needed a vocation that combined writing, reading, fulminating, and permission not to care about fashion.

She would have to be a professor.

She was, of course, torn between being an individual and being a typical woman: it was important to her to have a boyfriend, and she always had one. But when her college boyfriend, John Morrel, admitted that he didn't think any woman with children should have a career, that was the beginning of the end of that relationship. (Emily's desire to "have it all" was an unusual thing to express in the mid-1960s—but she had seen her mother's frustration).

Like so many women of her transitional generation, though, she could not commit herself fully to a Ph.D. After her 1965 graduation from Swarthmore, and advised by her professors to seek a Master of Arts in Teaching instead ("so you'll have something to fall back on"), she went to the M.A.T. Program at Johns Hopkins University. For the first time she was not living at home, or in a dorm: she shared an apartment with three other young women. They learned to cook, worked on relationships, raised a cat named Pooh, and embarked on careers: with her M.A.T., Emily taught English in Baltimore junior highs for three semesters, and hated every minute.

In July 1967, Emily married a Johns Hopkins chemistry graduate student named Bruce Toth. Also originally a New Yorker, Bruce had grown up in Portland, Oregon, had working-class parents, loved to cook, and was a great audience for others' witty sallies. He was also very tolerant: he liked both the Beatles and the Rolling Stones (most people felt they had to choose).

Their honeymoon, a month-long cross-country trek in a tiny Triumph TR-4, wound up in San Francisco for the "Summer of Love," a funny but awful time in which youngsters dressed in extravagantly colorful clothes, sang about peace and love, and scrounged drugs and food so they wouldn't die in the streets. The young Toths noted the contrast between appearance and reality and scurried back to graduate school— or he did.

Emily Toth began teaching at Morgan State College (now University) in Baltimore, a historically black school which was the only one that would hire a young woman. (Others said—sometimes overtly—that they'd rather have a man.) But the times were a-changin'. Morgan students were rebelling against bourgeois regimentation. They were growing Afros, and supporting Black Power; Emily was learning about black popular culture and a whole new world she'd known nothing about. She began to read African American literature (which had never been mentioned in any of her college literature classes), and she was enthralled.

Gradually she started seeing parallels between the position of women and the position of black people: limited, stereotyped, oppressed —yet expected to be lively, entertaining, and grateful. She brooded.

Meanwhile, teaching undergraduates the same things, over and over, began to pall. Itching for new challenges, Emily began taking night courses in the Master of Liberal Arts Program at Johns Hopkins. One professor, Elias Rivers, evidently saw himself as something of a talent scout, and suggested she apply to the new Comparative Literature Program and become a Ph.D. student. She did, but the program collapsed when its major professor, Paul de Man, decamped for a better offer at Yale. That allowed Emily Toth to seize the moment and devise her own program, through the Johns Hopkins Humanities Center.

She was the first out-front feminist graduate student at Hopkins, and it was tough. She was kicked out of Chaucer class for arguing with the professor about women; she was kicked out of a European literature class for declining to be the professor's "mistress." But the Humanities Center had as its major professor Dr. Richard Macksey, who was that rare academic genuinely interested in everything and welcoming to all. Thanks to Dr. Macksey's mentoring, Emily Toth minored in film, and was one of the first scholars to study Women in Film.

Still, graduate school was only a small part of her life: she was engaged in making a feminist revolution. At an anti-Vietnam War rally in 1969, she learned about a new women's group, Baltimore Women's Liberation, which eventually sponsored a journal, a book store, a free clinic, a day care center, and consciousness-raising groups in which women shared experiences and discovered that they were not alone. Their families were not the only ones with terrible secrets; they all had bittersweet mother-daughter conflicts in a culture in which women had been taught to hate each other. Everyone's husband needed to be pushed to do his share of housework and child care, and there were also many husbands who wanted to "smash monogamy"—i.e., commit adultery and call it a supremely political act. Their wives had doubts.

Her C-R group helped Emily to re-interpret the books she was reading in school: she saw how traditional ideas of romance could deflect women from independence and a professioanl life. When she gave speeches for schools and community groups for Baltimore Women's Liberation, she gained experience with hecklers (and that helped later with teaching). Meanwhile, many marriages floundered when the wives became intensely involved in C-R groups, questioning both the institution of marriage and their husbands' places in their lives. Emily and Bruce Toth's marriage was one of the few to survive the Baltimore C-R groups. They also decided they did not want children.

Years later Emily Toth learned that her C-R group had been infiltrated by a FBI spy, who reported back to headquarters that Baltimore Women's Liberation was a group of white middle class whiners who wanted their husbands to behave better. The infiltrator concluded that they presented no danger to anyone.

Through the women's movement, many women who had always wanted to write began to write seriously and provocatively—about women. Mary Jane Lupton, Emily Toth's Morgan State colleague and C-R companion, came up one day with a grand and unique book idea: a cultural history of menstruation. When she invited Janice Delaney, a graduate school friend, and Emily Toth to join her, a historic partnership was forged. They drew up an outline, got a New York literary agent, and assigned themselves the drafting of different chapters. Then they met once a month, in Janice's red room, to share drafts.

They knew about favorable environmental influence.

By the fall of 1972, Emily was reading the few dusty tomes she could find about menstruation and had just finished her Ph.D. exams, when she had a fateful encounter at the Midwest Modern Language Association meeting in St. Louis. First she met John Cornillon, promoting his wife's new book, and then she met Susan Koppelman (then

Cornillon), editor/compiler of *Images of Women in Fiction: Feminist Perspectives. Images,* the first book of feminist literary criticism, would transform the way women's literature was regarded, while the meeting with Susan Koppelman would begin a lifelong friendship characterized by gossip, humor, snideness, grandiosity, love of food, and cherishing of popular culture, including its most tacky and kitschy forms.

That spring, Emily Toth attended her first national Popular Culture Association meeting. PCA provided free housing for graduate students but when she arrived late, she found herself climbing into bed next to a sleeping woman she'd never met (who turned out, the next morning, to be a minister-in-training). They never saw each other again, but it was a fine introduction to the oddnesses of the growing field of Popular Culture, just recently created by Ray and Pat Browne and their colleagues.

Popular culture was, of course, too unconventional for a dissertation topic: even Kate Chopin, then unknown, was considered an unusual choice at staid Johns Hopkins. But Lawrence Holland, known as the kind member of the English Department, agreed to direct Emily Toth's dissertation on "'That Outward Existence Which Conforms': Kate Chopin and Literary Convention." Thanks, perhaps, to wide interest in *The Curse,* she had half a dozen interviews at the Modern Language Association convention, and was the first in her class to be offered a job: a non-tenure-track instructorship at the University of New Orleans.

It proved to be her only offer. Bruce, meanwhile, was teaching at a private school in Baltimore, and had essentially given up on his Ph. D. They decided to put her career first, knowing that Bruce would always get hired, because people couldn't stand to see a man without a job. (They were right.)

And so, in the summer of 1974, the intrepid Toths moved to New Orleans, where they rented an apartment along the Mardi Gras parade route. Emily finished typing her dissertation on her Hermes manual typewriter, in those pre-computer days, between parades in Mardi Gras 1975. Bruce taught at a small, eccentric private school which soon folded, while Emily was teaching massive, endless sections of freshman composition. But they fell in love with Louisiana culture and New Orleans food, and found themselves continually coming back over the next thirteen years. Meanwhile, Emily's first national publication, in the *Johns Hopkins Magazine,* was prophetic: called "The Job Market, MLA Style," it was a whimpering, black humorish piece about the oversupply of Ph.D.s. (Though she received tear-stained letters from unemployed Ph.D.s around the country, everyone was assuming that the job slump would be temporary.)

On the second try, her MLA interviews produced a tenure-track job, at the University of North Dakota, where the Toths moved in 1975. Bruce worked at the Human Nutrition Laboratory; Emily created the first courses in women and popular culture, including "Women and Film," "Women's Humor," "Mothers and Daughters," and "Love Stories." She had never been so free to teach what she chose, but Grand Forks seemed to be the coldest place on earth. The students, too, were quiet and austere. The garrulous Toths, who were short and dark and gestured a lot, were curiosities among the tall, blond, silent descendants of Vikings.

Yet when Emily Toth's first book appeared, all of Grand Forks seemed to celebrate what was truly an odd tome: *The Curse: A Cultural History of Menstruation,* written with Janice Delaney and Mary Jane Lupton. It was not at all a medical book, and it had chapters on such topics as menstruation in literature, psychology, anthropology, slang ("The Monthly Euphemism") and jokes ("Red Humor"). There were chapters, which Emily drafted, on the menstrual products industry ("From Rags to Riches") and famous menstruators in history ("The Menstrual Hall of Fame"). It was the first book ever to study menstruation in American popular culture, and it is still the only humorous one. (The public library in Waco, Texas, returned it to the publisher as "unsuitable," but it was published in translation in Germany, Holland, Denmark, and Japan.)

The Curse led to Emily's appearing on radio and TV shows, including several in St. Louis—which meant visits with her friend Susan Koppelman. The two quickly encouraged each other's research and questioning, especially in popular culture. They egged each other to create new knowledge, which included names for repulsive phenomena, such as "epistemological solipsism" ("If I don't know it, it doesn't exist"). Faced with the menace of creeping jargon, the discourse of high theory which was then beginning to invade literary studies, Koppelman and Toth decided on the criteria for any piece of interesting writing: gossip, humor, and new information. They knew their research and writing would change the world for women.

For the Toths, living in North Dakota proved too hard and cold, and Emily started job hunting again—this time, getting a tenure-track assistant professorship at Penn State. She was hired in the English Department in 1977, and tenured there in 1981; Bruce was, variously, an instructor in science for non-majors (a kind of "Biology for Poets"), or a research associate in biochemistry.

Penn State, in semi-rural State College, Pennsylvania, was very removed from the energy and popular culture of American cities. While urban areas were becoming more multicultural, Centre County, Pennsylvania, was overwhelmingly white, and three-quarters of the people in State College were between the ages of 18-22. It was an excellent place to raise children, everyone said. But to the Toths, who never intended to have children, it was a tedious town for grownups. There was no indigenous culture; the only community culture centered around sports; and the local restaurants and movies were all geared for teenagers.

As a result, faculty turned in on—and against—each other. Departments were famous for long-term ostracisms and feuds; photocopying machines broke down under the volume of outraged memoes; and there was an inbred savagery in some departments, notably English, that Emily Toth had never seen before. It was partly sexism, but mostly what she would call, years later, an endless posturing and contest over "Whose Is Bigger?"

The Curse had made her department head blush, but everyone was pleased with her second book, *A Kate Chopin Miscellany*. It was a collection of Chopin's unpublished writings, which Toth had edited long-distance with Per Seyersted, Chopin's discoverer, who lived in Norway. Chopin was not yet canonical, but at least she was "literature."

But then, just before tenure, Toth won a grant and a book contract to write *Inside Peyton Place: The Life of Grace Metalious,* for the twenty-fifth anniversary (1981) of the famous novel. She had gotten the idea on the day Elvis Presley died, and the book was to explore the roles of women in the 1950s—and especially how Grace Metalious, a feminist before her time, found little support for her unconventionality and drank herself to death before she was forty.

To some of Toth's powerful English Department colleagues, a book on the author of *Peyton Place* was "trash." They said so, and her tenure vote split evenly, half voting Yes, half voting No. Her chair voted yes, though, and so did college and university committees, and she did receive tenure—but was not promoted from assistant to associate professor for another two years. She had been in the department for ten years before she was assigned a graduate course to teach.

But being an outsider in the English Department had its advantages, for she could be loaned out to teach popular culture courses in American Studies and Journalism (the 1960s; cultural aspects of mass media; women and minorities in mass media). Isolation also meant more time, for one who wanted to write. Intrigued by the new historical romances of Kathleen Woodiwiss, Emily Toth set out—for the first time in thirty years—to write one herself. Her agent sold it as a Civil-War era combination of *The Group* and *The Awakening:* five young women coming of age in New Orleans, with romance and adventure, independence and passion. When *Daughters of New Orleans* came out in 1983, with a racy cover, and when it received a "Best Feminist Historical Novel" citation from *Romantic Times,* Emily Toth's designation as a creator of "trash" was secure for life.

She edited one collection of essays, *Regionalism and the Female Imagination,* and kept up a lively correspondence with Susan Koppelman and other "conference cronies": kindred spirits she met at academic meetings, especially in women's caucuses. Partly because she could stay with Koppelman in St. Louis (Kate Chopin's home for most of her life), Toth got two contracts to write Kate Chopin books—one a biography, and one an enlarged collection of Chopin's papers, diaries, and letters. On sabbatical in 1984, Toth also spent several weeks in Louisiana doing research, and fell in love, again, with the food and the unique Cajun-Creole culture.

She also continued to give papers every year at Popular/American Culture Association meetings. She wrote about women's humor and (with Susan Koppelman) devised new rules for it; she explained romances to the hardhearted multitudes; she gave advice about academic politics; and she dug up gossip about American writers, including contradictory eyewitness reports about F. Scott Fitzgerald's penis.

Emily Toth was also recognized—and put to work—in the Popular/American Culture Associations. From 1975-1977 she was an Area Chair, and was a PCA Vice President from 1976-1978 and a Council Member at Large, 1980-1982. In 1981 she was the first, and founding, President of the Women's Caucus for Popular Culture, which is now best known for the four annual awards (the only ones) honoring the best feminist studies of popular culture: the Emily Toth Award, for the best single-author book-length study; the Susan Koppelman Award, for the best anthology, multi-authored or edited book; the Jane Bakerman Award, for the best published article; and the Kathleen Gregory Klein Award, for the best unpublished article.

Although they sometimes clashed over women's issues, Ray Browne was often encouraging when Emily Toth would complain about her hidebound colleagues, whose disdain for women's studies and popular culture left her unrecognized and unrewarded. "Most academics are frauds," he would say, and Toth grew to agree with him.

With five books in print and two more under contract, she went on the job market again—and found the perfect match.

Louisiana State University's English Department was seeking a senior scholar in Women's Studies, and it was an up-and-coming department encouraging innovative writing and research. There were three times as many women professors as in Penn State's department, and they were delighted that Emily Toth was a novelist and a Chopin biographer.

The Toths moved to Baton Rouge in the summer of 1988, and did not look back. Emily became a full professor, at last; Bruce was a research associate in Biochemistry, and later in the Veterinary School. They celebrated their return by attending a small-town crab festival in Henderson, Louisiana—where a foreign film crew, seeing them waxing ecstatic over the food, photographed them as "exemplary Cajuns."

The Toths' triumphal return coincided, however, with the decline of Emily's parents. Her mother, a smoker most of her life, went through a decade of health crises until her death from emphysema in 1990. Her father suffered from Alzheimer's disease and lived in a nursing house for seven years before his death in 1995. And so, while Emily kept watch long-distance on her parents, *Kate Chopin: A Life of the Author of "The Awakening"* took five years longer than expected to write. Her mother did get to see the dedication and acknowledgment to her, but died the day the book was printed.

Kate Chopin was reviewed in most major newspapers in the United States and in England. Women reviewers recognized the underlying questions asked, about love and loneliness, about whether a mother-woman should choose a man or choose herself: they recognized that Emily Toth was creating a new kind of narrative. Male reviewers, however, were preoccupied with whether hers was the "definitive" biography, and questioned whether "gossip" (oral history gathered from descendants of those who knew Kate Chopin) could be considered a valid source of information about women's lives.

Kate Chopin did receive a Certificate of Commendation from the American Association for State and Local History, was chosen for taping by American Printing for the Blind, and was designated as a "New & Noteworthy Paperback" in the *New York Times Book Review* (November 7, 1993: 32).

A year later, Emily Toth published an edition of Kate Chopin's last story collection, *A Vocation and a Voice*. By then two cats, Beauregard and Bunkie, had joined the Toth household, and they watched while Emily tried to come up with a new book idea.

She rejoined the Romance Writers of America, and wrote a mystery/romance about Carville, the leprosy settlement in south Louisiana. Her agent shopped it around, but publishers all said no ("No romances for people with scales," they reportedly said). She wrote another New Orleans historical novel, about the 1890s lottery, which was also rejected—whereupon her agent dropped her.

Emily worked intermittently on her edition of Kate Chopin's private papers, which had been under contract with Indiana University Press since 1987. She finally finished it ten years later. Meanwhile, *The Curse* had come out in a second edition in 1988; audiences all over Louisiana were always eager to hear Emily speak about Kate Chopin; and filmmakers suddenly became interested in Grace Metalious and the 1950s. In 1997 Emily Toth appeared on camera in a History Channel documentary, *David Halberstam's "The Fifties,"* talking about *Peyton Place* and its author. That year she also sold the film option for her biography to Jigsaw Productions, Inc.

She felt she was recycling herself, while still grieving and refocussing, as one does in middle age. Her friend Susan Koppelman, who managed to publish books despite her own disabilities and intense involvement in taking care of sick relatives, was a consolation and inspiration.

For awhile, academic politics were a distraction: Toth served on the LSU Faculty Senate Grievance Committee for six years, the last one as chair. It was a time-consuming, mostly frustrating job in which procedures usually won out over justice or fairness. She tried, usually unsuccessfully, to mentor women newer to academia—but when she found them, it was often too late.

She brooded, and in 1992 began to write an advice column for academic women in *Concerns,* the journal of the Women's Caucus for the Modern Languages. Written in Question and Answer form, it featured "Ms. Mentor"'s answers, in a Miss Manners-ish voice, to questions about what an academic women should know: what to wear, what really goes on in hiring and tenuring, why lunch is important, when to gossip and when to snicker and when to sue.

Toth kept writing reviews for the *Women's Review of Books,* the *Baton Rouge Advocate,* and other newspapers and journals. She studied popular women novelists, especially Sandra Brown and Danielle Steel, and recognized that they were inimitable. Then she reviewed very favorably a University of Pennsylvania Press book by romance writers, called *Dangerous Men and Adventurous Women,* and met the Press's editor, Patricia Reynolds Smith, at the Romance Writers of America national conference in New York City in 1994.

Knowing that authors should always "Write about what you know," Toth and Smith came up with a book deal: *Ms. Mentor's Impeccable Advice for Women in Academia.*

Ms. Mentor's book, published in 1997 with a cover drawing by Nicole Hollander, would be designated for women professors, graduate students, recovering academics and people who love them. Ms. Mentor, said the cover, is "a brilliant and crotchety intellectual who never leaves her ivory tower" and "knows everything about women in academia."

In warm, irreverent, gossipy, blunt prose, sometimes indebted to Beavis and Butt-head as well as to Miss Manners, Ms. Mentor traipses through the stages of an academic career, from "Graduate School: the Rite of Passage," through the job hunt, the conference scene, "Slouching Toward Tenure," and finally "Emerita: the Golden Years." Ms. Mentor explains savage memoes, the sexist stutter step, E.A.T. (the Early Administration Trap), and (most famously) "peacocking"—the practice, by many male academics, of showing off their own knowledge during the question period after another speaker's presentation. Ms. Mentor noted this as an indirect form of display ("I Have a Penis!") and suggested that women carry, and wave, peacock feathers at such moments.

Readers recognized and welcomed Ms. Mentor's grandiosity: Martha Baker, reviewer for the *St. Louis Post-Dispatch,* hailed her point of view as "third person haughty." Susan Koppelman, meanwhile, recognized Ms. Mentor's manner as very similar to the ways she and Emily Toth had spoken with each other for years: leaving answering machine messages starting, "O Great One"; making lists of their own perfections and unique talents; and calling each other Empress. Ms. Mentor represented the culmination of their greatness.

Since the book encouraged them to send flattering messages and queries, readers raced (via e-mail) to assure Ms. Mentor of their adoration. The retired President of Penn State especially liked Ms. Mentor's warning faculty women to "Never diddle a dean." Other correspondents praised her humor and wisdom, and often asked advice themselves, in the formula she suggested: "I have this friend who has this problem . . ."

Emily Toth, via Ms. Mentor, had created a new character, the tart-tongued Miss Manners of academia. In December, 1997, a *Vogue* article by Elaine Showalter portrayed Ms. Mentor as an academic fashion maven who insisted on "frumpy." For the first and only time in her life, Emily Toth was asked for advice and sound bites about fashion.

Although she is collecting material for a sequel, *Ms. Mentor Bites Back,* Emily Toth's next book will be the long-awaited edition of Kate Chopin's diaries and letters, followed by a short biography-celebration of Chopin for the centennial of *The Awakening* (1999). She has been invited to write an advice column for the *Chronicle of Higher Education.*

As a pioneer in popular culture, Emily Toth has moved from menstruation to mentoring. She convenes meetings of the Women's Studies Consortium of Louisiana (which has no formal structure, meaning that she is Empress-for-Life); she creates circles of LSU women faculty to discuss authority, time management, and other problems; and she nudges women in her region, the South Central, to write and publish more. She escorts patients at her local abortion clinic; writes pointed letters to the newspaper in favor of battered women's rights; and is a secret eater/spy for a local restaurant critic.

Like most middle-aged women who've been lifelong feminists, Emily Toth plans to grow old loudly, and disgracefully.

Books by Emily Toth

The Curse: A Cultural History of Menstruation (expanded, updated edition). With Janice Delaney and Mary Jane Lupton. University of Illinois Press, 1988. Original edition: New York: Dutton, 1976; New American Library paperback, 1977. Translations: Rhodos (Denmark), 1976; Courage Verlag (Germany), 1979; Kodansha (Japan), 1976; Kooyker Wetenschappelijke Uitgeverij (The Netherlands), 1979.

Daughters of New Orleans (historical novel). New York: Bantam, 1983.

Inside Peyton Place: The Life of Grace Metalious (biography). New York: Doubleday, 1981.

Kate Chopin (biography). New York: Morrow, 1990; London: Random Century, 1991. University of Texas Press, 1993.

A Kate Chopin Miscellany (letters, diaries, essays). Associate editor, with Per Seyersted. Natchitoches, LA: Northwestern State University Press, and Oslo, Norway: Universitetsforlaget, 1979.

Kate Chopin's Private Papers. With Per Seyersted and Cheyenne Bonnell. Indiana University Press, 1998.

Ms. Mentor's Impeccable Advice for Women in Academia. University of Pennsylvania Press, 1997.

Regionalism and the Female Imagination (edited essays). New York: Human Sciences Press, 1985.

A Vocation and a Voice (Kate Chopin's last story collection). New York: Penguin Classics, 1991.

Forthcoming

Kate Chopin's Centennial Story (tentative title). University Press of Mississippi, 1999.

Daniel Walden

DANIEL WALDEN:
A PIONEER IN THE STUDY
OF AMERICAN URBAN AND ETHNIC CULTURE

Robert C. Doyle

When we enter the world of Popular and American Culture Studies, we learn from the outset that Ray Browne, John Cawelti, Russell B. Nye, Peter C. Rollins, and Daniel Walden were some of the people who blazed the tough professional trails by themselves, opened academic doors for others, and developed pathways for intellectual pursuits in an academic otherworld left unplowed to them by their predecessors. Where once disdain amplified an abundance of false myths about the culture of everyday life, and academic snobbery often had the upper hand at distinguished American universities, these unsettled men refused to be held back, sought out others with interdisciplinary philosophies, and took action. Each scholar knew that the essence of the profession is curiosity: Ray Browne led the way into detective fiction; John Cawelti took us all beyond Henry Nash Smith into the dazzling romantic world of the Western; Russell B. Nye took us into entertainment culture; Peter C. Rollins demythologized American popular film, and Dan Walden introduced Urban and Ethnic Studies into the fold. Ray Browne founded the Popular Culture Association with the idea of establishing an open scholarly forum; the others joined and stayed with him; and together they have produced mounds of work that set the standard for critical inquiry into the complex world of American popular culture.

This essay focuses on Daniel Walden, the scholar, the man, and the friend he has been to so many people with seminal ideas about the American experience.[1] When students in the Mid-Atlantic American Culture/Popular Culture Association compete for the Daniel Walden essay prize each year, knowingly or unknowingly, they enter a world in perpetual motion that started in the Jewish neighborhoods in Northeast Philadelphia in the 1920s and has extended to the stately Allegheny mountains in central Pennsylvania by the end of the century.

An old wise proverb says that beauty is neither in the coming nor the going but in the pathways. Dan Walden's pathways, like the man, have been diverse. Northeast Philadelphia was an exciting place to grow up Jewish. Life was hustle-bustle all the time. Individuals were always in a hurry. Yiddish was spoken by many people as a kind of *lingua franca* that linked old and new immigrants who may have spoken Russian, Polish, Hungarian, or German at home, and their synagogues served as cultural as well as religious centers for members and guests. Distinguished cantors sang their services with trained voices as clear as the bells in stately European cathedrals. People were far from wealthy and hard work dominated the time of nearly everyone in the neighborhood. Leisure, as one thinks of it today, was unknown, but somehow there was always school. On the way to school, young students discussed the Bible and political responsibilities; at weddings, there were much merriment and good-natured mischief, music and dance, and always arguments about life in the neighborhood. The affairs of everyday life bred a distinct cultural identity into each participant; from identity came association and pride, tempered by curiosity, thought, and literature. A combination of all these intangibles yielded a kind of intellectual whirling dervishness, from which one learned the meaning of commitment.

Being Jewish in Daniel Walden's mind, as a boy in Philadelphia, as an American soldier in World War II, an entertainer in New York and Europe, and finally as a scholar and teacher, became the subject in his 1974 book of the same title: "The experience of being Jewish," he wrote, "of living the warmness of community, of being a part of an organic, progressive community that has existed proudly and contributed mightily for thousands of years—this might be enough."[2] To be Jewish in one's soul, one had to grow up Jewish; this article is about understanding the nature of this unique and loving human commitment.

From 1936 to 1940, a young man named Daniel Weinroth attended Northeast (Philadelphia) High School, but the world was heating up. Beginning in 1933, Jews became easy targets of unparalleled oppression by Nazis and Fascists throughout Europe. In 1936, European Jews were forced to wear yellow Stars of David for easy identification in town ghettos, and in 1939, the oppression devolved into life without hope crowded in massive concentration camps. Hitler started his war in 1939 and spread the camp system east and west, wherever the army marched and wherever the rails led his dreaded SS. Like others in his generation, Dan knew that war was close.

In 1942, Dan Weinroth stood alongside millions of other American men; he was a soldier in the American army, not a "Doughboy" of a past generation going "over there" to make life better for the folks "over here," but a simple soldier inducted into the largest army ever amassed by the United States government. He knew why it was important to be there. By 1943, Jews began to die *en masse* in a genocide no one could ever imagine. Large armies require their soldiers to perform all sorts of duties. Some are imminently dangerous; others are not. Soldiers have few choices about the danger of their respective duties. Six days after D-Day in June 1944, he arrived in France, and for the next year, his unit fixed radar and communications equipment. By May 1945, when the murder ended in Europe, at least six million Jews had died alongside a total of eleven million innocents in "Operation Heydrich," the Nazi death camp system. After twenty months in the combat zone, Dan came home on a crowded troop ship, and like so many combat veterans before and after him, he was determined to begin a new life. He turned his genial efforts toward two seemingly unconnected visions: entertainment and education.

For a few million people, 1946 was a good year. Peace was at hand, and the World War II soldiers and their wives created the Baby Boom. Sergeant Weinroth joined other soldiers who turned themselves into a demobilized army of ambitious civilians, collected his G.I. Bill, and began school in New York, the "Big Apple," the place where world-class stars created world-class entertainment. He took courses in theater and voice, and a year later began performing summer stock in New Hampshire at the phenomenal rate of a play a week. There is an adage in entertainment that one makes one's own breaks. A little luck comes in handy from time to time though, and when the former Sergeant Daniel Weinroth, U.S. Army, become "Danny" Walden, singer and actor in New York, he found work. The year 1949 landed him in the chorus of *Annie Get Your Gun* with Mary Martin; a year later he played twenty-eight shows a week at the famous Roxy Theater with stars like Danny Kaye and Cab Calloway. A promising entertainment career was underway.

New York treated him well, but like so many professional entertainers in the past, he knew that one earned the real spurs on the road. It was in the middle of the Cold War; the agents of McCarthyism were seriously harassing entertainers for their politics, and "Danny" Walden began thinking about Paris. Every entertainer eyes someone in the business who just takes one's breath away, someone whose personality, as it were, explodes on stage. For "Danny" Walden, that someone was the French singer Edith Piaf. When he worked with her at the Versailles Club in the Upper East Side, he knew why folks called her the "Little Sparrow." She was pure magic on stage. In the meantime, more work came his way. The seasons of 1951 and 1952 soared and found him working as Cecco in *Peter Pan* with Jean Arthur and Boris Karloff, then it was off to the New York City Opera Company, membership in Actors' Equity, and the American Guild of Musical Artists. In 1954, Dan Walden was anything but jobless, and he still thought about Paris.

A major break came in 1955 when he was booked in *Le Boef Sur Le Toit* in Paris, an underground club, what the French call a "cave," situated on the Left Bank of the Seine River. Dan sang with a French band, and the audience wanted to hear a mix of American standards and French favorites. Back home in New York, he played the Sawdust Club with Teresa Brewer, one of the hottest singers in show business at the time. His show-business career had reached a major level, and there was no doubt of his talent. His ability to seize and develop opportunities showed others in the industry that "Danny" Walden was a strong up-and-coming talent, but something had happened in Paris that caused Dan Walden to take stock of who he was, where he was in his life, and where he was going. It was time for a change—there was something else out there for him—and "Danny" Walden, still unsure of the exact pathway, had to find it. Essentially and most importantly, "Danny" had to become Daniel again somehow.

City College of New York (CCNY) possessed an irresistible magnetism. University life and course work began to take primacy over the long and tiring nights' work singing in night clubs. In short order, Dan began to seek out social work off stage that in his mind provided more human service during the day than pleasing faceless club audiences on stage after the sun was nowhere to be seen. After he finally got a full-time job as a case work assistant for the Traveler's Aid Society and then at an information booth at Times Square, the transition became firm and a new commitment evolved into a life's work. In 1957, Dan Walden married Beatrice Schulman, and the Waldens began their new life together in New York. Marriage and social service, as valuable as they were, created only two components of this new life; its third part fit hand-in-glove with the exciting world of academics under the direction of his undergraduate mentors Professors Hans Kohn and Dean James Peace.

Dan Walden's intellectual achievements at CCNY, known affectionately as the "proletarian Harvard" among New York's working-class student body at the time, began in 1959 with his bachelor's degree and continued to graduate studies and a master's degree at Columbia University in 1961. It was during his senior year at CCNY and the first stage of his postgraduate studies, from 1959 to 1961, when Dan Walden's life as a scholar really began, and where his ideas about urban culture, ethnic and Jewish studies took shape. If one reflects on the period, better, if one lived it, the memories of new frontiers, service, youth, and renewed hope—the Kennedy myth in short—hung high in the popular gallery of ideas. At Columbia University, where prestigious scholarship and extensive publishing were in high demand, the Kennedy myth did not go unnoticed. Columbia was an idea factory, and luminaries like Richard Hofstader (his M.A. advisor) were writing major works that would be studied for the next several decades. Who had time for a thoroughly non-traditional, ex-G.I. graduate student from CCNY who could sing? Professor Hans Kohn did.

Even for 1958-1961, Hans Kohn was an unusual person with an unusual history, and perhaps, at his age slightly out of kilter at fast-paced City College of New York. Like Walden, Kohn was also a veteran of wartime service, but he served in a different war, in a different uniform, and, from an American perspective, on the other side. During World War I, Kohn was drafted into the Kaiser's Army and found himself fighting Russians. Taken prisoner on the eastern front, much of his war was fought quietly behind barbed wire until the Russo-German Armistice of 1917. After his war, Kohn went home and discovered that rebuilding one's life after a great deal of suffering and loss was nearly impossible. Extreme nationalism took root in postwar Germany and generated a new form of the political right; radical socialism did much the same on the German left. Both were anti-semitic at the core, and Germany, as well as much of Europe in the 1920s, began its down-slide into the abyss of intellectual, cultural, institutional, and political chaos. For Jews like Kohn, European National Socialism became the ultimate oppressor. For Germany, Nazi lies took hold of the land of Goethe and Schiller in a death grip so strong that it destroyed a nation. For the war veteran and intellectual historian Hans Kohn, it was time to leave.

Of all the professors at CCNY at the time, Kohn was the first important influence on Dan Walden's academic future. From Kohn, Walden learned to identify, fear, and oppose irrational nationalism. Simultaneously, Walden became an interdisciplinarian when he synthesized a profound interest in the African-American experience with his thinking about European Intellectual History and the fundamental conflict between nationalism and internationalism. More importantly, he learned firsthand to appreciate the values of good teaching and solid scholarship. Under Joseph Borome's tutelage, he published his first scholarly article, "The Contemporary Opposition to the Political and Educational Ideas of Booker T. Washington," in the *Journal of Negro History* in 1960, in which he set the tone for much of what would come later. He wrote with more than a little foresight. "[T]he sad fact remains that even today [1959] this nation has not achieved the self-evident truths of liberty and equality for all its citizens . . . though the direction is undeniably positive."[3] Later in their careers, Professors Kohn and Walden amplified this theme when they joined forces to publish *Readings in American Nationalism,* an anthology of readings designed for students in the Vietnam era to consider positive and negative political power in terms of the inputs and outcomes of American nationalism from colonial times to the 1960s. They remind their readers that, "We in America need watching and self-control even more than our adversaries, if only because we have greater capabilities."[4]

By 1961, after writing his thesis, "Anti-Intellectualism in the Period of Jacksonian Democracy," and with a master's degree in hand, it was time for another change. There were other interests to pursue and more essential skills yet to be developed. Professor Kohn urged Walden to continue his studies, not in American Social and Intellectual History at traditional Columbia, but in the social interpretation of American culture with Professor Henry Bamford Parkes in the American Civilization Doctoral Program at New York University.

Parkes saw that Dan Walden had talent, curiosity, and a sincere desire to be a substantive part of the academic community. After Walden completed his doctoral apprenticeship, Parkes directed his doctoral student toward the writings of W. J. Ghent, the populist and intellectual socialist writer who published *Our Benevolent Feudalism* in 1900 and continued his work through the 1920s. What Ghent had done was worthy of study. As a populist, Ghent feared governmental power and influence that spiraled from a center, especially when it dominated the lives of common people. In other words, Walden finally made the leap that for him made a difference. Under Professor Henry Bamford Parkes, Dan Walden made his entry into the social interpretation of American culture. In 1963, the year that ended the Kennedy myth, Michigan State University hired him in its Department of American Thought and Language, and a year later, after writing his dissertation "W. J. Ghent: Populist Socialist Writer, 1870s–1920s," New York University's Graduate School conferred its doctorate on him.

Michigan State was only the beginning. In 1966, the Waldens began a life-long association with Penn State, when Professor Walden received an appointment in the English and American Studies Program at the Capitol Campus in Middletown, Pennsylvania. It was a year of political upheaval in American society: the Vietnam War was heating up, and thousands of American soldiers were fighting the Vietcong and the North Vietnamese Army in a place by and large unknown to the general public. At home, the antiwar movement was growing: the Students for a Democratic Society (SDS) organization was expanding on campuses around the country; and ethnic and African-American citizens were struggling for recognition and civil rights. In the midst of all these troubles, Ray Browne, Dan Walden, and the aforementioned others formed the Popular Culture Association and later the American Culture Association.

It may have been an exciting time—there was certainly no lack of funds in academic circles—but it was a time of genuine concern for the welfare of the Republic as well. Things were not well, and Penn State needed new approaches to satisfy student demands for relevant courses that addressed urban problems and concerns. The University turned to Dan Walden to help address these burgeoning social problems, and in 1967, over interactive microwave TV, he introduced "The American Negro Experience," into the curriculum as Penn State's first Ethnic Studies course. An innovation to solve an immediate problem, this course certainly broke ground; more importantly, with time it gave birth to what eventually became a plethora of courses in that field in American Studies, History, English, and the Department of African-American Studies.

By 1968, the United States was seemingly tearing itself apart. The beginning of the Tet Offensive in Vietnam showed conclusively that the Vietcong meant business and were nowhere close to defeat, regardless of what American government officials might have said. The war and its claim to so many American lives seemed to be terribly wrong, and President Lyndon B. Johnson refused to consider the Democratic Party's nomination for another term of office. Martin Luther King, Jr., was shot in Memphis; Robert F. Kennedy lost his life to an assassin's bullet and died in San Francisco in the arms of former Penn State football player Roosevelt Grier. The Democratic National Convention first shredded and then dissolved into an event more reminiscent of a civil war than an exercise in American democracy. With the Democratic Party in shambles, the way was cleared nationally for the Nixon presidency and all the problems of his era in the White House. Without a doubt, it was a time of upheaval, protest, social consciousness, and bitter feelings.

During the period, the faculty and student body at Penn State's main campus were unhappily polarized because of the succession of national catastrophes, and Penn State asked Dan Walden to come to the rescue yet again. Beginning in the fall 1968, although Dr. Dan Walden could never hope to stop a war in Vietnam, he brought his ethnic studies approach to University Park. In fact, he taught it at Capitol and University Park at the same time. At University Park, he joined forces with an African-American faculty member in the English Department, Charles Davis, a man better known as an Emily Dickinson scholar rather than for African-American literature and culture. The two colleagues combined their interests and produced an anthology called *On Being Black*. Not only was the book a success on its own, selling 135,000 copies, Professor Davis changed directions in his intellectual life to African-American literature and experience. African-American and Ethnic Studies was given life at Penn State. In 1972, a second book in this series appeared, *W.E.B. DuBois: The Crisis Years,* and Dan Walden joined intellectual forces with Kathryn Newman, the dominant force in the formation of the new Society for Multi-Ethnic Literature in the United States.

In 1974, Dan Walden followed the lead created by *On Being Black* with a new anthology called *On Being Jewish,* a book designed for use as an introduction to Jewish literature in Penn State's Comparative Literature Program. A year later, he started *Studies in American Jewish Literature,* a new journal supported only by subscriptions, which still continues.

From the 1970s into the present, Walden has been Editor-in-chief of *Studies in American Jewish Literature* and produced a volume of *SAJL* each year, published *Twentieth Century American Jewish Fiction Writers* (1984), was series editor for Peter Lang Publishing, Inc. for two series, wrote numerous articles and chapters in African American literature and culture and in Jewish American literature and culture, was Director of the American Studies Program at Penn State for 13 years, initiated one of the first Black American Literature courses in the country in 1967, initiated one of the first American Jewish courses in the country in 1970, initiated one of the first interdisciplinary multicultural courses (American Studies 405, "Ethnicity and the American Experience") in the country in 1972, gave talks at every national PCA/ACA convention, helped refound the Middle Atlantic PCA/ACA and set up the Daniel Walden Graduate Paper Award, and taught thousands of undergraduates and hundreds of graduates.

After thirty-two years at Penn State University, Dan Walden retired August 30, 1998. He will continue to teach once a year, free, for several years, because he wants to and because Penn State welcomes him body and soul. The future belongs to Dan and Bea. It will be interesting to see what will develop. It is certain that he will not slow down. Among the books on which he is now working are a collection of his essays from 1960 into the present, titled *Walden Ponders,* and a book called *Conversations with Chaim Potok.*

Notes

1. I confess that Professor Daniel Walden is one of my dearest friends. Most of the personal data here comes from our interactions over the years, along with two directed interviews conducted in July and August 1996, and Carolyn Ruwitch Kendall, "A Real *Mensch,*" *Town & Gown Magazine* (Mar. 1993) 70-74, 76, 78, 80.

2. Daniel Walden, Introduction, *On Being Jewish: American Jewish Writers from Cahan to Bellow* (Greenwich, CT: Fawcett, 1974) 29.

3. Daniel Walden, "The Contemporary Opposition to the Political and Educational Ideas of Booker T. Washington," *Journal of Negro History* 45 (Apr. 1960) 103-15. This paper was submitted for consideration in 1959 for the J. Salwyn Schapiro Prize Contest. My source is Dan Walden's personal manuscript of this early article, 11.

4. John K. Fairbank of Harvard University in a speech to the American Historical Association, quoted in Hans Kohn and Daniel Walden, eds., *Readings in American Nationalism* (New York: Van Nostrand Reinhold, 1970) 10.

CONTRIBUTORS

Regina Calvin, a native Hoosier, is a free-lance writer with a special interest in regional literature.

Robert C. Doyle, after his naval service and activity as a professional musician, earned his dostorate in 1987 at Bowling Green State University. He taught American Studies at Pennsylvania State University, at Westfälische Wilhelms-Universität-Münster as a Fulbright scholar, and as a Visiting Professor of American Civilization at the Université des Sciences Humaines de Strasbourg II. His books include *Voices from Captivity, Interpreting the American POW Narrative* (1994) and *A Prisoner's Duty, Great Escapes in U.S. Military History* (1997).

Michael Dunne, co-editor of *Studies in Popular Culture,* is the author of *Metapop: Self-referentiality in Contemporary American Popular Culture.* In addition to scholarly journals, his work has appeared in two other boks published by Popular Press: *Comic Crime,* edited by Earl Bargainnier, and *All That Glitters: Country Music in America,* edited by George H. Lewis.

Gary Hoppenstand is an associate professor teaching in the Department of American Thought and Language at Michigan State University. He has published numerous books and articles on topics ranging from nineteenth-century American literature to popular culture studies. His textbook, *Popular Fiction: An Anthology* (Longman, 1997), was the recipient of the Popular Culture Association's "Ray and Pat Browne National Book Award." He has also served as vice president of the Popular Culture Association.

Maurice Hungiville is presently associated with the Michigan State University Press as a consulting editor.

Michael K. Schoenecke is an associate professor of English at Texas Tech University. He completed his Ph.D. in 1980 at Oklahoma State University. He has published on such diverse topics as film, sport, architecture, and music.

Stephen Tatum is associate professor of English at the University of Utah, where he teaches courses in American literary and cultural studies. He is the author of *Inventing Billy the Kid,* as well as articles and essays on western American literature, film, and history. His essay "The Solace of Animal Faces" (*Arizona Quarterly*) received the 1994 Don. D. Walker Prize for the best essay published that year in western American studies.